AMERICAN WAYS OF LIFE

American Ways of Life

☆ ☆ ☆ ☆ ☆ ☆

GEORGE R. STEWART

NEW YORK / RUSSELL & RUSSELL

TO J. D. H. AND R. A. H.

These have been long in the earth, they know the seasons,
They know by the stinging of flies when the rains come,
They smell the snow on a dry wind, they are wise
In the changing of gales when the shape of the moon changes,
They stir in their sleep at night when the tide turns:

Only they speak in the tongue of another country.
There are names in their speech of fruits unknown in these valleys.
Also their gods are carved with the muzzles of jackals,
And their proverbs are proverbs made in a dry place:
Their festivals do not keep the days of the sea.

From: Archibald MacLeish, Land's End.

CONTENTS

AMERICAN WAYS OF LIFE

CHAPTER 1

LAND AND PEOPLE

As a beginning, let us momentarily make use of a device of science fiction, and imagine a "historical" event that never occurred. . . . During one of the vigorous and expansive periods of the Chinese Empire, one of their navigators (who might have been named Ko Lum Bo) conceived the idea of sailing eastward from China and thus arriving at Ireland, which was known to be the farthest outpost of Europe. The Chinese wished to reach Ireland, it may be believed, because they had heard tales that those barbarous islanders made a certain drink called Wis Ki.

Ko Lum Bo made his voyage, and discovered a country that he supposed to be part of Ireland, although he was disappointed in not finding any Wis Ki being manufactured by the natives.

During the course of the next two centuries the Chinese colonized this country, eventually discovering it to be not Ireland, but a wholly new continent. Nevertheless they continued to call the natives Irish, or sometimes Red Irish.

The Chinese colonists introduced their own well-established

ways of life. They continued to speak Chinese, and to practice their own religion. Being accustomed to eat rice, they
still ate it, as far as possible. Vast areas of the country were
terraced and irrigated as rice paddies. The colonists continued
to use their comfortable flowing garments, and pagodas dotted
the landscape. In short, the civilization was Asiatic and not
European.

Yet it could not be wholly Asiatic. The Chinese adopted
from the natives the valuable food plant known as Irish corn.
They also made other adjustments to the land itself. For instance, landing on the shores of San Francisco Bay with their
domestic animals, especially their pigs, they found that the
country, as they advanced inland, was largely open grassland
and desert. Since such land was much better suited to sheep
than to pigs, the colonists came to depend more upon sheep,
and gradually lost some of their taste for pork. When they
finally came to the forested eastern part of the country, they
entered a region much more hospitable to pigs than to sheep.
But by this time they were so well accustomed to raising
sheep that they continued to do so.

Thus, in the end, a student of their civilization would conclude that it showed the influence of two factors. Much of it
resulted from what the colonists had brought with them, and
the rest sprang chiefly from the influence of the land itself. . . . At this point let us drop science fiction. . . .

Like an individual's character, a nation's way of life may be
conceived as the result of environment and heredity. The environment of a nation consists of the land that it inhabits, the
seas that border that land, and the air that sweeps across it.
The heredity of a nation, at any given moment in its history,
consists of the sum total of the blood strains and acquired
habits of its people.

An individual's environment and a nation's may be considered essentially the same in their nature, continually changing with time. Whereas, however, an individual's heredity is to be conceived as being immutably fixed from the beginning, the heredity of a nation changes with every new immigrant and emigrant.

This present book is twofold in its purpose. It attempts to present certain aspects of life in a particular nation, with special reference to the features that may be considered distinctive; and at the same time, to show how these distinctive ways of life have arisen historically, as the result of heredity and environment.

2

Of the two prevailing influences, that of environment is the simpler to explain. Here we can include all the influences of the land itself—its size, continental nature, topography, soil, climate, native plants and animals. Thus, we eat comparatively little fish—obviously, in part at least, because the great majority of our people, inhabiting a continental country, are far removed from the oceans. Similarly there is a strong influence of the environment in our heavy eating of pork, in our fondness for iced drinks, and in many others of our ways of life, as it will be the business of the succeeding chapters to demonstrate.

Scarcely had the colonists come ashore from their ships when they found that the land could not be wholly ignored. They might wish to remain English or Dutch or Swedish, but sheer necessity often forced an adaptation. Thus, at Jamestown, lacking beer and ale, they drank water rather than go thirsty; later, in want of food, they ate the Indian corn rather than starve.

Generally we may say that it was necessity, but sometimes necessity pointed the same way as inclination. Many a man in the colonies, and later on the frontier, ceased attending church, primarily because there was no church to attend. But also, he may have gone to services in the more settled country because of social conventions, and so could welcome the chance to attain his freedom.

Certainly, also, the land sometimes drew people to its ways because they found those ways more attractive. The Indian mode of life, for instance, exercised a great charm. Not only did some Americans "take to the wigwam" in the past, but also, even at the present time, the tradition of an occasional lapse into primitive life remains a strong one. We have only to remember the Boy Scouts, and the thousands of business-men who—like that typical American, George F. Babbitt—go yearly into the woods for a couple of weeks, to sleep in the open, slap mosquitoes, travel by canoe or on horse, hunt and fish, grow beards, talk male talk, and in general attempt to give themselves back to the Indians.

The land also worked in more subtle ways. By influencing particular events, it made finally inevitable the adoption of new ways of thought and of life. Thus, indirectly, it had its influence even upon our religion.

By influencing particular events, the land exercised its sway in various ways, particularly through what we may call the intermediary mechanism of the frontier. The influence of the frontier upon American ways of life is everywhere admitted. But the frontier itself, as it existed in our history, could not have so existed except under the particular circumstances of our land—its size and continental sweep, its greater extension from east to west, its climatic conditions, its great forests, its Indian tribes.

By and large, indeed, the frontier and the land itself began to exert their greatest influence only after the settlers had left the coastal regions and begun to penetrate inland and lose touch with the ocean and the European commerce that it bore. A comparison may be made with the conditions of World War II. The troops of an invasion force, landing under the support of naval gunfire, often had comparatively easy going at first. But as soon as they moved inland and lost naval support, they had to advance on their own and to solve their own difficulties by adapting to what they met.

So it was with the colonists. We need give only one illustration. . . . As long as the colonists remained close to tidewater, rum was their chief strong drink. When the frontier had advanced far enough inland to make transportation a problem the colonists began to manufacture their own strong drink from locally grown grain, and thus became whiskey-drinkers. Other factors were involved, as will be explained in a later chapter, but the co-ordination of whiskey-making with the distance of the frontier from tidewater seems fairly close.

The Indians may be considered a special factor of the environment. At first thought, this grouping of the Indians with the trees and animals may seem disrespectful and suggestive of race prejudice. It is, in fact, just the opposite. It recognizes that the influence of the Indians upon our way of life is of moment, and is quite out of proportion to the inconsiderable strain of their blood that persists in the modern American nation.

The story of Squanto, one of the most moving and symbolic tales of our history, illustrates the whole matter in small compass. This Indian, who after strange adventures had learned to talk English, became an interpreter for the settlers at Plymouth, and William Bradford calls him "a special instrument sent of God for their good beyond their expectation." He taught them how to raise the Indian corn, "showing

them both the manner how to set it, and after how to dress
and tend it." Having taught the colonists this and much else
in the course of about fifteen months, Squanto took sick,
"bleeding much at the nose," and died. He thus left no
hereditary imprint upon the English colony.

What can be said of Squanto can also be said in general for
his people. Having transmitted some skills and taught some
lessons, they died off—either in war with the white man or by
infection with his diseases. The Indians are thus best to be
considered as part of the environment.

On the whole, however, the environmental influence upon
our ways of life, even including the influence of the Indians,
is less important than the hereditary influence. The reasons
are easy enough to point out.

First of all, the land itself did not harshly demand changes.
Its climate differed somewhat from that of northwestern
Europe. Also it was heavily forested, whereas the European
forests had mostly been cut. Otherwise the colonists found
on our eastern seaboard a natural environment that was remarkably like the one they had left.

They themselves were highly conscious of this similarity.
"Much like England!" is a common refrain in the early de-
scriptions. In the forests the colonists noted many familiar
trees—oaks, ashes, maples, elms, pines, cedars. The animals
also were mostly either those, such as deer and foxes, with
which they were familiar, or else they were such as not too
long before had roamed the English forests and were still remembered in legend and story, such as wolves and bears. Even
for life in the streams a Dutchman could write: "The river
[Delaware] has a great plenty of fish, the same as those in our
fatherland—perch, roach, sturgeon, and similar fish."

John Smith, coasting the shore in 1614, observed that parts
of it looked like Devonshire, and named the whole region

New England. He may have done so partly for propaganda and partly for patriotism, but still he had a basis of reality, such as he would have lacked if he had been sailing the coast of Labrador or of Guatemala.

Even more important than the similarity of the land to northwestern Europe was the firm-rooted resolution of the colonists to remain European—generally, no doubt, an unconscious resolution, but probably all the firmer for being unconscious.

At the time of the settlement of the colonies European civilization was well founded, long established, strong, confident, and even bigoted and intolerant. By and large, the individual colonists had no wish to cease to be Europeans. Some, to be sure, felt the charm of the Indian way of life, and lapsed into it. But the very use of the word "lapse" indicates that such a procedure was considered a falling away.

The overwhelming majority of the colonists held hard, as any group of people may be expected to do, to their already established customs and modes of thought. Personal habits are not willingly changed, and in America as elsewhere we find this mere personal conservatism to be reinforced by sentiment, nostalgia, patriotism, race prejudice, and even religion. The colonists thus continued to speak European languages, wear European clothes, follow European religious practices, and build houses that were as much as possible like European houses. They even brought their European place names with them, and lived in towns called Plymouth, Boston, New Amsterdam, and Norfolk. In 1619 the inhabitants of a Virginia settlement which had been called Kecoughtan petitioned the Assembly to be allowed "to change the savage name," and it accordingly became Elizabeth City.

3

The hereditary factor is not only stronger but also much more complicated than the environmental. First of all, we must distinguish between the earlier and the later waves of immigrants.

The older immigration extended from the beginning to about 1840. It is notable chiefly for its great unity and homogeneity. Such an idea must be maintained in spite of certain superficial variations and in spite of a modern tendency to emphasize the variety of the American stock from the very beginning. Even during this early period, it is true, the basically English population was interpenetrated by other groups. There were many of the other stocks from the British Isles —Welsh, Scottish, Irish, and particularly Scotch-Irish from Ulster. In addition there were large numbers of Dutch and Germans, and smaller groups of Swedes, French, and Swiss. Even before the Revolution there are also records of Jewish immigrants, especially from Portugal, and even of an occasional Scandinavian, Bohemian, and Pole. In addition, there were Indians and large numbers of Negroes. Finally, certain areas were originally settled by French and Spaniards.

Anyone thus claiming a great diversity for our early population would seem, at first glance, to be able to make a good case. The strength of the argument, however, disappears upon more careful scrutiny, at least in so far as the development of our way of life is involved. In the first place, the areas settled by the French and Spanish were not absorbed until rather late, after the Revolution, and remained peripheral and comparatively without influence. The Indians, as has already been indicated, are to be considered an environmental, not a hered-

itary factor. The Negroes, though numerous, were definitely
kept apart, and so transmitted little of their own ways to the
Americans.

Even so, we may still seem to be left with a considerable
mingling of peoples. But this variety, too, fades under closer
scrutiny. With few exceptions the colonists of European
stock were of northwestern European origins, and there can
have been, racially, only negligible differences among them.
Even in their cultural backgrounds they differed little. They
were heirs of the European Middle Ages, of the Renaissance,
and of the Reformation. They were Christians by tradition,
and nearly all were Protestants.

Naturally the groups differed somewhat, one from another,
and displayed some clannishness. They were conscious of their
differences, often more conscious of differences than of resemblances. Thus a Pennsylvania governor of 1718 was already
voicing the cry that the American conservative has echoed
ever since. "We are being overwhelmed by the immigrants!"
he said in effect. "Will our country not become German instead of English?"

Nevertheless, from the perspective of two centuries and
from the point of view of the modern world with its critical
problems of nationality and race, the differences existing
among the various colonial groups fade into insignificance.
We sense, comparatively speaking, a unified population. In
the political realm, indeed, there were divergences that might
lead even to tarrings and featherings, but racially and socially
and religiously the superficial differences were much less important than the basic unity.

Considered, then, as a unit—a somewhat variegated unit,
if you wish—this early population has been of great importance
in shaping our ways of life. Most strikingly, its predominating
language has become our predominating language. We still

operate under the Constitution and by means of the governmental machinery established before the population was much
diversified. In fact, scarcely one of our present ways of life
fails to show strong influences of the original customs and
habits that these early people not so much originated as
brought with them out of the common northwestern European heritage.

Because the early customs were so well unified, the attempt
to attribute specific features of our ways of life to this or that
group is difficult. Obviously we speak the English language
because it was spoken by the English colonists, but it was also
spoken by the numerous Scotch-Irish, and by the great majority of the Scots, Irish, and Welsh.

The Dutch were among the earliest settlers, and came in
good numbers. Their contribution to our life is certainly important, and is indicated by the large number of prominent
men who have borne Dutch names. But in their ways of life
the early Dutch differed so little from the English, Germans,
and other colonists that attempts to determine specific Dutch
contributions are likely to end up by suggesting that their
fondness for deep-fat frying has given us the doughnut—a
pleasant food, certainly, and a typically American one, but
only a minute detail in the pattern of our life.

The Scotch-Irish have been credited with "whiskey, the
Presbyterian church, and our independence from Great Britain." The last, however, is obvious hyperbole, even though the
Scotch-Irish were ardent Revolutionaries. Even the others
may be considered doubtful. A few Presbyterian churches were
established before the beginning of Scotch-Irish immigration.
As for whiskey, there is evidence that "Carolina corn" was
being manufactured as early as 1682, again well before the
coming of the Scotch-Irish. They are also credited with the
introduction of the Irish potato, but this too is not literally

correct. About all that it is possible to say surely is that the Scotch-Irish made Presbyterianism important, aided in the Revolution, and established the potato as a popular food and whiskey as a popular drink.

Thus in general the influence of this early American population can be considered as a unit. Only now and then can it be analyzed and attributed specifically to one or another of its groups.

The newer immigration began after 1840. First came the Irish, and soon after them the Germans. Then the great Scandinavian immigration got under way. All three of these groups were northwestern European, and so introduced nothing that was racially new and little that was culturally different. The most notable innovation was that nearly all of the Irish and many of the Germans were Roman Catholics.

After 1880—and to continue until the end of mass immigration—the sources of immigration shifted to southern and eastern Europe. Now for the first time there was a shift not only in the nature of the racial stock but also in the cultural background. In religious affiliations the new immigrants were largely Roman Catholic, Orthodox Catholic, and Jewish. In their customs, in everything from their food habits to their appreciation of the arts, they differed considerably from the older population. Moreover, they arrived in such millions and had such large families after they arrived that they now compose a very considerable part of the American population.

As the result of this later immigration, the hereditary background of the people of the United States has shifted greatly. If the British-Protestant element, the so-called Anglo-Saxon, can be put at 75 per cent in the Revolutionary period, it must now be reduced to less than 50 per cent. Has the question asked by the governor at such an early date at last been answered in the affirmative? Have the later immigrants made the country over after their own image?

In general the answer to the question would seem to be a negative. Remarkable as it may seem at first thought, the continual flow of immigrants does not seem to have destroyed the cultural domination of the early tradition. That the situation really is such, the later chapters of the book may serve to demonstrate. The manner in which this somewhat surprising result was enabled to occur may be presented now.

In the first place, the Americans—that is, the established inhabitants of any particular time—held the ground, and were a vast majority. In any one year the number of immigrants was only a very small percentage of the whole population. Moreover, these immigrants differed among themselves, and so in no sense presented a united front. On the other hand, the Americans possessed an established body of customs—a way of life. They had an ideology, expressed in the Constitution and in many other writings. Economically, they held the property. Politically, they held the power, and the immigrant was not even able to vote until after he had been naturalized and therefore somewhat absorbed into the American pattern.

Moreover, few of the immigrants entered the country with any idea of hostility or antipathy to it. The vast majority of them were not trying to make the United States different, but were welcoming the chance to make themselves a part of what was already there. Their case was different from that of the first colonists. Those early-comers had looked upon the Indians as heathen savages, to be assimilated or exterminated, but not to be imitated or joined. The later immigrants, though they might come from ancient and proud and highly civilized countries, were seldom in a position as individuals to look down upon the civilization of the United States, and they generally looked up to it. They therefore, to a very surprising degree, tended to lose their racial or national habits and ways of thought, sometimes by necessity, sometimes for convenience, sometimes by actual desire to become one of the dominating majority.

In the third place, the continuing successful progress of the United States aided this absorption. If the country had been slow to develop and had begun to lack confidence, the immigrants might have been less willing to learn American ways, and the Americans themselves might have begun to take counsel from the newly arrived foreigners.

It is therefore false to assume that the cultural heredity of the United States is to be appraised statistically by a mere counting of heads of immigrants according to their point of origin. The symbol of the melting pot, such a favorite one in American history, is in fact a startlingly bad one. Immigrants are not mere lumps of metal, elemental and unalterable, to be mingled with the molten mass and inevitably to change its whole constituency in proportion to the amount thrown into the pot. A better figure of speech would be to speak of the "transmuting pot." We need not assume that the original metal was gold. Let us call it merely "the American metal." As the foreign elements, a little at a time, were added to the pot, they were not merely melted but were largely transmuted, and so did not affect the original material as strikingly as might be expected. Their racial background was of course unchanged, but culturally and psychologically they generally became American.

4

Although the life of an individual may be said to be wholly determined by his heredity and environment, still that indi-

vidual is likely to have his own creative ideas. These doubtless in some way spring from heredity and environment, but
for practical purposes they may often be better treated as
something new and unique. In the same way a people may
have its own "native developments."

In the evolution of the American ways of life, these native
developments are particularly strong in the field of recreation. They are to be found also, however, in language, in
names, in religion, and in most of the fields. Since native developments spring from the people, they might seem to lie
closer to the hereditary than to the environmental influences.
On the other hand, they sometimes seem to be connected with
the land. About all that we can do is to conclude that, if a new
development arises that cannot be surely attributed to the influence of the land or to some custom brought in with the
immigrants, then we may consider it to be the result of an
essentially creative process.

Every new idea must obviously arise in the mind of an individual; there is no place else in which it can arise. Theoretically, therefore, we may say that every native development is to
be credited to some individual. In some instances, these individuals are known. Thus we are certain that James A. Naismith
invented basketball. But what ingenious frontiersman, spurred
perhaps by lack of barley or rye, conceived the idea of making
corn whiskey? What housewife made the first blueberry pie?
If monuments are ever erected to such heroes and heroines,
the inscriptions will have to be as anonymous as that to the
Unknown Soldier.

Many of our customs must have sprung from numerous
ideas, and thus have arisen by a kind of evolution, or folk
process. Baseball is an instance. Although its invention has
been credited to various individuals, it did not come suddenly
into being, as basketball did. On the contrary, it developed

slowly out of primitive games played with ball and bat, and though it can certainly be said to be American, it cannot be attributed to any one American.

Patriotically, we can wish to attribute as much as possible to these native developments, but actually the close resemblance of most of our customs to previously existing European customs makes us realize that the creative factor has not been as strong as we might wish.

5

Finally, the influence of "international ideas" must be considered. By analogy with the life of an individual, such ideas correspond roughly to the influence exerted upon an individual by his own contemporaries, and so may be broadly considered environmental.

In all ages ideas have spread from one people to another, and this has been particularly true in modern times. In the United States, for instance, there is a very strong French influence in cookery. This stands in little proportional relationship to any immigration from France, although some individual chefs came to this country. But in general the popularity of French cooking was induced by magazine articles and books, especially by cookbooks, and by returned travelers. It spread, not by being carried about by French people, but by being propagated as an idea. In the same way golf and skiing are popular American sports, not primarily because of Scottish and Scandinavian immigration, but because the ideas were introduced and spread.

In what are sometimes called the higher levels of civilization—such as government, law, religion, philosophy, and the arts—the influence of ideas has long been recognized as highly important, and the history of ideas has become a major field of study. Often the influence can be attributed to individual thinkers, and no one would doubt the importance of the contribution to American thinking and even to daily life of such men as Locke, Darwin, and Freud. Much less study has been devoted to the more earthy matters that are the subjects of most of the following chapters, and frequently we shall have to be content to note the apparent influence of such ideas without knowing from what individual or even from what country the ideas originated or what was their precise medium of transmission to the people of the United States.

Because of the mingling of hereditary and environmental factors, with the additional complications of native developments and the influence of international ideas, the history of certain of our ways of life is extremely involved and complex. Others display a history that is less difficult to unravel. The simplest story of all is probably that of language, and with it we therefore begin.

CHAPTER **2**

LANGUAGE

The people of the United States call them-
selves "Americans," but speak "English." The anomaly is interesting, and so is the three-and-a-half-century-long linguistic
history that explains it.

On the whole, however, as compared with the development
of our other ways of life, the development of our language
is simple. We speak English because that was the language
of the great majority of the colonists. Other colonists and
later immigrants speaking other languages, environmental influences, native developments, international ideas—each has
affected American English in interesting ways; but even in
their total effort they are of relatively minor importance. In
the language, therefore, we have an extreme example of a way
of life that may be termed hereditary and has remained comparatively stable.

In the seventeenth century, at the time of the settlement of
the American colonies, English was already a highly developed
language. It had therefore no need to borrow heavily from

other languages with which it came into contact. The early colonists had many dealings with Indians who spoke various languages, and also with speakers of Dutch, German, French, and Spanish. They imported as slaves many Negroes still speaking different African languages. Traces of all of these can be found in our present American English, but they are only traces, and the original English of the colonists was not much altered by these contacts.[1]

From the very beginning, moreover, English was the prevailing speech in most of the colonies, and in 1664 it became the official language of all of them. Thus from the very beginning English has been dominant, and its domination has steadily become stronger.

As the years have passed, the language has in fact come to illustrate excellently the principle of the "transmuting pot." The immigrants arrived, at an average yearly rate of less than one per cent of the already existing population. Many of these immigrants themselves spoke English, and the others spoke various languages, so that even this small fraction was divided. As a result, the immigrants have always found it to their comfort and advantage to learn English. Generally speaking, they did so as rapidly as possible. Those of the first generation—particularly the women, immured in their homes—often failed to learn English well, but the second or third generation had usually lost all trace of a foreign origin. An occasional group,

[1]This statement must be taken, of course, as applying only to the development of the language in America. Upon the English language considered as a whole, French has had a tremendous influence. But probably not more than a few dozen French words have actually come into use because of contacts with the French on this continent, and in comparison with the many thousands of words that crowd our dictionaries this number can scarcely be said to constitute more than a trace. In other phases of language, such as grammar and pronunciation, the influence is harder to appraise, but is probably even less important.

such as the closely knit Pennsylvania Germans, clung tenaciously to their original speech, but they formed the rare and comparatively unimportant exception. Although a considerable majority of the present citizens of the United States are probably sprung from non-English-speaking stock, still no one could well argue against the usual statement that the United States is an English-speaking country.[2]

It is not, of course, 100 per cent English-speaking. Some tens of thousands of Indians still speak their own languages. A single state, New Mexico, is largely bilingual, and a considerable proportion of its citizens still speak Spanish only. All along the Mexican border, in fact, much Spanish is spoken, but this language maintains itself largely by continued migration, legal and illegal, across the border. Some French is still spoken in Louisiana. There are also, especially in the larger cities, foreign districts where languages other than English are spoken. These last, however, are the result of comparatively recent immigration, and are maintained by continuous arrival of new immigrants. There is nothing to indicate that even in a small way these languages attempt to rival the prevailing one.

[2]Curiously enough, from the very beginning, Manhattan Island seems to have been the most polyglot place in the country. In 1646 Father Jogues reported of Manhattan and its environs: "the Director General told me that there were men of eighteen different languages." One has difficulty in imagining what the eighteen could have been, even allowing for some Indian and African languages. The Director may have made separate languages out of some dialects, thus perhaps separating Walloon from French. The continuing polyglot nature of New York City has done much to create the false impression of the United States as a country where many languages are spoken and where broken English is common. This is often the first impression of foreign visitors, who commonly land in New York. Frequently they also leave with this impression, having never got far enough into the country or stayed long enough to overcome the first impression. Over vast areas of the country foreign languages are rarely heard, and even broken English has become increasingly uncommon since the restriction of immigration in 1921.

DIALECT MAP (Based on vocabulary)

DIALECT MAP
(Based on vocabulary)

Such a map as this must be interpreted with caution. If the test had been pronunciation, the relationships of the various regions would probably be different. The heavy black lines have been drawn only by inference. In addition, the lines as they can be drawn on such a small map exaggerate the sharpness of changes and produce an oversimplification. The map, moveover, is based on the speech of people born and brought up in one particular area, and so makes no allowance for recent migration, such as the great movement from regions 3 and 4 into 1 and 2. Since large cities have been much affected by such migrations, the map chiefly reflects the language of the country and the small towns.

Regions 1, 2, and 3 represent the colonial dialects and their extensions. Region 4 is a mingling of 2 and 3 with the former somewhat predominating. Historically, it began with the heavy migration southwestward from Pennsylvania and Maryland in the latter eighteenth century, mingling with a westward-moving migration from the eastern parts of Virginia and the Carolinas. Region 5 is dominated by 2, but shows some influence of 1 and a still slighter influence of 3.

The map may be considered to show primarily the routes of migration from Atlantic to Pacific. It also shows the breakdown of colonial regionalism, and the mingling of the colonial stocks in the West, together with a growing domination of the speech of the middle colonies.

They all seem to be dying out, rather than to be developing and spreading.

English is indeed so dominant that, nationally speaking, there is no linguistic problem. Except possibly in New Mexico, language is not a political issue. Some organized groups encourage the study of their own languages in the schools and colleges, but in their cultural nostalgia they do not attempt to displace English as their first language.

The language in the United States is moreover remarkably well unified. Traditionally, it has usually been considered as existing in three main dialects—that of New England, of the South, and of the great region comprising the Middle Atlantic states, the Middle West, and the Far West, which is often called General American. Recent researches are indicating that the situation is somewhat more complicated geographically. The differences among the dialects are, however, not very striking. They are less than the differences existing among the dialects of France, and less even than exist in the varieties of English spoken within the small confines of Great Britain.

The differences also are probably becoming less. The distinctive New England dialect has been largely submerged in the populous centers of Massachusetts, Rhode Island, and Connecticut. Southern speech, also, is almost certainly growing closer to General American because of modern methods of communication. Even fifty years ago a child might grow up in a southern town, seldom be twenty miles away from it, and rarely hear any speech except that of the neighborhood. Now a southern child is likely to have radio, TV, and motion pictures, and on them all will hear mostly a dialect that is not his local one. If a comedian in New York or Hollywood begins using a new slang word or popularizes a new use of some old word, people in Georgia are just as likely to take it up as people in Massachusetts. Visit Yellowstone or any other non-southern tourist center, and observe the numerous cars from southern states. All those Southerners drove across "Yankee" states to get there, and talked to people on the way. If a Southerner is drafted, he nearly always (because Southerners are a minority) serves his time in an "outfit" composed mostly of "Yankees." Isolation is the mother of dialects, and the South is now no longer isolated.

In the matter of vocabulary, one has difficulty in seeing how new southern words can now originate, and remain southern. In the first place, there are few specifically southern conditions remaining to give rise to new words. Besides, granted that new expressions will originate in the South as elsewhere, there is nothing to make them spread as far as the present dialectal boundary and then stop. Modern communication and transportation being what they are, a new word coined in Memphis is just as likely to get to New York or Denver as rapidly as to Atlanta. Even old southern words, it would seem probable, have a tendency to spread to the country as a whole, or to die out.

There seems also, rather surprisingly, to be no organized movement for the preservation of southern speech. The cultivated Southerner is proud of his manner of language, but he has not codified it or organized for its preservation.

As a result of the tremendously unifying effect of modern means of communication, we may therefore consider it likely that the language of the United States not only will continue to be English, but also will become more and more unified.

2

In connection with our linguistic history, one fact is thus overwhelming in its importance—our present language is essentially that brought to American shores by English-speaking immigrants. The changes that have occurred since that time, either by natural evolution or by external influence, are comparatively minor.

How closely our language resembles that of even the first English immigrants is readily shown if we reprint a few sentences of simple writing by one of them. In so doing we can justifiably modernize the spelling, for in the seventeenth century orthography had not been standardized. We quote from George Percy, who landed with the Virginia colonists of 1607 and wrote a brief account of his experiences:

The savages bear their years well, for when we were at Pamonkies, we saw a savage by their report was above eight score years of age. His eyes were sunk into his head, having never a tooth in his mouth, his hair all gray with a reasonable big beard, which was as white as any snow. It is a miracle to see a savage have any hair on their faces. I never saw, read, nor heard, any have the like before.

The passage has an archaic flavor, as in the use of the word score, and the way in which its words are put together seems a little queer. But it is readily understandable. One is even interested to notice that the "mistakes" in grammar such as the omission of a who and the uncertain reference of having and their are much the same as an untrained writer makes today— and as an earl's son, Percy was more trained to the sword than to the pen.[3]

If, then, the language of the original colonists was merely the English of England, why then does ours differ somewhat from theirs today? Three reasons can be offered.

First, the people of Great Britain in the seventeenth century spoke different local dialects. What we now consider to be standard English for England developed from the language of

[3]If we could hear Percy read this passage, we should notice a considerable difference in pronunciation.

London and the near-by counties. But the settlers of America came not only from that region but also from many others. New England was settled largely from the eastern counties. Pennsylvania received a heavy immigration from the north of Ireland. English as it came to be spoken in New England and much of Pennsylvania thus naturally was not the same English that developed as the standard in England. For instance, in what we consider typical British English of today, the final r has been lost. It is, however, partially preserved in General American, possibly because the Scotch-Irish of the eighteenth century preserved that sound, as they still do in Ireland.

A second cause for the differences between the two countries lies in mere isolation. Language is always changing. When two groups of people speaking the same language are separated and remain in comparative isolation, change continues in the language of both groups, but naturally it does not continue in the same direction and at the same rate with both of them. The languages thus tend to become different.

Third, the language in the United States has been subjected to various influences that have not affected the language in Great Britain—the environment, the languages of other early colonists and of the later immigrants.

3

In effecting the comparatively minor changes that have appeared in the language since the seventeenth century, native developments have probably been the most important factor. Fortunately, some of these have run parallel to developments in Great Britain, so that the languages have not separated as much as they might otherwise. These parallel developments can be explained largely by the fact that the two languages were never completely separated. Immigrants, books, and travelers in both directions did something to minimize the separation.

As a good example of this parallel development the pronunciation of such a word as *tea* may be taken. In the seventeenth century this was apparently pronounced *tay* throughout all the English-speaking world. It has now been changed except in Irish dialect.

In such a word as *bath*, however, the Americans preserved the old pronunciation, and the British changed. As a result, we write a Britisher's pronunciation of this word as *bahth*.

Spelling also differs, largely as the result of the changes introduced by Noah Webster. Because of him Americans write *honor* and *center* instead of following the British custom of writing *honour* and *centre*.

The forms of words and the usages of words also changed. Sometimes, for instance, the Americans regularized a verb, so that *thrive-throve-thriven* came to be usually *thrive-thrived-thrived*. Most Americans, also, have stopped using the verb form *lend*, and have come to use *loan* as a verb as well as a noun.[4]

Vocabulary shows interesting changes and a considerable number of them. Sometimes the Americans merely kept the old forms or meanings while the British dropped or changed them. The most notable example is in the use of the phrase "I guess," which in the United States usually means "I think" and thus preserves the older meaning. Another example is the common American affirmative "yeah." This seems to be noth-

---

[4] In this connection the wartime use of the term *lend-lease* is interesting, and would indicate that the term itself was supplied by the British or by some American with strong British background. *Loan-lease* would represent more common American usage.

ing but a native development of the old form "yea," which was particularly beloved by the Puritans and the Quakers, preserved in slightly changed form with us, but lost before the encroachments of "yes" in Great Britain.

On the other hand, with okay the Americans made the innovation. This expression seems to have arisen as a popular abbreviation of Old Kinderhook, the nickname of Martin Van Buren, during the presidential campaign of 1840. It is thus a wholly native development. It is, however, rapidly spreading throughout Great Britain, and so may soon cease to be any means of differentiation.

Another factor working toward change in the language has been the rapid development of civilization in the past two centuries. Unfortunately, no international committee made any effort to standardize the new terms that constantly had to be invented and developed. Thus when it comes to automobiles we have the unnecessary differences shown in such word-pairs as hood-bonnet, truck-lorry, and gasoline-petrol. In the same way, American usage favors motion picture, moving picture, or movies, and British usage runs to cinema, or flicks.

Sometimes developments seem to take place by the route of slang, without any particular reason that can be assigned. Occasionally the results can even be embarrassing. When an Englishman remarks that he is "getting a good screw," he means that he is being paid well, and when an English girl says casually that she is "knocked up" she merely means that she is tired out.

Environment, also, produced changes in the language, or at least gave directions to native developments. We have lost such topographical words as heath and down, chiefly because no such features existed along the heavily forested eastern seaboard, and thus the words that every immigrant must have known fell out of use and were forgotten in the second or third generation. Along with them went the words for the kind of plants that grow in such places—*bracken, furze, whin,* and *gorse.* In exchange, the colonists picked up and manufactured new words for new experiences. Thus to identify new "critters" they coined *mud hen, garter snake,* and *copperhead.* To speak most accurately, such differences are in thing rather than in word. If an Englishman sees a copperhead in a London zoo, he undoubtedly has to use the American word. Still, a word once established begins to have a career of its own, and so the figurative use of *copperhead,* especially at the time of the Civil War, is characteristically American.

The same distinction—a difference in thing, not a real difference in language—applies to most of the words taken over from the Indians. Here we have, among many others, *hickory, persimmon, squaw, papoose, hominy, pone.* Again, such words move on to a figurative use more easily in the United States than in Great Britain. *Squaw* may come to be used to apply to women generally, though in a somewhat derogatory fashion. We can easily develop a proverbial simile "tough as hickory," and nickname one of our heroes "Old Hickory."

In some instances, in fumbling for a new word for a new thing, the Americans actually created a real difference between the two branches of the language. For instance, there existed in America two large species of the deer family with which most of the English colonists were not familiar. In the end one of these came to be known by its Indian name as *moose,* and the other as *elk.* The awkward thing is that *elk* in the older English usage meant, and in the present British usage still means, what an American means by *moose.* But what we call *elk* the British call *red deer,* or *stag* for the male. This has created a nuisance for the naturalists, who sometimes use the term *wapiti* to indicate the American elk. So far, however, our B.P.O.E. has not become the B.P.O.W.

4

Elk, moose, and other names for animals, form a very illustrative group by which to demonstrate some of the problems that the new environment produced for the language. The wild animals were of great importance and interest to the colonists, and many of them are mentioned in the earliest accounts of settlement. The majority caused no linguistic headache. When an animal was about the same as one that the colonists knew at home, they naturally called it by the same name—*fox, deer, squirrel, bat, otter, badger, frog,* and many others. Slight differences were ignored; many American foxes were gray, not red, but they could come under the general heading, even so. Similarly, the old names were easily applied to many animals that had once been native to England, were still native to parts of northern Europe, and were known to Englishmen by tradition. Here we have *wolf, bear,* and *beaver.*

When the colonists encountered an entirely new animal, there was also generally no problem about a name. Then they simply took a name that the Indians used. Thus John Smith mentions beasts that were called *aroughcun* and *opassom,* from which we have *raccoon* and *opossum,* and eventually *coon* and *possum.* Sometimes the colonists, over the course of a generation or two, treated such Indian words by the process known as folk etymology, to make them seem more like familiar English words. In this way, out of words that were wholly Indian to begin with, they made *muskrat* and *woodchuck,* again for animals for which English had no word.

Woodchuck, however, had a rival name that some of the English either coined descriptively or got by translating a Dutch equivalent. This was *ground hog.* The two names still continue to be used in different parts of the country. Each has worked well into American consciousness. The one has given us the folk saying:

> How much wood would a woodchuck chuck
> If a woodchuck could chuck wood?

The other has given us a name for Ground-hog Day.

Another animal also, so to speak, stuck halfway between, and ended up with both an Indian name and an English one. The *skunk* was new to the colonists, and that name for it is Indian, as we would expect. But there was also an English animal of somewhat similar nature, even having a bad smell, though by no means such an overwhelming one. So some colonists, especially in the South, called the new animal *pole-cat*, and many Americans still do so.

The English polecat was also known as *fitch* or *fitchew*. In America the colonists found an animal much like this. Apparently they began to call it *fitchew*, but the word then developed an *r* at the end, as words easily do. Doubtless the process of folk etymology helped, and eventually the animal came to be known as *fisher*. The trouble is that this does not describe the animal, and as a zoologist complains indignantly: "Who named the fisher? It does not fish!"

The colonists, however, not being trained as naturalists, made other zoological mistakes also. At least, these are generally called mistakes, though that is not a good word to use. The situation was that in the English of that time many words were used with broader application than zoologists later found convenient. The scientists are the ones that changed the rules, and are really—historically, at least—in error. Some of these "mistakes" caused no trouble. Thus the English had a dialect word for a hawk or hawk-like bird that the colonists applied to a bird that was not known in England. So we have *buzzard*.

To describe another native animal, which also was unknown in England, the colonists did not take an Indian word. Rather strangely, they used an Italian word that had worked into English, and called them *buffalo*. Everyone got along very happily for a hundred years and more until the scientists decided that the animals were not buffalo, and in the bumptious way that some scientists have they decided that it was not "proper" to say *buffalo*. You should say *bison*. This was highly presumptuous, for the people as a whole make the language, not any special group for their own convenience, and in a democracy, particularly, the majority ought to rule. In the *buffalo-bison* matter the majority (being ninety-nine to one at least) has continued to rule in any case. Before the taxonomists got to work, *buffalo* had got too deeply entwined with American thoughts and feelings. A long time is going to pass before Buffalo, N.Y., becomes Bison, N.Y., before we talk of Bison Bill, and before we try to make the song over into:

Oh, give me a home where the bison roam.

In the meantime the *buffalo-bison* distinction is rather useful, for it serves to identify any man who says *bison* as the pedant that he is likely to be.

The height of confusion occurred with the largest of the cat family that the colonists encountered. The English knew next to nothing about big cats, but from legends and travelers' tales and books, including the Bible, they were familiar with a number of names, all drawn from the classical languages—*lion*, *tiger*, *leopard*, *pard*, and *panther*. In addition they had a wholly English expression, *cat of the mountain*, which was shortened to *catamountain* or *catamount*. They therefore had no need to borrow an Indian word, but they could not agree on what these big American cats really were. *Leopard* and *pard* seem to have been the only terms *not* used; apparently the idea of spots was strong for those animals ("Can the leopard change his spots?"), and one thing certain about these new cats was that the adults were unspotted. Toward the north the colonists seem to have decided that these cats were a kind of lion, and so called them. In Carolina and southward the usual word was *tiger*. In between, people more commonly said *panther*. Besides, the word *catamount* was used here and there and vaguely, to refer to the small wildcat as well as to the larger animal. Eventually *panther* came to be the most commonly used, and it was simplified to *panter*, and by folk etymology into *painter*. (A zoologist might also complain: "Who named the painter? It does not paint!")

As if things were not bad enough already, shortly after 1800 two learned names were introduced, and writers began to put the beast down as "properly" a *puma*, or *cougar*. Both of these were from South American languages, though why those not particularly up-and-coming Indians should know the "proper" name for such a wide-ranging creature is something that only a scientist would know. About the same time the frontiersmen of the Far West began to use the term *mountain lion*. Probably their contacts with the Mexicans had something to do with their reviving the old name, for the Mexicans regularly call the animal *león*. Even after this, however, the learned term *cougar* became popular and established itself in the Pacific Northwest.

Thus, in reading books or even in present-day conversation, you have to know that the same beast may be meant, whether it is referred to as *lion*, *mountain lion*, *tiger*, *panther*, *panter*, *painter*, *catamountain*, *catamount*, *puma*, or *cougar*. But you must know also that *tiger* may mean *jaguar*, and *catamountain* and *catamount* may mean *wildcat*.[5]

[5] In later times two western animals caused difficulties. We are still uncertain whether to say *bighorn*, *mountain sheep*, or *bighorn sheep*.

An exceptional case such as this is interesting as showing what might have happened. The fact that it did not happen and that the language remained so much the same throughout all the colonies shows both how well the language was established before the time of colonization and also how little, on the whole, it changed on American soil.

5

The influence of the non-English-speaking colonists, like that of the land and of the Indians, is not of great importance. To the Dutch we are indebted for the characteristically American *boss*, and because of Dutch influence, it may be, an American crew refers to its commander informally as *skipper*. French contacts along the frontier gave *portage*, *cache*, and *prairie*, along with a good many other words. The early Germans kept largely to themselves, but supplied *sauerkraut*, thing and word, along with *hex*, and a few others.

Contact with the Spaniards was the most fruitful of all. Even in early times, Spanish words or Indian words in Spanish form supplied a large number of terms—*hammock*, *tomato*, *barbecue*, *pickaninny*, *quadroon*, *mosquito*. After contact was established with the Spaniards in the Far West, well after 1800, many more Spanish words were adopted—among them, *ranch*, *lasso*, *lariat*, *buckaroo*, *rodeo*, *arroyo*, *chaparral*, and *mesa*.

The influence of African languages is slight. The list of com-

---

In earlier times it was sometimes known as *tayé*, *my-attic*, *argali*, *cimarron*, *ibex*, and *ahsahta*. We are also doubtful as to *antelope* or *pronghorn*, and this animal was earlier known as *cabri*, *mountain goat*, or simply *goat*. Again we should note that neither of these animals was known in the English tradition.

monly used words does not run much beyond *yam, gumbo, okra, voodoo,* and *zombie.* Even these were mostly borrowed through Spanish or French and not directly.

The influence of later non-English-speaking immigrants is also slight. As yet, at least, most words so taken over have scarcely passed beyond the status of localisms or slang. In New York City, for instance, a certain number of Yiddish expressions have circulation, but most of these would not even be recognized in other parts of the United States. *Kosher* and *kibitzer* would be exceptions.[6]

Even the tremendous German immigration of the mid-nineteenth century did not introduce any large number of German words. Most of the few that were so supplied are, interestingly, concerned with eating and drinking—such as *lager, wienerwurst, frankfurter, delicatessen,* and *hamburger.* Three words that have become very American—*bum, loafer,* and *hoodlum* —seem to indicate that these Germans were not as industrious as they are sometimes represented to have been, or else that their references to Americans were not complimentary. As with many other terms, however, there is doubt as to the origin of these three.

The influence of the heavy Irish immigration after 1840 is difficult to appraise because nearly all these Irish spoke English from the beginning. Real Irish words (that is, Celtic) that have worked themselves into our common language are as rare as hens' teeth, and always seem to be doubtful in their background. Two of the better candidates are *shanty* and *shenanigan.*

A more difficult matter to appraise is whether the influence

[6] Even *kosher* is by no means universally known. A certain kind of olive sold in California is known as *kosher.* At a ranch where such olives are grown and packed I asked what made them so. "Oh," was the reply, "it's just a name!" The individual, though intelligent enough, was wholly ignorant of the meaning of the word.

of these many thousands who spoke first a foreign language and then broken English has in the long run subtly affected our pronunciation and grammar, so that some of the effects that are here attributed to native developments are actually the result of this contact with foreign languages. H. L. Mencken, the great collector of material on what he termed the American language, had a dislike for anything that can be called native American, and attributed a great influence to various immigrant groups. But if this influence had been as strong as he would make it out to be, we should expect more striking evidence from the vocabulary. With vocabulary affected only to a negligible extent, we can hardly believe that the less easily appraisable effects are important.

Certainly much more striking in its effect upon our vocabulary is the influence of international ideas. *Beer-garden*, for instance, may well have come in with German immigrants, but *kindergarten* was introduced at the idea level, from study of German experiments in child education. The vocabulary of the automobile—a whole study in itself—displays French words that were certainly not introduced because of any heavy migration from France. Here we have notably *chassis, garage,* and *chauffeur.*

In more recent years the tremendous development of a new scientific and technical vocabulary has also tended to be international. Some of these words originate in the United States and spread to other countries, and with others the reverse is true. Many of these words enter the common vocabulary. We have only to think of *moron, ego, introvert,* and all the other products of modern psychology. These technical words are generally adopted into the language of Great Britain and into other languages also, and thus tend to make our speech rather less than more distinctive.

6

On the whole, the sum total of the combined influences working to differentiate American speech from British speech has not produced two languages, but has merely managed to give a certain flavoring for American speech as against British, and vice versa. The question really to be considered, then, is perhaps not "Why do the two manners of speech differ?" but rather "Why does American English not differ more than it does? Why is it so much like British English?" Some suggestions can be made.

First there has been little connection between nationalism and language in the United States. Just as there is no concerted and organized movement for the maintenance of Southern speech, so there has never been any strong movement to express American nationalism by making its language more different from that of Great Britain. On the contrary, the tendency has generally worked in the other direction. Many of our "best people" have cultivated some approximation of British usage, and our schools have diligently taught Shakespeare, Milton, and the other great writers of England.

Some individuals, indeed, have worked for a more specifically American language, and one of these had a considerable influence. This was no less a person than Noah Webster. Possibly his interest was not entirely without personal and financial background, for as the compiler of the first important American dictionary he was in competition with the makers of dictionaries in England, and could expect a better reception if people in the United States were conscious of their language as something separate. But Webster honestly thought that after the independence of our country its language would rapidly diverge from that of Great Britain. This was not a bad judgment as of that time, but he could not predict the rapid increase of communication in the nineteenth century. Believing as he did, however, he saw no harm in trying to help the movement along. Webster, however, must be counted as an exception. In general, Americans seem to have preferred to keep close to the language of the older country, or not to be concerned about the matter one way or the other.[7]

A second reason for the resemblances between American and British English is to be found in the close communication that has always been maintained between the two countries.

British books have always been widely read in the United States; during the last century at least, American books have been widely read in Great Britain. Even in the days of the sailing ships there were trade and travel. British actors visited the United States. With the improvement of steamships, millions of American tourists visited Great Britain. There is scarcely need to list again all the modern developments of communication—phonograph, telephone, radio, motion pictures, television. All of these, without having been specifically intended for such a purpose, have been of tremendous importance in holding the English language together.

Finally, as a unifying influence, must be mentioned the cul-

[7]In recent times H. L. Mencken, both in practice through his own writing and in theory through his widely read American Language, has been the most important single influence toward differentiation. On the other hand, the influence of H. W. Fowler, an Englishman, has probably been even greater, in the opposite direction, than that of Mencken. Even his volume The King's English was influential, in spite of its title. His later Modern English Usage is a work of reference that has attained the authority of a Bible with many Americans, especially professors and editors. Any writer trying to employ a particular American usage is likely to have Fowler quoted against him, and to be forced to exercise a good deal of firmness to be allowed to be American. I write from experience.

tural interdependence of the two countries. Not only were the two included as parts of a rapidly unifying world civilization, but they were also two of the most closely connected parts of that civilization. The very fact that they could understand each other's speech tended to draw them more closely together and therefore to make them understand that speech even the better. Any change in the civilization of Great Britain together with the words describing it was likely to be transferred immediately to the United States, and vice versa. Under such conditions any great divergence of the two languages became difficult.

The differences between the two branches of the language are sometimes troublesome, but are also stimulating and are likely to give a distinctive flavor. When an American reads in *Macbeth* that the witches meet on a "blasted heath," he may not know what a heath is, much less what a blasted one may be. But perhaps for that very reason the vagueness of that suggestion makes the place seem more strange and therefore a better meeting place for witches. On the other hand, perhaps some of the charm that Whitman has always exerted on British readers has been in the American flavor of his language, in such a line as "I loafe and invite my soul."

A more tricky situation arises when a word arouses the wrong suggestion on the opposite side of the Atlantic. When Keats wrote: "She stood in tears amid the alien corn," an American reader almost inevitably has the image of a girl standing in a field of broad-leaved, tasseled plants, perhaps even taller than she. But Keats undoubtedly had the image of a girl standing in a wheat field.

A similar instance occurs with the word *shepherd*. In the story of the Nativity the three magi, or kings, or wise men, undoubtedly symbolize the top level of society, and the shepherds, who also come to adore, symbolize the lowest class. This distinction would have been obvious to an Englishman at the time of the translation of the King James Bible, and it is still probably understood in that sense by the English generally. But in the United States something has happened. Since the eastern seaboard was not a great country for sheep, no special workers were known as shepherds, and the word went out of common use, and gradually came to have a faraway and romantic suggestion. When, after a century and more, sheep-keeping again became a special task in the western part of the United States, the word *shepherd* had apparently become so suggestive of the Bible and of poetry that it did not seem suitable, and the new word *sheepherder* was coined. In the western United States this word has much the same connotation as the word *shepherd* had for a seventeenth-century Englishman. By substituting *sheepherder* in the story of the Nativity the average American will get a good deal better idea of the original intention.

In late years there has arisen a tendency to speak of "the American language." Even in some European countries the term is now used, especially in conversation with an American. But the term does not have linguistic justification, and in addition the inhabitants of the United States have no historic right to pre-empt the use of the word *American*. We should remember also that the Romans, although they came to dominate the world much more than the Americans have yet done or seem likely to do, still always spoke Latin, not Roman. What is probable, however, is that the term *English* will not mean British English, as has often been true in the past. On the contrary, there will probably be a tendency to use the term *English* definitely to include the speech of the United States, and therefore to distinguish American English and British English.

There is, of course, no question of either branch being more "correct" than the other. Neither, as far as anyone can tell, is better than the other, and there is no standard even by which a superiority is to be determined, except possibly a test of effectiveness, and in this respect the two are probably equal.

In the future, the relative prestige of the two branches will doubtless be determined by their civilized activity, probably not by mere numbers or power. At the present time, though British English has the prestige of antiquity, American English has the prestige of the greater political influence and probably of a greater sum total of creative activity. But the situation may change.

The language spoken in the United States has been determined chiefly by the hereditary factor. Though influenced slightly by the land, by languages spoken in the land, by native developments, and by international ideas, American English still remains essentially English, and the speech of the English colonists. The situation is thus thoroughly simple. To observe the development of a somewhat more complicated way of life, we proceed to a consideration of American religion.

CHAPTER 3

RELIGION

For a comparion and contrast with language, religion in the United States offers many points of interest. In language, the environmental factor has been small; in religion, it has been a great force. Like language, religion has been tremendously influenced by the original northwestern European immigration; unlike language, it has also been almost equally affected by the later immigrations, and to a considerable extent by native developments. There is a final point of utmost divergence. In language the transmuting pot has worked with high efficiency; in religion the conception of a transmuting pot, or even of a melting pot, can scarcely be said to exist.

Any discussion of religion in the United States must begin with two disclaimers. . . . First, the actual beliefs of our people offer too delicate a problem for the historian to approach, and he must be content with an external appraisal by means of church affiliations. In this connection even personal statements mean rather little. Many people "belong" to some church without having anything but a minimal idea of its doctrines and without letting its moral precepts noticeably affect their lives. Many others state, merely because of family tradition, that they have a certain affiliation, although they rarely or never attend services or show any other evidence of religion.

Second, statistics issued by the churches themselves are difficult to interpret. Some churches report only members definitely on the rolls; others report large numbers of children. For such reasons some churches present the number of their members exact to the final digit, and others are content with an estimate to the nearest ten thousand. Some denominations offer only an obvious guess, such as "two hundred thousand."

To be safe, therefore, the best that one can do is to begin with a primary three-way division.

1) A very large number of people, approaching a half of the population, have no church affiliation at all.

2) A very large number of people, approaching a half of the population, are included, by the various methods of counting and estimating, as "belonging" to some Christian denomination.

3) A very small number, about one per cent, belong to other than Christian denominations, and of these nearly all are of Jewish faith.[1]

Even this simplest of all possible classifications shows the complexity of our religious situation. It appears even more startlingly complex when we consider the constituency of the

[1]As of January, 1953, with a total population for the country of about 160,000,000, the number claimed by the churches, including Jewish congregations, was 81,355,494. This is a padded figure in that some churches use a method of counting that includes many people having no essential connection with the church. But the figure would be larger if the Protestant churches included children associated with them but not "members." Balancing overestimates against underestimates, one may be able to take the actual figure as fairly accurate. The estimated figure for the Jewish congregations was 1,485,000. Jehovah's Witnesses keep no membership roll, and the Church of Christ, Scientist, releases no figures. (See World Almanac, 1953, p. 705.)

half of the population which have here been merely termed Christians. The actual number of sects in the United States is, in fact, not definitely known. Estimates run from two hundred to more than three hundred. The actual figure is of little importance, since it must be constantly changing as old sects die out and new ones are organized. In size these sects run from great churches with many millions of adherents to the Primitive Friends, who in 1952 mustered but one congregation of nine members. This extraordinary complexity is the chief external feature of religion in the United States.

2

Historically, this presentation of religion may well begin with some explanation of why Christianity has so predominated. This is one of those "self-evident" facts that historians generally fail to consider, but actually the United States might well have been non-Christian. We have only to consider the interesting date, 1492. It is not only the date of the discovery of America, but is also the date of the fall of Granada, the last Mohammedan kingdom in Spain. The failure of the Moors to discover America is merely another "accident" of history. They held an advantageous location—in fact, the very country from which Columbus sailed. They were for several centuries highly prosperous; they had skilled geographers and bold seamen. If they had discovered America, they might well also have colonized it, so that it would have become a land of the Crescent and not of the Cross. The early Puritan settlers commented that New England had been preserved as a Protestant refuge. They might just as well have congratulated themselves that it had been providentially preserved from Islam and held available for Christianity. Looking at the matter in the long perspective of history, we might well say with the Duke about Waterloo: "It was a very close thing."

To pass to actuality, the problem is to explain the existence in the United States of the almost equal division between those who nominally at least are Christians, and those who are unchurched.

To begin with the seventeenth century, when the colonists began to arrive, membership in a church was approximately synonymous with existence, for any European. He might, like Falstaff, have forgotten "what the inside of a church is made of," but he had an affiliation, nevertheless. In England, he was a member of the Church of England, unless he was one of the few who still maintained their traditional Roman Catholicism, or unless he was one of the few extremists who had definitely separated themselves from the Established Church. Even an atheist generally remained a member of the Church, since it asked little or nothing of him, and was a useful agency for maintaining social and political unity, and since an open break with the Church might get him into hot water.[2]

Under such a system the Established Church and even some of the others contained a great number of merely nominal members who rarely or never attended a service, who neither knew nor heeded its doctrines and moral precepts, and who as far as personal convictions and feeling were concerned had not much more of them than a rabbit or a sea gull. For all that,

---

[2] Atheists have had a bad break in the United States ever since Wingfield, the first president of Virginia, had to defend himself against that charge. Even though an American may quite readily say that he has "nothing to do with churches," he will rarely say that he is an atheist. The term "religious preference" has come into use. A person may thus indicate, when filling out forms, that he "prefers" one sect to another without stating that he actually "accepts" any—much as if a man might state that he preferred drowning to hanging, although not really enamored of either.

they may have been good citizens, and what is certainly beyond
doubt is that numbers of them migrated to the colonies.
When they came ashore, the land—we may say—took them
over. The Church of England, to be sure, sent some of its ministers. One of them—"good Mr. Hunt, our preacher"—landed
with the very first colonists at Jamestown.

(All honor to Robert Hunt and his like. He preached first
under the shadow of an old sail attached to trees. Later he
preached in a "homely thing like a barn." In a fire on January
17, 1608, he lost his books and everything except the clothes
on his back—yet none did "ever see him repine." A few months
later he was dead.)

The Church of England, however, was split by dissensions at
home, and soon there was civil war. The attitude of the colonial
governments often came to be that of the governor of Virginia
in 1692; when he was reminded that the colonists had souls to
be saved, he snapped out, "Souls! Damn your souls! Make
tobacco!"

The Pilgrims, you might think, must have been better off,
but in some ways it was even worse. During the first two years
there was no minister there, and no one received the sacrament. Even when the company sent them a minister, he
turned out to be a Church of England man, and there was
nothing but trouble with him until they sent him home.
Finally they got a good Separatist minister, but that left all the
Non-separatists (like Captain Miles Standish) outside the
Church.

With the Dutch in New Netherland religion had even less
auspicious beginnings than in Virginia and Plymouth. During
the first few years of the colony there were apparently no
church services at all. In 1626 informal services were being
held, but a real minister did not arrive until 1628.

Of the early colonies only Massachusetts and Connecticut

seem to have maintained some kind of efficient religious organization.

When the colonists began to spread out and settle in the back-country, religion lapsed still further. Travel being what it was in those days, people tended to lose all touch with a church. It is rather amusing to find that this problem was recognized as early as 1632. Such a crisis then occurred in Plymouth Plantation, and William Bradford lamented: "This, I fear, will be the ruin of New England, at least of the churches of God there."

Even in Massachusetts this scattering was seen to be a peril. Johnson, writing about 1650, tells how the settlers got out of touch with the Church:

The husbandman, whose over-eager pursuit of the fruits of the earth made some of them many times run out so far in the wilderness, even out of the sweet sound of the silver trumpets [obviously figurative language] blown by the laborious ministers of Christ, forsaking the assembly of the Lord's people, to celebrate their Sabbaths in the chimney-corner—horse, kine, sheep, goats, and swine being their most endeared companions.

This scattering of population made the maintenance of churches particularly difficult in the southern colonies where there were few towns. Many travelers commented upon the lack of religion in the South. Jasper Danckaerts noted in 1679:

The lives of the planters in Maryland and Virginia are very godless and profane. They . . . have neither church nor cloister. Sometimes there is some one who is called a minister, who does not as elsewhere, serve in one place . . . but travels for profit, and for that purpose visits the plantations through the country. . . . You often hear that these ministers are worse than anybody else, yea, are an abomination.[3]

[3]Although the great majority of early ministers were God-fearing and conscientious, we find also a good many mentions of unministerial ones, such as the Swedish Lars Lokenius, described in 1657 in a Dutch ac-

In 1704 the Reverend John Blair tried to act as a minister in North Carolina, but found the population so scattered around that he could accomplish little: "I rode one day with another, Sundays only excepted, about thirty miles per diem in the worst roads that ever I saw; and have sometimes lain whole nights in the woods."

Even when Southerners gathered together into a town, they displayed little evidence of religion. William Byrd commented of Edenton in 1728: "I believe this is the only metropolis [capital city] in the Christian or Mahometan world, where there is neither church, chapel, mosque, synagogue, or any other place of public worship of any sect or religion whatsoever."

In the backwoods districts along the North Carolina-Virginia line Byrd found conditions even worse, if possible. The people did not know Sunday from the weekdays: "any more than Robinson Crusoe did." Yet, a generation or two before, the ancestors of these people had been attending church on Sundays and doffing their caps to the vicar every day. In the forest all this had changed—not because the descendants were more vicious than the ancestors, but merely because there was no church to attend and no vicar for hat-doffing. The land was determining.

After the middle of the eighteenth century the situation improved a little, but up to that time, as W. W. Sweet puts it in his *Story of Religion in America*, "Only a small percentage of the population were members of the colonial churches."

Many of our older historians, who must have been a rather

---

count: "This Lutheran preacher is a man of impious and scandalous habits, a wild, drunken, unmannerly clown, more inclined to look into the wine can than into the Bible. He would prefer drinking brandy two hours to preaching one; and when the sap is in the wood his hands itch and he wants to fight whomsoever he meets."

pious lot, seem to have passed the matter over. Most Americans grow up with the idea, vaguely absorbed in school and from reading, that in colonial days everyone was godly and churchgoing. This has the result of making the thoughtful person believe that at some time there must have been a great defection from religion, to produce the half of our population that is at present unchurched. But this condition goes back, not so very different, clear to the beginning. The ancestry of the unchurched may or may not be honorable, but is at least ancient.

The great, unorganized mass that is the unchurched cannot, however, trace its ancestry back to European sources. It originated on this side of the Atlantic, and resulted from the conditions of the land itself. In the great forest no churches were standing and no ministers waiting. The people came ashore and got a head start of the ministers and the churches.

Moreover, a good many of the people, so to speak, kept ahead of the ministers all the way across the continent. A frontier community was likely to be a decade old before it boasted a church. Even if a Methodist circuit rider had turned up before that time, he could not do much, on his occasional rounds, except fight a delaying action against the Devil. If there had not been so many sects, it would have helped, but the day of the union church scarcely arrived till the twentieth century.

Agricultural communities were a little more godly than mining camps, but of the latter, in California, it has been maintained: "First the saloonkeeper, then the gambler, then the newspaper editor, and then the minister." Some cynics have even held that the prostitute arrived in third or fourth place.

The churches, none too wealthy even in the more settled communities, often did their best to send out missionaries. As an example, the story of the churching of California after 1849 is a magnificent one, particularly as regards the work of the

Catholics and Methodists. But there, as everywhere else, it was all another case of too little and too late. It could not have been otherwise. Lacking unity, centralization, and official sanction, the churches deserve praise for having done even as well as they did. In spite of their comparative failure, Sweet comments: "The greatest achievement of the American churches has been the extension of their work westward across the vast stretches of the continent." But he adds: "keeping abreast with the restless and ever moving population," a conclusion that seems too optimistic.

The total results of the failure of the churches to keep up with the settlement may be startlingly shown in many ways. For instance, we think of the Irish as being staunchly Catholic, their religion reinforced by strong sentimental and nationalistic forces. Yet considerable numbers of Irish names will be found among the unchurched and on Protestant rolls. These latter probably represent cases in which an Irish immigrant was unchurched, and then later—either he or a descendant—returned to a church, but not his ancestral one.

If we take typical Irish names and check them in a list where religious affiliation is given, the defection even of the Irish is striking. In a recent volume of Who's Who, of people named Kelly, Kelley, Casey, and Sweeney (all good Irish names), only 28 per cent listed themselves as Roman Catholic. Of the others, 23 per cent were down as members of Protestant churches, such as the Episcopalian, Presbyterian, and Methodist. Finally, 49 per cent declared no religious affiliation at all. Some of these last are perhaps to be counted as Catholics, but they can scarcely be very strong Catholics if they did not think it worth-while so to state when preparing their biographies for Who's Who.

3

So far, this discussion of our religion has chiefly been concerned with demonstrating that the proportion of the unchurched was as large in early times as it is now—if not, indeed,
larger. Just as necessary, however, it is to demonstrate the historical background of the other half, those that are listed in the
church rolls.

There was also, certainly, this other side of it in the colonies.
Far in the backwoods, the Devil might prevail, but godliness
had its strongholds in the towns and villages, especially in New
England. There is an old saying: "Where a man's bread is,
there is his fatherland." It could just as well be worded:
"Where a pious man goes, there he takes his church." And
many pious men and women came to America.

That is about all there is to the history of the colonial
churches. Church of England people came to Virginia, and so
there was a Church of England there. Separatists came to New
England, and eventually we have the Congregational Church.
Presbyterians from northern Ireland and from Scotland came
to New Jersey and Pennsylvania, and from there spread into all
the back-country toward the South. So we have the Presbyterian Church. A few English Catholics came to Maryland and
spread over into Pennsylvania, establishing a Catholic toehold.
Quakers and German sectarians settled in Pennsylvania. Where
the Dutch settled, they established the Dutch form of Protestantism. The interesting point is that all these churches had
originated elsewhere, and merely came into the colonies with
the immigrants.

The proportions, moreover, must have remained about the
same. All the churches lost members to the great mass of the

unchurched, as the frontier advanced. The smaller and stricter churches doubtless held on to their members better than the large and loose ones did. But the fact that there were, at the time of the Revolution, many more Congregationalists than Catholics means essentially, not that the Congregationalists had converted more people in the colonies or had lost fewer, but merely that more of them had come across originally in the ships.

The era of the Revolution is a very important one, and we can do well to take a look at the religious situation of that time and in connection with the Revolution itself.

First of all, there were the Deists, who were very few in numbers and are perhaps to be considered merely a part of the unchurched, since they had no organization of their own and merely held to a belief in God. In spite of the smallness of their numbers, they exercised a large influence, and supplied a good deal of the ideology through a few men—especially Franklin, Jefferson, and Paine.

The Church of England showed its connections by its name, and this connection was not in name only. Among its members were included the people who were most English by tradition and sentiment. Many of them, including nearly all of the clergy, remained Loyalists. This church thus suffered heavily both in numbers and in prestige, especially when the Loyalists emigrated by many thousands. Nevertheless, from the old Church of England came some of the most notable of the Revolutionary leaders, including Washington himself.

Washington's own position in the Church is interesting, and is wholly characteristic of colonial times. He attended church, but did not consider himself a member and did not take communion. In any other part of the Christian world at that time a man of his temperament and social position would certainly have been a church member.

The two great Revolutionary churches were the Presbyterian and the Congregational. From them came the secondary leaders and a great mass of the fighting men in the Continental Army. Shoulder to shoulder with them marched the unchurched, along with men from the smaller churches—Methodists, Baptists, Lutherans, and Catholics.

The conscientious objectors of the time were supplied from the Quakers and the smaller German sects, among whom Pacifism had always been an article of faith.

In religion, as in politics, the results of the Revolution were important. The old Church of England, now become the Episcopalian, was in a much weakened position. The Congregationalists and the Presbyterians were strong, almost dominant, in numbers and prestige. Since the war, like all wars, had had a demoralizing effect, the unchurched were more numerous than before. Of minor importance at that time, but destined to have important results in the future, was the improved position of the Catholics. Under the astute leadership of Charles Carroll of Carrollton they had joined strongly in the Revolution, and had fought in the army. Like the Nisei in World War II, what had been a small and suspected minority emerged from a war, having given bloody proof of their desire to be Americans. From that time on, religious and political discrimination against Catholics grew weaker.

4

After the Revolution, history resumed its interrupted course. Again the ships began to dock at New York and Philadelphia and a dozen other ports, and again the immigrants, pouring ashore, either kept their old religion, or took the opportunity to break away from churches altogether. Nevertheless, this post-Revolutionary period supplies the most notable exceptions in this general process—in the growth of the Methodists and the Baptists.

Methodism had originated in England as an offshoot of the Church of England in the middle of the eighteenth century. About 1765 two lay preachers brought it to the colonies. A decade later the Methodists numbered only a few thousand, chiefly in Maryland and Virginia. At the beginning of the Revolution they were somewhat embarrassed by the strong Toryism of their English founders, the Wesley brothers. As the war progressed, however, the American wing triumphed, and the Methodists became strongly devoted to the Revolutionary cause. At the end of the war they quickly organized as a wholly American church, and were ready for the future. This future was to be a great one.

In those post-Revolutionary years, the Methodists became pre-eminently an evangelizing and proselyting church. Demanding no high standard of education among their ministers, the Methodists required zeal and vigor. Like foraging hussars, their circuit riders swarmed across the backwoods districts, stopping at every log cabin, not to plunder, but to offer the gospel. They preached an optimistic theology of salvation by good works, and such a theology—that a man should be saved by his own efforts—appealed to the American frontiersman. Probably of even more importance, Methodism offered an emotional warmth, and a proselyting zeal that was infectious. In 1780 there were fewer than 9,000 Methodists; a generation later it was a major church.

Unlike the Methodists, the Baptists had been present in the colonies from the beginning, or very close to it. Their center was in Rhode Island, but for nearly two centuries they remained a small church. They supported the Revolution vigorously, and afterward were ready for their great expansion. Like the Methodists, they were proselyters, and they profited by considering that "the call" was more important for a preacher than a training in theology and Hebrew. The Methodists had their circuit riders, but the Baptists had their farmer-preachers. These latter supported themselves by their own labors during the agricultural season, and then went out to spread the gospel during the rest of the year. Within a generation the Baptists, too, became a leading denomination.[4]

Any pressure can be expected to move more easily to fill a vacuum than to push back other pressures. In this way the Methodists and Baptists grew, not by converting Presbyterians and Congregationalists, but by moving into the vacuum left, particularly in the South, by the weakening of the old Church of England. The two churches also grew by taking over great numbers of the unchurched frontier people. The growth of these two churches eventually transformed the South from our least religious into our most religious region. Also by becoming strong in the South, the Methodists and Baptists brought Christianity to the slaves. At the present time seven eighths of Negro church members are of these two denominations.

This post-Revolutionary growth of these two major churches, important though it is, is only an exceptional manifestation of a native development. Immigration still remained the dominating influence. Down to 1840 newcomers were chiefly from Great Britain and northern Ireland, and thus were

[4] In spite of being a humorist, Mark Twain is not to be disregarded as a realist, and his picture of the farmer-preacher Silas Phelps in *Huckleberry Finn* (Chapter 33) is a thumbnail sketch worth remembering: "He was the innocentest, best old soul I ever see. But it warn't surprising; because he warn't only just a farmer, he was a preacher, too, and had a little one-horse log church down back of the plantation, which he built it himself at his own expense, for a church and schoolhouse, and never charged nothing for his preaching, and it was worth it, too. There was plenty other farmer-preachers like that, and done the same way, down South."

traditionally Protestant. After 1840, when southern Irish began
to dominate the immigration, the Catholic Church spurted
ahead. After 1848 thousands of German Catholics arrived, and
still later came the inpouring of Italians, Poles, French Cana-
dians, and Mexicans.

Another church to grow greatly because of late-nineteenth-
century immigration was the Lutheran. Between 1870 and
1910, 1,750,000 Scandinavians poured in. Actually, however,
history repeated itself in this detail also, and only a small proportion of these newcomers joined their hereditary Lutheran
Church—or, apparently, any other. According to estimates,
only 7 per cent of the Danes, not more than 20 per cent of the
Swedes, and less than 30 per cent of the Norwegians established relations with any church.

For our smaller churches the story is the same—both as to
growth through immigration and as to failure to absorb any
large proportion of the immigrants. . . . Until 1867 there was
no Greek Orthodox church in the United States. At that time
a large enough number of Greek immigrants had assembled
in one spot to make the formation of a church possible. After
1890 Greek immigration soared, and the Church now claims a
membership of one million. Such a figure as this last, however,
is particularly instructive. If this church claims (1952) 320
congregations, but a total of one million members, there must
be about three thousand members for every congregation. The
million must, therefore, represent an estimate of the total
number of Greeks in the United States, and the potential
rather than the actual participants. The conclusion must be
that the Greeks, like other people, have largely drifted into the
mass of the unchurched. That the Church, however, should
count them as members is not altogether without reason. In
Greece itself membership is taken for granted, and the church

66 AMERICAN WAYS OF LIFE

authorities in the United States are apparently making the same assumption. Here, however, it is probably unwarranted. In the United States, these unchurched Greeks, if they or their children or grandchildren return to religion, will be just about as likely to show up as Roman Catholics or Baptists.

The older churches—those that had seen the country through the hard years of the Revolution and the young republic—did not view their own comparative submergence with entire equanimity, although in general they accepted it supinely. They sent out a few missionaries to labor among the immigrants. In 1867 the Baptists had forty-seven workers among immigrant Germans, Dutch, French, Welsh, and Scandinavians. But in that decade of the sixties nearly three million immigrants landed, and such a comparatively small effort by a major church indicates the hopelessness of the attempt. The Baptists and Methodists had some success among the Germans and Scandinavians; the Presbyterians, among the Italians. But in all periods the great masses of our immigrants have either kept to their traditional churches or drifted away from churches altogether.

5

In the main, then, the complexity of the religious structure of the United States arises chiefly from immigration and from the conditions of the land itself; native developments, however, have also been of importance. This could, indeed, hardly have been otherwise. The colonies were peopled by Protestants, and chiefly by the more radical sectarians who represented the very "dissidence of dissent." The birthright of our Christianity was therefore the idea of the "come-outer." No one could expect that people with such a tradition would cease to proliferate into new sects just because they came to another country. In fact, probably no year has passed without the preaching of some new gospel.

Nevertheless, the total result in the history of world religion is as yet negligible. In more than three centuries no Zoroaster or Buddha or Mohammed has arisen. No new faith has begun to count its adherents by the tens of millions and to spread a new color over the map of the world's religions. From the point of view of a neutral observer, such as a Taoist or an atheist, the striking facts about these new developments are their great number and their slight differences one from another.[5]

In the early nineteenth century, for example, the followers of Thomas Campbell and his son Alexander split from the Presbyterians, joined with the Baptists for a while, withdrew from the Baptists taking some thousands of members along, united with a church calling themselves simply "Christians" and incorporating many former Methodists, and now form a body known officially as the "Disciples of Christ," numbering nearly two million members. Yet all this ferment sprang from what now seem minuscule theological causes, and at no point in the history would any of the "Campbellites" have thought of themselves for a moment as non-Protestants, much less, as non-Christians.

Somewhat more radical as religious leaders were Joseph Smith and Mary Baker Eddy. Yet their two very American churches proclaim their Christianity, even in their official

[5]Some argue that the last three centuries have not been highly "creative" in religion anywhere, and that there has been more religious forment in the United States than there has been elsewhere. But this is doubtful. Baha'ism has perhaps affected the lives of more people than either Mormonism or Christian Science. In a negative sense, the influence of both the French Revolution and the Russian Revolution has been profound.

names, as the Church of Christ, Scientist, and the Church of Jesus Christ of Latter-Day Saints.

Dissent and separatism have continued to be characteristic of religion in the United States down to the present time. As the older and larger churches become more prosperous and conservative, the tendency has been for their less educated members to break away, and found some new church, dedicated to more literal belief in the Bible and to more emotionalism in church services.

Judaism also has followed the prevailing pattern, and has split into several American branches. Roman Catholicism still seems to present a united front, and thus to afford an exception to the rule. Actually, however, it has not wholly escaped. In Arizona a few thousand Papago Indians are known as Sonora Catholics, and go their own ways. Other schisms have also occurred. The Ukrainians in their homeland accepted the Pope, but were allowed certain unorthodox practices, such as a mass in their own language and a married clergy. When many Ukrainians entered the United States, they wished to have their old customs, but such heresies could not be allowed, once the Ukrainians were living closely with other Roman Catholics. The result was showdown, and many of the Ukrainians separated, to become the Ukrainian Orthodox Church of America. A somewhat similar history resulted in what is probably the most fully and specifically named of all our sects— the Carpatho-Russian Greek Catholic Orthodox Christian Church, U.S.A.

In connection with the multiplication of sects, the influence of the land itself should not be forgotten. Its very size and emptiness permitted sects to find room for survival. A striking example is the flight of Roger Williams from Massachusetts in 1636, to find refuge in the forests along Narragansett Bay and thus make possible the establishment of the Baptists. Even more spectacular was the migration of the Mormons to Utah in 1847. In a smaller country many sects might well have been wholly suppressed.

The influence of international ideas has on the whole been of negligible importance. This is only to be expected. The last three centuries have not been notable for the development of major religious ideas anywhere in the world. Within the last century the Salvation Army (originating in England) and Baha'ism (originating in Iran) furnish examples of religious bodies that have established themselves in the United States essentially not by immigration of people but by immigration of ideas. The influence of such a non-American theologian as Karl Barth may also be noted, but can certainly not be claimed as a major factor.

As of more importance might be cited the international influence of Deism, Darwinism, and other ideas of the eighteenth and nineteenth centuries which caused a drift away from the churches throughout the Christian world.

6

Certain other general features of our religious history call for brief comment. . . . One of these is the strong tradition of religious freedom without which the extreme multiplication of sects would have been difficult or impossible. From our present vantage point, if we look back at the religious intoleration of the early colonies, we are likely to think that religious freedom was achieved only late and with difficulty. We must remember, however, the situation in other countries at the same time—as in Spain, where the Inquisition was in full power. Relatively speaking, religious freedom was characteristic of the colonies even from the beginning. This was truer in practice than in theory. Laws to restrict religious freedom might stand on the books, but such laws were difficult to enforce in loosely organized frontier communities, and frequently little attempt was made to do so. Moreover, one effect of the large numbers of unchurched citizens has always been to make more difficult any persecution of one particular sect.

A second general feature is the prevailing moral flavor of our Christianity. Partly because religion is a personal matter and not a mere concomitant of citizenship, church members in the United States, on the average, have taken their membership somewhat seriously and have regulated their living by their religion. The most striking example is the split of three major churches, North and South, because of slavery. Frequently it is held up as a religious scandal that such a schism should have occurred. Granted that in some ways this is true, the split shows a high religious ideal.

Slavery may originally have been an economic question but it became a social question, and then a moral one. Having become a moral one, it inevitably, in America, moved to the position of a religious one. The Catholics could not divide because their main policy was decided outside the United States. The Episcopalians did not split, for they represented, more than any other Protestant sect, the tradition of the somewhat easygoing established church. The Congregationalists did not split because they had little southern representation. But with Presbyterians, Baptists, and Methodists, the rift was wide and complete. Neither side would compromise with what it vehemently considered to be the Mammon of Unrighteousness. Regrettable as the catastrophe may have been, it shows that our great churches considered their religion a seven-day business, not merely a parade for Sundays, and the extremity and violence of the action are thoroughly American.

It might also be pointed out that, while the church and

state have been separated in the United States, the government has never been anti-religious or anti-church. On the whole, as between the churched and the unchurched, the government has swung toward the former. Nearly all presidents have made a point of attending religious services, and he would be a bold politician who would openly proclaim himself to be without church affiliation. Many of our coins bear the inscription "In God we trust," although there is no specification of what the attributes of this God shall be or what church He favors. One of our stamps bore the faces of four chaplains. The not infrequent pronouncement: "This is a Christian country," seems to meet no refutation from any of the unchurched, or even from the Jews.

In general, the unchurched are also the inarticulate. Partly this is because they have been traditionally drawn largely from the less educated and lower classes. Partly it is because they are unorganized, having by necessity only a negative bond, which can scarcely be called a union at all. Partly it is that from the Revolution onward, the great Protestant sects have been strongly nationalistic, so that an unreligious attitude can often be made to seem somewhat un-American. Thus the attempt of an atheist to be given a turn to speak over the radio, on the grounds of freedom of religion, is likely to meet frenzied resistance. Similarly, when a letter in a correspondence column mildly points out that "religious freedom" also means "freedom to have no religion," there is a great raising of hackles. If the writer had declared that he wished to become a Mohammedan or reinstitute the worship of Olympian Zeus and therefore invoked his constitutional rights of religious freedom, he would merely have been stating a commonplace and would probably not have been honored with a single reply. It is noteworthy that in the recent un-American activities investigation (1953) many different groups were accused, but only when the churches were said to be harboring disloyal elements was the reaction vigorous and effective.

Nevertheless the stupendous mass of the unchurched, extending from the highest to the lowest of society, can never be forgotten. In one sense, the existence of this tremendous number of people without religion is the most characteristic feature of religion in the United States.

7

Some further comparison of our linguistic and our religious history is of interest. If we take some early date, say 1700, we find the status of the two somewhat similar. Though English is everywhere official, the linguistic situation is complicated. Dutch is spoken widely in New York and New Jersey. A few Swedes, unable to speak English, still linger by the Delaware. German is the prevailing language in large parts of Pennsylvania. Other groups speak Welsh or French. Even English is spoken in a variety of dialects. By comparison, the religious situation of 1700 is less complex. Practically every citizen is either a member of a Protestant sect, or else looks back to the time when he or his father was a member of such a sect "in the old country."

As time went on, however, the linguistic situation became simpler until it finally approached unity, but the religious situation increased in complexity. The reasons for our linguistic unity have already been presented, and so have some of those for our religious diversity.

Still another reason for this diversity lies in a traditional American (or possibly universal) attitude toward religion. From the very beginning we did not really expect a man to change his faith. Religion was something you died for, not something you let yourself be argued out of. Shifts between such theologically close churches as the Congregational and the Presbyterian were of course accepted. In marriage it was assumed that the wife followed her husband from one Protestant sect to another. But for a grown man to allow himself to be deliberately converted from Methodism to Episcopalianism or from being a Friend to being a Lutheran suggested something fickle in the man himself, possibly even shady. The same attitude can be seen in the not uncommon feeling of a "cradle Catholic" toward a convert. Thus, while an original linguistic diversity progressed toward unity, an original religious diversity remained, and even grew more diverse.

Another closely related feeling contributed to prevent the early churches from absorbing the immigrants. Often churches did not want others to enter their chosen group. They did not seek converts, and even feared that the outsiders on entering their congregation would corrupt it. In many sects, membership was a kind of aristocratic privilege, to be attained only by the few who were deemed worthy. In an attempt to increase membership without corrupting the inner sanctum, Congregationalism once established a so-called Halfway Covenant, permitting a kind of second-class church membership.

In summation, we can say that the complicated religious situation of the present United States springs chiefly from hereditary factors. Not only the early immigration, as with language, has determined the results, but also the more recent and still continuing immigration. In addition, the influence of the land has been important. Native developments have played a secondary role. International ideas have not counted for much.

To anticipate the next chapter, we may compare the history of our religion with the history of our food. The two show much in common. Just as we have great variety of churches, so we have of foods—and, with both, chiefly because of immigration. Just as we assume that an American named Joe Fuselli probably likes spaghetti and that an American named Wan Fong probably eats a good deal of rice, so we go by churches.

The analogy, indeed, is not perfect. The same man may with equanimity eat spaghetti on Wednesday and rice on Thursday, but he can scarcely so shift from Catholicism to Confucianism. In short, the problem of spaghetti vs. rice, of "alimentary freedom," is unlikely to rise to the level of a major political problem. But a question of the future in our religious history may well be whether any sect, having grown strong under a system of religious freedom, will bring sectarianism into politics toward the end of restricting that freedom for others, including the freedom of the unchurched not to believe.

CHAPTER 4

FOOD — 1

In the development of our language and religion, the environment has been of minor importance; in
food it has exercised a strong influence. The reason is not
difficult to see. Early colonization occurred under primitive
conditions, and food was often a primary consideration. The
colonists were often under the necessity of eating what was
available, and this might mean eating the food of the country,
or going hungry. Once they had begun to eat it, they often
developed a liking for it. On the other hand, food habits are
tenacious, and some of these were carried from the old country
with the immigrants.

The situation is therefore involved. In American food there
is a large environmental element mingled with a large hereditary element, and the two are often so intimately mingled
as to be scarcely separated with certainty. To present a complex subject more clearly, we shall first consider meats; next,
cereals and various miscellaneous foods.[1]

[1]The focus will be chiefly upon foodstuffs, rather than upon cookery.
The two, however, are not always easy to separate, and so the methods
of food preparation will occasionally be presented.

To demonstrate our present habits of meat-eating, a table serves most readily. In 1950, according to the Bureau of Agricultural Economics, the average citizen of the United States ate, in pounds:

Beef and veal....................	70.9
Lamb and mutton	4.0
Pork	68.8
Fish	11.5
Chicken	27.0
Turkey	5.0

Even a cursory glance at the table reveals certain striking facts. First quantitatively, the total consumption of meat is extremely high. This may be considered primarily an environmental factor, for in proportion to the number of its inhabitants the productiveness of the United States is extremely large. But this liking for meat may also be considered, to some degree, an inherited trait. The British Isles, and northwestern Europe in general, possess considerable expanses of excellent pastureland, and the people of those regions have always been able to eat more meat, especially beef, than the people of such a region as the Mediterranean basin.

Of even more interest, however, are the proportions that the various meats bear to one another. To begin with, we should note that certain meats are lacking altogether from the list, their consumption being so small as not to be considered worth recording. There is no listing for goat flesh or for horse meat. Others are lower than might be expected—lamb and mutton, and fish. But beef, pork, and chicken are extremely high, and so too is turkey in comparison with its consumption in most countries.

As for the reasons for these distinctions, the simplest thing to do would be merely to conclude that the people of the United States happened to like beef and pork better than lamb, or else that these meats happen to be cheaper. But various more basic reasons can be suggested.

Some of these are environmental. In a continental country the consumption of fish is likely to be low. Before the improvements of modern transportation and refrigeration, in fact, many districts of the United States scarcely knew fish at all, and could therefore develop no habit of eating it. Traditionally and even now, the consumption of fish varies greatly with regions, being greatest along the seacoast. New England, close to the Newfoundland banks, could make the codfish an important part of its diet. The areas around Chesapeake Bay and New Orleans could also be famous for their seafoods. But these districts form only the fringe of the country. Even a few miles inland, under primitive conditions, fresh fish must have been a comparative rarity, and the difficulties of transportation made even salt fish expensive.

But there is also a hereditary factor—to be seen most strikingly in the absence of horse meat from the table. This absence cannot be for reasons of health, for horse meat is nutritious. It cannot be for any sound reasons of unpalatability, for many peoples eat horse meat with gusto. It cannot be economic, for horse meat is so cheap that it forms the basic ration of many American dogs. It cannot, finally, be environmental, for horses thrive over great areas of the country.

Almost certainly, the absence of horse meat from our diet can be put down as a hereditary quality. The peoples of northwestern Europe have not traditionally eaten horses, though the custom has developed in France and elsewhere rather recently. Some have suggested that this taboo is a mixed-up remnant of pagan religious scruples—that horses were sacred to Odin. More likely, the prohibition may have arisen because horses were originally too rare and expensive and too valuable for warfare. In any case, though nowhere supported by law or religion, the American objection to this meat has been traditionally almost as strong as the Jewish objection to pork.

Incidents could be collected to prove the point. . . . During one of the "starving times" a few years after the first settlement of Virginia the chronicler records the eating of a mare, but he does so in the same sentence that tells of incidents of cannibalism, and he apparently considers the one to be about as unnatural as the other. More than two centuries later, during a time of short rations on the California frontier, a very hungry man was served up a tender "filet of filly," which he supposed to be beef and ate with great relish. After he had finished, some joker showed him the mane and tail of the animal that he had just been eating, and in revulsion he vomited up his whole badly needed meal.

2

To consider, however, meats that are actually eaten, we should approach the matter historically. . . . The first colonists found the Indians, except for an occasional eating of dog, wholly dependent upon game for their meat. Aside from a little salt meat that they may have brought with them, the colonists were also dependent on game for their meat ration. But the early colonists were not born frontiersmen and trained hunters, and to such people a game supply is highly unreliable. After starving along through the late summer of 1607 and making do on sturgeon, oysters, and crabs, the Jamestown colonists suddenly had a surfeit of meat in the autumn when the rivers were covered with swans, ducks, and geese, and even the woods were full of "divers sorts of wild beasts as fat as we could eat them." Then came a starving time again.

But a feast-or-famine regime is as unhealthy for a community as for an individual and anyone could see, after this year, that domestic animals were necessary to insure a steady supply of meat. Besides, though they could eat "aroughcuns and opassums" if necessary (that is to say, coons and possums) they must have hungered for beef and pork and good chicken-pasty —not to mention milk and eggs. As Johan Printz, governor of New Sweden in the early years of that colony, put the matter with a bluntness that becomes eloquence: "It is impossible to colonize the land without cattle."

But what animals should they bring? As far as meat was concerned, the English had depended chiefly upon cattle, sheep, and swine, but also made use of goats and domestic fowls. These creatures have all been associated with man for so long that we think of them as naturally, given the necessary care, living almost any place a man can live. But actually, in their native habitats, they differ considerably, and in the primitive conditions of the new colony these differences were of importance.

Cattle take most naturally to a country of mingled woodland and grassland; they thrive in well-watered and even swampy pastureland. Sheep, on the contrary, need dry grassy uplands. Goats are browsers, and do best neither in forest nor on grassland, but in brush country. Swine are forest lovers, and also take well to swamps. Chickens also were originally jungle fowl, and therefore adapt themselves to a forest, or at least to its edges. Both swine and chickens, moreover, have that great advantage that man also shares—they are practically omnivorous.

Remembering that the eastern United States was originally a thick forest, and placing this against the natural habitat of the various domestic animals, we can easily see the influence of environment, doubtless even on our present meat-eating habits.

A low-lying forested country, almost wholly lacking in grass, was hostile to sheep. England was one of the great wool-producing countries, and the first English colonists made attempts to introduce sheep. "Some sheep" are mentioned as being in Virginia in 1609, but apparently they did not flourish. A listing of the stock of a Virginia plantation in 1623 includes poultry, hogs, cows, goats, and horses—but no sheep. Sheep were brought to New Netherland about 1625, but in 1650 an observer mentions cattle and swine, but not sheep. A few were brought to New England in 1633, but there also they do not seem to have been successful. The settlers who emigrated to Connecticut in 1635 are recorded to have taken with them their horses, cows, and swine—but again no mention of sheep.

The forest was inhospitable to them, not only because it supplied little grass, but also because it harbored wolves, which were more destructive to sheep than to the other domestic animals. The story is the same everywhere. Even as late as 1666 a eulogist of Maryland was forced to confess that the colony could not "boast of her plenty of sheep here, as other countries . . . Few desire them, because they commonly draw down the wolves among the plantations."

Eventually the forests were cut back and the grass grew, and eventually the wolves were reduced in numbers or exterminated. In 1642 it was noted of Massachusetts: "the Lord hath been pleased to increase sheep extraordinarily of late," and their number was estimated at three thousand, but this was only a quarter the number of the cattle even yet. By 1661 New England was exporting sheep to New Amsterdam. A report on Carolina for 1682 read: "they [sheep] thrive very well, the country being so friendly to their natures"—although in such vague statements we must, as always, suspect the optimism of the land developer. In any case, by the time the land had been rendered hospitable to sheep, many colonists had got out of the habit of keeping them and of eating mutton.

Apparently as a substitute for the unsuitable sheep, the colonists tried goats. In Virginia an actual count reported eighty-eight of them in 1617. Goats, and also domestic rabbits, were introduced into New Netherland before 1625. Goats came early to New England also. A French ship unloaded six at Charlestown in 1630, the first year of the Massachusetts Bay colony.

Living upon twigs and leaves instead of grass, goats could do better than sheep in the forests. They were also more able to take care of themselves against wild beasts. But, like the sheep, the goats could not really fit into the American environment. The Connecticut emigrants apparently did not think it worth-while to take any of them along. By the middle of the century it was reported of Lynn, Massachusetts, that "Goats which were in great esteem at their [the settlers'] first coming, are now almost quite banished." Environmentally, the goat was really neither here nor there. In the forest he could get along, but not thrive particularly. Once the forest was cleared, the land went to grass, not to brush, and so was better suited to cattle and sheep than to goats.

Just as England was good sheep country, so it was good cattle country, and the English were accustomed to having "neat-cattle" as the common term then was. They soon brought bulls and cows to all their colonies, and these apparently managed to get along well enough. Serious difficulties were that they were large and so were difficult to transport across the ocean, and that they bred slowly. Though 100 cattle were landed at Jamestown in 1611 alone, only 128 were counted in 1617. The chief reason for this slow increase is probably that the colonists found themselves too hungry for beef and veal, and so killed off animals that they should have kept for breeding purposes. Such a possibility is strongly suggested by legislation of 1619 that forbade anyone to "kill any neat cattle whatsoever, young or old, especially kine, heifers, or cow-calves" without permission from the governor.

In New England three heifers and a bull were landed at Plymouth in 1624 as "the first beginning of any cattle of that kind in the land." In 1625 the Dutch successfully supplied New Netherland with cattle, and other animals also, by means of ships especially equipped for oceanic transportation of livestock.[2]

Once the breeding stock had been built up, the cattle flourished, and later colonies were stocked from the already established ones. The story of New Sweden is illustrative. Before Governor Printz arrived in 1643 the colony had only two head of cattle. Three more arrived in the same ship with Printz. In that year or the next, he managed to purchase seven oxen and one cow from New Netherland, though at a high price. Printz, who obviously loved his cows, again reported officially in 1647 —the original five had increased to ten, and the purchased cattle were now fourteen oxen and one cow. In this year he expressed hopes of buying cattle in Virginia, good evidence that the herds there had prospered.

By this time the cattle industry was definitely on the upgrade. A description of Carolina in 1666 declares that the

[2]These were very ingeniously constructed vessels. Each carried about fifty horses and cattle, each in a separate stall, with a floor of sand. Water was carried under a kind of false deck, so cleverly contrived that visitors to the ships could not discover where it was stowed. Thence it was pumped up for use. Besides the larger animals, the ships carried swine and sheep, and also plows and other agricultural implements. The passengers were mostly country people, who doubtless worked for part of their passage by taking care of the animals.

marshes and meadows supplied excellent pasturage for cattle, and suggests that the number of cattle was considerable. A note on Pennsylvania for 1683 reads: "Here is also plenty of cow-cattle." By 1698, it was reported for the same colony: "some farmers have forty, some sixty, and from that number to two or three hundred head of cattle." By 1700 obviously, cattle breeding had been well established, and Americans were assured of a steady supply of beef.

But if the success of the cattle in the colonies may be called satisfactory, that of the swine can only be termed spectacular. Their possibilities had been demonstrated even before the coming of the English. In 1539 Hernando de Soto landed in Florida with a well-equipped exploring expedition of Spaniards. He brought ashore also, as his own personal property, a small herd of swine. These were driven along with the expedition, which in the course of the next three years traversed a circuitous path of several thousand miles. De Soto allowed no swine to be killed, keeping them as a food reserve. Nevertheless, many of them must have died of natural causes or been stolen by hungry Indians or Spaniards, even at the risk of their own skins. Yet, when de Soto died, the herd amounted to seven hundred head!

Pigs had been common in England ever since Anglo-Saxon times when England itself had been a forested country. Doubtless also, some of the English leaders had read of the success of the Spaniards with swine in the New World. "Three sows" arrived at Jamestown with the First Supply in 1608, only a year after the foundation of the colony. They were accompanied, we may infer, by an indispensable but unspecified boar. Each sow must have littered twice in the first year, for at the end of that time the colonists rejoiced in a herd of "sixty and odd pigs." These were transported to an island some seven miles from Jamestown, still known as Hog Island. The pigs must soon have overrun its narrow limits. Only eight years later, in that same census of 1617 that enumerated 128 cattle and 88 goats, the pigs have got beyond counting, and the notation is merely "innumerable numbers of swine."

From the first, these pigs had been allowed to forage for themselves, and they took naturally to the Virginian woods and swamps. They met little competition, for there were no native pigs. They ate anything and everything—roots, berries, persimmons, nuts, acorns, snakes, the eggs and younglings of ground-nesting birds. They multiplied with great litters of ten or twelve. The winters were not severe enough to bother them greatly.

The problem, in fact, was to keep track of your pigs and see that they did not run wild. Many of them certainly did so. Indians picked off some of these strays; wolves and panthers accounted for many others. But the fecundity of the sows assured victory over such odds. Besides, the half-wild pig is a formidable animal. Thomas Ashe, describing Carolina in 1682, declares: "when the stock [of wild swine] increases and grows strong, the older surround the younger, and boldly oppose, and oftentimes attack their invaders." An early Virginia edict forbids anyone "to hunt deer or hogs without the governor's leave," as if hogs, only a few years after their first importation, were just as much wild animals as deer. Nevertheless, even though they ran wild, these swine were a potential food supply.

In New England swine multiplied also, though there the heavy snows and long-continued cold weather made them more dependent on men for shelter and food in the winters. Everywhere toward the South swine rapidly attained the same success that they had met in Virginia. In 1644 one boy was enough to take care of the Swedes' cattle, but for their swine they assigned two men and a boy. Our already cited description of Carolina in 1666 noted "hogs find so much mast and other

food in the woods, that they want no other care than a swine-
herd to keep them from running wild." Before long, indeed,
many escaped the swineherds, and in 1682 Thomas Ashe
noted of the swine of Carolina "great numbers forsake their
own plantations, running wild in the woods."

Along with a few dogs, chickens have the honor of being the
first domestic creatures brought to Jamestown. They must
have come on the first ships in 1607. Wingfield, the first
president, who left Virginia in May, 1608, records with pride
that "I had by my own housewifery bred above thirty seven
[chickens]." All but three of these, he tells, had gone into the
pot before he left, and doubtless most of those belonging to
other colonists had also failed to survive the starving time.

Nevertheless, there were enough cocks and hens left to serve
for breeding stock. A year later the record runs: "Near five
hundred chickens brought up themselves, without having any
meat [food] given them." From this time on, chickens—frequently foraging for themselves, at least in the summer—were
a regular accompaniment of any colonial settlement.[3]

The story of the turkey is more complex. Wild turkeys were
common in the American forest, and provided one of the most
plentiful supplies of game. But domestic turkeys had already
been introduced into England during the sixteenth century.
Readers of Shakespeare may remember the turkeys mentioned
in Henry IV, Part I. Our modern domestic turkeys are the
descendants of domestic ones brought across from England,
rather than a tamed race of the native wild turkey. The earliest
mentions of turkeys used for food refer to the wild birds, but
tame ones are noted at Jamestown in 1614. Wild turkeys,

[3]Needless to say, the production of eggs kept many a hen out of the
pot during times of short rations. Fried eggs for breakfast is an old
American custom—"eggs," because everyone kept hens, and "fried" because that was the commonest method of frontier cookery and because
there was usually some ham or bacon to grease the pan with.

however, remained a principal food supply for the frontiersman until well after 1800.[4]

Ducks and geese seem never to have been very important in England. Geese, in particular, are more characteristic of eastern Europe. Although domestic varieties were soon introduced into the colonies, and although wild varieties were common, neither of the birds has ever been among our important foods.[5]

3

On the whole, neither the influence of later immigration, nor native developments, nor international ideas seem greatly to have affected our meat-eating habits. The early northwestern European hereditary traits are evident and important in setting the taboo against horse meat, and probably in establishing a preference for the more popular meats. But the land itself has exerted an even stronger influence. This has been important in taking away any chance there was that we should be eaters of fish, mutton, or goat flesh. It has made turkey one of our national dishes. By enabling us to have an abundance of beef it has made us beef-eaters. Most striking of all, by receiving hospitably the fast-breeding and omnivorous chicken and pig, the land has assured that those two meats should be perhaps even more characteristic of our food than is beef. "A chicken

[4]Josselyn, however, writing about 1670 of northern New England, states: "some of the English bring up great store of the wild kind, which remain about their houses as tame as ours in England." Perhaps the English turkey, doubtless of Mexican ancestry, did not thrive so well in the Far North.

[5]Peacocks, pigeons, and domestic rabbits were brought to Jamestown within the first decade. Although none of these became economically important, pigeon pie remained a favorite dish down through the eighteenth century. William Byrd, in his diary, frequently mentions it.

in every pot" can become a political symbol, and *Chicken Every Sunday* the title of a popular book. "Pork chops" has become a phrase by which the labor unions symbolize economic advantage. The two even meet in alliance, and one of the most typical of our dishes is ham and eggs.

In all probability the figures already cited for chicken and pork are actually too low. Every year millions of chickens pass from yard to table without ever being recorded as statistics, and the same is true for numerous hogs on farms, and even in small towns, throughout the South and Middle West. Comparatively few cattle and sheep are thus slaughtered.

Throughout our history, in fact, heavy consumption of pork has been the general American tendency, especially among the less well-to-do. William Byrd of Westover, a leading Virginia gentleman of the early eighteenth century, has left us copious records of his meat-eating habits in his own diaries. He enjoyed a great variety—beef, veal, mutton, pork, fish, chicken, turkey, pigeon, game of many sorts. But when William Byrd went out to survey the boundary line between Virginia and North Carolina he found the inhabitants eating only pork. He wrote once of "a true Roanoke entertainment of pork upon pork, and pork again upon that," and again, "I made a North Carolina dinner upon fresh pork."

In addition to being easy to produce, pork has had the great advantage of being easy to preserve. It is, in fact, perhaps the only meat that may be made more palatable, as ham and bacon, by being cured.

Naturally enough, beloved though it is, pork has remained a plebeian dish. For a dress-up dinner an American chooses turkey for Thanksgiving or Christmas, and otherwise seems to alternate between fried chicken and beefsteak. Thus, indeed, one would interpret the phenomenon that along the highways of the land ten thousand restaurants proclaim chicken and steaks in neon lights. So also when prisoners are returned from Korea, a grateful republic offers its sons beefsteak, although some of them—especially if from south of the Mason-Dixon line—would undoubtedly prefer pork chops.

CHAPTER 5

FOOD—2

Equally as complicated as the history of our use of meat is that of our use of grains. . . . Traditionally, the English of the seventeenth century, like the other northwestern Europeans, grew four kinds of "corn"—wheat, barley, rye, and oats. The colonists brought seed with them, and set out to cultivate the old crops in the New World.

The first time, they must have strewn the precious seed with misgiving and fear. As farmers, they knew that weather and soil must be propitious. And who could know all the locusts and worms that America might bring forth, and what mysterious blasts and blights? Some of the more superstitious, or even some of the more religious, must have feared the hostile power of Hobomoko, the devil of the Indians, or of those nameless devils that sometimes, so it is recorded, could be heard roaring in the woods.

Occasionally there was failure, as when the colonists planted wheat at Plymouth in their first spring—"but it came not to good, either by badness of the seed, or lateness of the season, or both." And then their chronicler adds, as if to allow for stranger causes: "or some other defect."

Fortunately, however, there was no basic difficulty. Soil and climate were favorable, and the new grains encountered no unduly hostile insects or diseases. One is appalled to think what a difference it would have made in American life if these four grains, or even if wheat alone, had been found to be subject to some universal blight, as the European grapes were subject to phylloxera.

In most of the colonies some of the European grains were grown from the very beginning. The "corn" that the Jamestown men planted in their first spring was almost certainly European grain, doubtless of more than one kind, although because of the use of the word "corn" most Americans would incorrectly assume that it was maize. Wheat and barley are specifically mentioned as being raised in Virginia in 1614. The Plymouth people, as has been mentioned, also planted European grain at their first opportunity, and the settlers of Lynn, Massachusetts, put twenty acres into barley and oats their first year. As early as 1628 there was "winter grain" in New Netherland (which would have been wheat and rye), and "summer grain" (which may have included barley and oats too). By 1642 a writer describing that colony could report: "Our Netherlanders raise good wheat, rye, barley, oats," and from that time onward, certainly, we may consider that the four common European grains were fully naturalized in the colonies.

A complicating factor, not paralleled in the case of the domestic animals, was the possession by the Indians of one very valuable grain. The colonists became familiar with this "Indian corn" by getting it by gift or barter, or by stealing it from Indian storehouses, as the pious Pilgrims did on Cape Cod. From the Indians the colonists learned its culture. In every colony it soon came to be widely cultivated, and in most places it became the chief food crop.

Before long the colonies were raising six staple grains as

opposed to their traditional four. The last to appear was rice, which became an important money and food crop.

2

As with meats, the present situation can be most easily presented by a table showing the average *per capita* consumption in pounds for the year 1950[1]:

Wheat	136.3
Barley	1.6
Rye	1.5
Oats	3.0
Rice	5.0
Corn	33.2

The case of the grains may be presented by the consideration of each varity separately.

1) *Wheat.* As the table shows graphically, wheat is now the pre-eminent American grain for human consumption. The average American eats about three times as much of it as he eats of all the other grains combined. Wheat is important partly for environmental reasons, that is, much of the United States is admirable wheat-growing country, and the productivity of wheat is high. But also there is a hereditary influence. The English traditionally considered wheat to be the best of grains. Chaucer's Wife of Bath mentions barley bread as good enough for common people, and wheat bread as what a person would naturally take if he had the choice.

But much barley was raised in England, and eaten by human

[1]These figures include various food products, such as corn syrup and breakfast cereals, but do not include grain consumed in the form of beer and whiskey, or corn eaten as a vegetable or canned. Nor do the figures include grain that has been fed to animals and thus eaten by human beings indirectly.

beings. Why the Englishman thus preferred wheat but raised large amounts of barley may seem a little difficult to explain. Probably he raised barley for rotation of crops and also as a kind of insurance, because it might make a crop in years when wheat failed. Also, tradition being so strong a factor in farming, he may have raised barley because that was what he had always done.

But in the colonies tradition was broken. During the first hard months at Jamestown the regular ration is described as having been a kind of porridge: "half a pint of wheat, and as much barley, boiled with water." The colonists, however, considered this to be extremely poor fare, and altogether there is no indication that much barley was ever eaten on this side of the ocean. Barley offered few advantages, and the English colonists were able to gratify their liking for wheat bread.

Whether wheat is actually the best grain for human consumption is not the question. The American is a wheat-eater because the Englishman, along with most of the Europeans, considered wheat to be most palatable, and also because the American land is well suited for growing it.

2) *Barley.* The case of barley has really been presented in connection with that of wheat. The two have been rivals in Western civilization ever since the beginning of agriculture. In the United States, for human consumption, the question seems to have been decisively answered. Of the peoples who have contributed largely to the formation of the American nation none have been particularly devoted to the eating of barley. In the United States the average person consumes most of his small ration unknowingly as malt combined with other foods. Barley itself he knows as something that he encounters as a few grains at the bottom of a plate of soup. The amount of barley grown is actually a quarter as large as that of wheat, but almost all of it is consumed by animals or in liquid form as beer.

3) Rye. Although the amount of rye eaten by the American people is about the same as that of barley, this represents a much larger proportion of the total production. There is, however, little environmental reason why rye should be either grown or eaten. It is a kind of poor relation of wheat and barley that will make a crop far north and on poor soils. Traditionally, the English had little attachment to rye, which is not particularly suited to their island and is not much cultivated there. The Dutch had more liking for the grain, and it was even more a favorite with the Swedes and Finns who settled on the Delaware. As late as 1682 it was recorded of these latter: "The people generally eat rye bread, being approved of best by them."

In later times also the use of rye has been associated with certain national groups, especially the Swedes, Germans, and Russians. As a result, its products generally carry such suggestions even in their names, as with pumpernickel, Swedish rye-crisp, and Russian rye bread. The influence of these later immigrants has been strong enough to establish a general liking for rye bread as a relief from the monotony of wheat bread, and the question "White or rye?" is a standard one at most American sandwich counters. Still, even in our so-called rye bread, the amount of wheat is much greater than that of rye.

4) Oats. With oats, the situation is strikingly different. Twice as much of it is consumed as human food as of barley or rye.

Oats, like rye, is a northern grain, but thrives in wet climates. It was thus well adapted to the British Isles, and was much cultivated there. In most of Scotland and Ireland wheat did not do well, and oats was the prevailing grain. Out of necessity, therefore, the Scots used it in various forms of porridge and oatcakes. A famous passage in Froissart's Chronicles describes the use of oatmeal by the Scottish borderers of the fourteenth century. Just as the Swedes and Finns stuck by rye even when wheat was available—because they liked it—so the Scots did with oats.

But the eating of oats was a good English custom too. In the eighteenth century Dr. Johnson made his famous joke about oats being fed to horses in England but in Scotland supporting the people. History shows, however, that Dr. Johnson was wrong about this matter, as about so many others. From the beginning of the Jamestown colony oatmeal is mentioned. About 1613 the Spanish spy Molina wrote a letter describing the colony, and the only European grain that he mentions as being eaten is oats. In a 1623 list of supplies to be brought by each immigrant, one fifth of the cereal ration for the year is in oatmeal. This early use of oats must, however, have been sustained and augmented by the immigration of Scots and of the even more numerous Scotch-Irish.

What we may call a native development may also have been of some importance. . . . During the eighteen-nineties one of the greatest of early advertising campaigns stimulated the sale of the trade product Quaker Oats. One pound of this breakfast food was declared to make "as much bone and muscle as three pounds of beef." Who knows but that such a campaign may have had more influence than all the Scots that ever came out of Scotland?

5) *Rice.* Rice cannot be grown in northwestern Europe, and was known there only as a luxury at the time of the first colonization. Its culture was introduced into Pennsylvania and South Carolina about 1685. It is mentioned as important in Pennsylvania as late as 1698, but its culture died out there and it became exclusively southern. Especially in South Carolina it came to be a leading money crop, and naturally it was also eaten. Rice remains, however, of minor importance in the

American diet, only somewhat exceeding oats. This is all the more remarkable in that the environment in much of the United States is suitable for rice and that it is a highly productive and nutritious crop. Its failure to become a really popular food is probably attributable to its late introduction and to the lack of European tradition. In the South, where it was first known and has been chiefly cultivated, it is eaten much more heavily than in the North.

In the United States, rice is only doubtfully to be considered a cereal at all. It is commonly classed as a semi-vegetable, comparable to the potato. Rice and bread may be served at the same meal.

6) *Corn.* Although its consumption is less than a quarter that of wheat, the average American would probably consider corn our most typical grain. In another sense this is certainly true, for the production of corn is about three times that of wheat. The corn, however, is largely consumed by animals.

The history of the word itself is of interest and significance. In English it once meant an actual grain of any kind, and we still speak of barleycorns. It was, however, specialized in England to mean the common kind of corn, that is, wheat. When the colonists encountered the strange "corn" grown in the Indian fields, some of the more learned among them called it "maize," which was what the Spaniards called it, or "Turkish wheat," as it is still called in Italy. Rather curiously, the colonists did not take over any Indian word for it, although they adopted "hominy" and "pone" for two of the forms it assumed. Instead, they commonly called it "Indian wheat," or "Indian corn." This last was the one that stuck. Gradually, moreover, as Indian corn became the most commonly raised grain, it came to be known simply as "corn."

There is no need here to go back into the long and controversial history of the maize plant. All we need to remember is that at the time of the colonization the Europeans found the Indians of our eastern seaboard cultivating corn in their fields. Naturally, to begin with, many of the colonists did not care for this Indian corn as a food, for many people cherish deep-rooted food prejudices. Whether they liked it or not, however, was of little importance. All too often it was eat corn or go hungry. Corn, obtained from the Indians, saved the James-town colonists in their starving time. Having thus been forced to overcome any prejudices they might hold, they found it to be a good food.

Before long it became the chief cereal food for many colonists, just as pork became their chief meat and, for the same reason, that is, that corn produced more for less labor. An anonymous writer describing the foodstuffs of Maryland in 1634 begins with the native grain, declaring: "In the first place I name corn, as the thing most necessary to sustain man," and what he goes on to describe is Indian corn. Actually, in its eating of corn, the United States occupies a halfway position. It eats a great deal more than England and most other countries, but much less than a country like Mexico. The amount of corn used as human food would, however, rise appreciably in the statistics if green corn and canned corn were included there.

In many ways, corn is a somewhat old-fashioned American food. It is more heavily used in the South, which has been less affected by the late-comers. Corn is more associated with the country districts than with the city, and with more primitive areas than with more highly developed ones. To many New Yorkers, for instance, such terms as *pone, Johnny cake, corn dodgers,* and *cornmeal mush* would suggest the language of a historical or regional novel.

Nevertheless, corn still occupies an important position in

the American diet, and it continues to do so largely because of its great capacity for being cooked in various ways. Whereas almost all the wheat goes into the form of flour, and then appears on the table as a breadstuff, corn is Protean. Apparently it has always been so. A writer describing Carolina in 1682 mentions corn bread and biscuit, roasted green corn, parched corn, and corn cooked in several different ways with milk. He also mentions various drinks that may be prepared from it. Actually he has hardly made a beginning, for he does not record hominy and mush, unless some of his milk dishes used the grain in those forms. He also fails to mention succotash, boiled green corn, rye-and-corn bread, hasty pudding, and much else. At the present time corn also appears on the table as canned corn, tortillas, tamales, fritters, corn soup, and corn syrup. As cornstarch it supplies a useful cooking ingredient. It gets to the breakfast table in various forms of "dry cereal," to the cocktail party as parched corn, and to the baseball game and circus as popcorn.

Being thus ubiquitous and universal, corn has come to have a sentimental and symbolical value far exceeding that of wheat. Ears of corn appear as architectural ornaments, especially in the national Capitol. In the Pulitzer Prize comedy *Of Thee I Sing* the heroine's ability to make corn muffins is considered a transcendent American virtue. "Corn-fed" is an epithet to describe a thorough, though somewhat provincial, American. In modern slang, the same bucolic suggestions have caused corn to become a word meaning any simple but tried-and-true form of entertainment, such as might presumably appeal to the taste of country people—but the term need not be wholly derogatory, and the expression "good corn" is allowable. In our poetry, corn may stand as a symbol almost coextensive with the United States itself. In Stephen Vincent Benét's

Western Star the eating of corn is made the symbolic act by which the colonists cease to be European:

> And those who came were resolved to be Englishmen,
> Gone to the world's end, but English every one,
> And they ate the white corn-kernels, parched in the sun,
> And they knew it not, but they'd not be English again.

The extent to which corn has become involved with the American way of life may be gauged by its imprint upon our language. In Mathews's *Dictionary of Americanisms* the entries under corn and its compounded words such as corncob and corncracker cover seven pages.

With cereals, as with meats, we have thus a mixed situation. A strong hereditary influence shows in the predominance of wheat, and a strong environmental influence in the secondary position of corn. The slight but continuing use of oats and rye has a demonstrable hereditary backing. So, negatively speaking, does the comparatively small use of rice. A falling-off in the use of barley since the time of the first colonists may perhaps be called a native development, but it is also environmental, since there was no need to make use of a second-choice grain in a country so well adapted to wheat.

3

With vegetable foods other than grains, the situation is equally complex. The colonists brought with them the seeds of their common garden plants, and apparently found no difficulty in growing them. Within five years of the settlement of Jamestown the Reverend Mr. Whitaker reported: "Our English seeds thrive very well here, as peas, onions, turnips, cabbages, cauliflowers, carrots, thyme, parsley, hyssop, mar-

joram, and many other whereof I have tasted and eaten."
Bradford, describing New England in 1654, presented the situation in verse:

> All sorts of roots and herbs in gardens grow,
> Parsnips, carrots, turnips, or what you'll sow,
> Onions, melons, cucumbers, radishes,
> Skirrets, beets, coleworts, and fair cabbages.

He also mentions berries, pears, apples, cherries, plums,
quinces, and peaches.[2]

In addition, a strong environmental influence was exerted
in this area of American foodstuffs through the Indians. Besides their corn, the Indians cultivated various varieties of
beans, pumpkins, squashes, and melons. They made use of the
native nuts, of persimmons, and of blueberries, huckleberries,
and cranberries, with which the Europeans had not previously
been familiar. They also knew the trick of making maple syrup.

The new varieties of beans were of special importance. In
England, although beans were known, they were generally
considered a coarse food, fit chiefly for horses, and peas were
widely used. The year's food ration for an immigrant to early
Virginia included two bushels of peas. The widespread use
of beans is thus to be considered environmental. From the
Indian custom of baking their beans comes the popularity of
"Boston baked beans." From this source also may probably be
traced the Southern fondness for butter beans and black-eyed
peas, which are more like beans than peas, in spite of their
name. Succotash shows its Indian origin both in its name and
in being composed of corn and beans.

[2] The successful adaptation of so many Old World plants and their
immunity to New World diseases is remarkable. Of all the plants and
animals brought to America, the European grape fared worst, and after
that the sheep, and man. More than half of the immigrants to Virginia
in early times died within the first year.

As typical American dishes that we would not have except for this environmental influence may be mentioned—waffles with maple syrup, pumpkin pie, huckleberries with cream, blueberry muffins, pralines, and turkey with cranberry sauce. During World War II blueberry pie was sometimes cited as a symbol of the American way of life.

Various groups of immigrants have also left particular marks upon our food habits. With the Negro, for example, three favorite foods may be associated—watermelon, peanut, and sweet potato.

The watermelon is of African origin, and was probably brought to America by slave ships. Various accounts mention its being grown by the Indians, but if this is what we know now as watermelon, the seeds must have been introduced by contact with Spaniards. The peanut is Brazilian in origin, but was taken thence to Africa by the Portuguese, and probably reintroduced into the West Indies and thence to the territory of the United States by the slave trade. Its close association with the Negroes is shown by the existence of two colloquial names for it—pinder and goober—both African in origin. The sweet potato followed the same general route as the peanut, and also shows its association by the African origin of its alternate name, yam.[3]

The sweet potato suggests the Irish potato, or—as it is generally known—merely the potato. It is a far-traveled plant. Having originated in Chile, it was cultivated in Peru by the Incas, and thence taken by the Spaniards to Spain and returned to Florida. From Florida it was brought by the buccaneer Hawkins to England and thence to Ireland. As the Irish potato it made its fourth transatlantic passage, and was cultivated in

[3]Though not an important food, okra or gumbo should doubtless be added to this list. Both the words are of African origin, and so is the plant itself. Peter Kalm, in 1748, noted that okra "is reckoned a dainty by some people, and especially by the negroes."

Pennsylvania as early as 1685. The English, however, were apparently not particularly fond of it, and only with the immigration of the Scotch-Irish in the early part of the eighteenth century did the potato become important in the American diet.

With the introduction of the potato the basic foodstuffs of the United States, and most of the food habits also, were established in a form from which they scarcely altered for more than a century. Only with the development of railroad transportation, refrigeration, and canning, all after the middle of the nineteenth century, was there any important change. By these aids, seafood was made available to the whole continental area. The other great addition consisted of the tropical and semi-tropical fruits—oranges, lemons, bananas, and pineapples.

4

Thus far, American foods have been considered chiefly as springing from hereditary and environmental sources, more strictly speaking. It remains to consider the influences of other factors.

Native developments have been of considerable importance, but generally these have been closely connected with environmental factors. An example is the influence of the frontier upon American foods—the frontier itself being, as has been pointed out in Chapter 1, a result of the environment. Frontier cooking, in its basic stage, was merely what we should now call "campfire cooking." It was cookery, moreover, with a minimum of utensils. Our tradition of fried foods, at which gourmets wring their hands, is thus easily explained. Here lies also another cause for the importance of pork, for of all meats it takes most kindly to being fried. The great American tradition of hot bread is also to be explained most easily in terms of the frontier. Frequently there was neither time nor equipment for the preparation of a real bread. Such expedients as corn bread and biscuits, quickly prepared and eaten while still hot, solved the predicament. Possibly a Scotch-Irish or Scottish influence may be postulated here, for of all European countries Scotland with its many kinds of scones seems to come closest to our biscuits and hot rolls. In this kind of cookery a strong regional variation is observable, and the South has sometimes even been described as "the hot-bread country."

The torrid summers of much of the United States have also been reflected in various native developments of foods. Most notably, the manufacture of ice cream has become almost a major industry.

The general environmental feature that the country was always larger than the people could fill has been reflected in the high cost of labor and the increasing disappearance of domestic servants. As a result, labor-saving devices for the home have become more common, and of such devices for food preparation we can mention pre-cooked breakfast foods, biscuit and cake mixes, canned foods, and frozen foods. The same situation leads also to emphasis upon the original good quality of the food, which thus being so good to begin with does not need much elaboration in the cookery. Thus may be explained the American's fascination by the beefsteak. A French or Italian cook can take an insignificant piece of veal, and by sufficient elaboration of sauces may transform it into a dish fit for a gourmet, but in so doing he has expended more time and labor than the American housewife feels justified in doing.

As a native development we may mention faddism in foods. Such fads usually represent a kind of primitivism. On the one hand, people advancing out of the frontier stage call for whiter bread, more refined sugar, imported delicacies, and a generally greater finish and sophistication. On the other hand, the reformers arise, somewhat like the prophets of Israel, calling for more primitive foods—if not literally for locusts and wild honey.

One of the earliest and most notable of these food reformers was Sylvester Graham, who flourished in the eighteen-thirties and forties. As the *Dictionary of American Biography* states so succinctly as scarcely to be bettered: "He advocated bread at least twelve hours old, made of the whole of the wheat unbolted and coarsely ground, and also recommended hard mattresses, open bedroom windows, cold shower baths, looser and lighter clothing, daily exercise, vegetables, fresh fruits, rough cereals, pure drinking water, and cheerfulness at meals." Obviously his general platform was a return to the Spartan simplicity of the fathers. He was so successful that graham bread, graham crackers, and graham flour (written without capital letters) are still regular articles of trade in any American market.

What might be called "commercial faddism" has already been illustrated in connection with oats. Similar campaigns have been conducted, and still are being conducted, for meat, bread, oranges, raisins, and many other foodstuffs. The success of any given advertising campaign may or may not be notable, but in the aggregate they must have considerably affected the contemporary diet of the American people.

Equally conscious and equally important, but more altruistically founded, is the vigorous campaign for education in food habits that has been carried on during the past generation. Calories, vitamins, and proteins have been rendered, no longer scientific abstractions, but household words with a reality as plain as that of butter or eggs. Not only the dangers of over-eating, but also the advantages of proper food selection have been brought home to the American people, as to no people in the past. No other people have ever become so self-conscious about their eating. An interesting result is that one notices in the United States fewer obese people than in Europe, in spite of the more abundant food.[4]

5

A fitting conclusion to this discussion of native developments might be a defense of native American food and cookery. In recent years a legend has arisen that Americans lived on a gloomy diet of fried pork and soggy saleratus biscuits until they were rescued by French cookbooks and Italian immigrants. People who propagate such a legend have probably been so unfortunate as never to eat a really good native American meal. Such a meal depended upon good material, simply prepared. It was a heavy meal, as befitted the people of a hardworking time and country. But it offered considerable variety. Breakfast, for instance, was designed to give a man a good start toward a morning's labor in the hayfield, not merely to get him to the office where he would sit till noon in a swivel chair. One might expect home-canned fruit, home-cured bacon fried with new-laid eggs, buckwheat cakes with maple syrup, hot biscuits with butter fresh from the springhouse, honey in the comb, coffee with cream. He who has never experienced such a meal has missed something of the American heritage, and he who feels himself slightly sickened at even the thought of

[4]About 1940 I heard a railroad official remarking that one of his gangs of section hands had been complaining about their food—they said they wanted more vitamins! "Chr—st!" he added. "A few years ago those guys had never heard of a vitamin!" The incident not only illustrates the food-consciousness of even one of our lowest economic groups, but also shows how readily scientific food research passes over into food-faddism. These section hands probably had only the vaguest idea of what vitamins were, and certainly no real knowledge of whether they were receiving the proper kinds of vitamins in the proper amounts.

such mountains of substantial food should ask himself whether he is perhaps merely too weak to be allowed to enter into such a paradise.

Most Americans traveling in Europe, even among all the delicacies of European chefs, have begun to hunger for their own foods after a while. That American of Americans, Mark Twain, recorded these longings in a full-page, double-columned listing near the end of A Tramp Abroad. He began with radishes and ended with "All sorts of American pastry." Being Missouri-bred, he specified many dishes "Southern style," here including hot hoecake, hot egg bread, hot light bread, hot biscuits, bacon and greens, and—inevitably—fried chicken. Among the many general American dishes that he listed, we may note porterhouse steak, fried oysters, hot buckwheat cakes, roast turkey, cranberry sauce, hominy, boiled onions, and green corn both "on the ear" and "cut from the ear and served with butter and pepper." He specified "American toast," and identified several dishes by special locales, for example, Boston bacon and beans, Virginia bacon, San Francisco mussels, and black bass from the Mississippi River. He was not above some of the backwoods dishes, such as possum, and coon. Finally, for dessert, he whetted his appetite with the thought of apple dumplings, peach cobbler, and five kinds of pie.

6

International ideas have influenced American food chiefly through the introduction of French cookery. After the alliance in 1778 all things French became popular, the cookery along with the rest. The émigrés who fled after the Revolution were not numerous, but they helped spread the vogue of French cookery. One of these was no less a person than Brillat-Savarin, the very demigod of the gourmet.

French cookery, being lighter, more elaborated, and more sophisticated, was in harmony with the general development of American civilization away from the primitive. On the contrary, its very elaboration and its emphasis upon painstaking preparation were out of harmony with the high cost of labor in the United States and the general lack of domestic servants. As a result, French cookery has influenced American cookery from the top downward, but has not basically changed it. Its influence is to be seen in the expressions "French fried potatoes" (frequently known as "French fries"), "French dressing," and "French pastry." It is to be seen also in the considerable number of commonly used but only half-assimilated French words—*bouillon, consommé, purée, fricassee* (which has lost its accent), *mayonnaise, pâté* (which has also become patty), and *hors d'oeuvres* (which I have heard called merely "derves.")

7

Much more important than the influence of international ideas has been the influence of the continuing immigration.

On the whole, these immigrants have brought with them very little in the way of new foodstuffs. The use of olive oil—and hence of other vegetable oils, with a consequent decline in the use of lard—may be attributed partly to the influence of French cookery, and partly to heavy Italian immigration, and to other causes as well. An increase in the popularity of the potato can be attributed to Irish and German immigration. The decline in the use of corn and its consequential relegation to being an old-fashioned food are probably to be connected with the immigration of vast numbers of Europeans from countries where corn was not used.

The influence of later immigrants is to be seen more in methods of preparation of basic foodstuffs, than in foodstuffs themselves. Italian fondness for spaghetti and macaroni merely confirms the American use of wheat, but uses wheat in a new form. Tamales, tortillas, and chile con carne continue, under new forms, our traditional use of corn and beans. Liverwurst—German, as the word shows—puts into palatable and preservable form a part of the animal which under older conditions had to be eaten fresh.

As regards foods, the transmuting pot has functioned at a somewhat halfway efficiency. The immigrant has not kept his old food habits as he has kept his religion, but neither has he wholly adopted the American way of life as he has with his language. The result has been a complexity that is scarcely less than that of religion.

This complexity is perhaps best shown by our restaurants. In a European city there is usually little contrast among restaurants. Generally speaking, they serve the food of their own country, prepared in its particular fashion. But for anyone going out for a meal in an American city, the first question must ordinarily be: "What kind of restaurant?" If there is anything such as an ordinary American restaurant, it will offer some traditional American dishes such as steak or fried chicken and hot biscuits, with an overlay of French soups and salads. But there will also be such a thing as "Mammy's Shack" specializing in southern dishes, and restaurants that are more specifically French. This is only the beginning. Beyond this you have your choice of Chinese restaurants, or of Italian, or of Mexican, German, Russian, Armenian, Japanese, Hawaiian, and Kosher. In recent years restaurants offering Swedish smörgåsbord have become highly popular.

Even in American homes you are likely to be served dishes showing various foreign influences, not at all connected with the ancestral background of that particular family. The canning industry has produced such anomalies as canned chop suey, canned tamales, and canned frankfurters.

In view of all this, the complaints about the "standardization" of American food seem strange. If standardization is to be interpreted as meaning a restricted diet with unvaried cookery, it exists only if we look at some small segment of the American population. Doubtless the food of a not very prosperous Iowa small-town family tends to get into a rut, and so does the food of a third-generation Italian family of San Francisco. But if we look at the country as a whole, the remarkable fact is the tremendous richness and variety of its diet. Necessity, reinforced by environment, especially on the frontier, led the early American to eat almost everything that was edible. The constant in-flooding of immigrants, with continual intermarriage, kept the American continually experimental and tolerant in his food.

Potato cookery offers an excellent example. Any American traveling abroad is constantly struck with what seems to him the poverty-stricken lack of imagination with which "foreigners" treat potatoes. The English and the Swedes merely boil them; the French with their unending "French fries" use little more imagination; the Spaniards, the Italians, the Greeks, all do only one or two or three things with a potato. In the United States you find potatoes, whether in restaurants or in the home, treated in about every way that any foreign country treats them, and in some others. Perhaps the most characteristically American is the baked potato—an obvious hangover from a potato baked in the ashes of a campfire. The American has no objection to a boiled potato, although he does not, like the Englishman, think this is the only way in which it can be approached. French fries are common, but not almost universal, as in France. In addition, we offer potatoes roasted with the meat, baked without skins, mashed, fried, scalloped, hashed brown, and creamed. Potato chips represent almost a national dish. There are potato salad, potato cake, potato fritters, potato croquettes, potato soup. There is even potato bread. Mark Twain, in the list already cited, included potatoes in five different ways—Saratoga, mashed, boiled in the skins, new potatoes boiled without the skins, and "early rose potatoes, roasted in the ashes, Southern style, served hot."

Obviously this great variety of potato cookery is not due to any special American genius, but results from frontier experimentation enriched by the continual introduction of new ways of preparation by immigrants.

8

In conclusion and for transition, we may consider the tomato. . . . Originally American, it was taken to Europe by the Spaniards, but thought to be poisonous and grown ornamentally. Italians in the eighteenth century discovered its good qualities, and it has become so characteristic of their cookery that one wonders how they managed before they had it. It was brought to the United States in the mid-eighteenth century, and grew slowly into popularity, aided by the introduction of French cookery. Among his special American dishes Mark Twain listed sliced tomatoes with sugar and vinegar, and stewed tomatoes. The recent tremendous popularization of canned tomato juice is a notable development. At some time, moreover, the Americans began to make the tomato sauce that they called ketchup or catsup—or often, by folk etymology, catch-up.

Its history is involved and obscure, and worthy of the researches of a Ph.D. candidate. The word itself seems to be eventually Chinese, but has passed through a Malay form. Something called ketchup, an article of the Indian trade, appeared in England as early as 1690, but it apparently had nothing to do with tomatoes. It seems to have been a sauce having some ancestral connection with the brine in which fish had been pickled, and it sounds altogether nauseous. From England the word and the thing doubtless came to the colonies. Whatever it then was, it came to be a regular condiment in the eighteenth-century kitchen. Gradually the word must have come to mean merely a highly seasoned sauce, and the recipe for making it was changed, doubtless by slow steps.

Eventually it came to be a tomato sauce, flavored with sugar, vinegar, onions, and spices. The word is spelled in either of two ways, apparently at the whim of the manufacturer. The product, moreover, is specified as "tomato ketchup" (or "catsup"), as if other kinds were available, though they never are.

However spelled, the product seems to fulfill some basic American dietary need. Mark Twain included it in his list of foods for which he hungered. It differs from most of the originally foreign foods by existing at the lower rather than the higher levels. In a "good" restaurant, it will not be put on the table, and even to ask for it seems crass. The cheaper the restaurant, the commoner the ketchup bottle, and in many a hash-house and beanery it appears on the table as regularly as the pepper and the salt, to be as freely used. It is the *vin compris* of the American workingman, serving to make an ordinary meal more palatable—and by this bridge we pass to a consideration of American drink.

CHAPTER **6**

DRINK

Food could be brought in the ships; drink
was a problem. The early colonists were drinkers of beer and
ale, but the small ships of the seventeenth century had no
room for the transport of the hundreds of barrels that would
have been necessary to supply a whole colony with drink for a
year. Besides, everyone knew that life could be supported—
albeit vilely, and scarcely in a Christian manner—on water.
So the early colonists always faced at least a year of water-
drinking, and were thus, in this respect at least, reduced to the
level of the native savages.

To give the colonists their credit, they seemed to have settled
to this water regimen with fortitude and resignation, as if
realizing that a New World was not to be conquered without
extreme sacrifice. But they seldom made any pretense about
liking the stuff. As one of the Jamestown men wrote, "Our
drink was water; our lodgings, castles in the air." He added
that such drink and lodgings, coupled with hard work, would
have made them miserable in their native country, or any other
place in the world. In the same passage he accuses President

Wingfield of secretly guzzling the reserve supply of wine and brandy. As late as 1620 it was stated of the Jamestown colonists: "the greatest want they complain of is good drink."

The Puritans—modern misconceptions to the contrary notwithstanding—did not conceive piety as involving drinking habits, and their attitude toward water was that of their time. Bradford notes that those who were preparing to sail in the *Mayflower* looked forward to the drinking of water as one of the perils of colonization. A shore party from the *Mayflower*, scrambling through the thickets of Cape Cod, became very dry in the throats: "But at length they found water and refreshed themselves, being the first New-England water they drunk of, and was now in their great thirst as pleasant unto them as wine or beer had been in for-times." This sounds as if they liked the water, but we should note the phrase "in their great thirst." A little while later, as Bradford records bitterly, the colonists "were hasted ashore and made to drink water, that the seamen might have the more beer." Other quotations from his *History of Plymouth Plantation* might be cited to prove that the Pilgrim Fathers, though they could drink water with resolution, did not like it.

The same seems to have been true everywhere. Among the Welsh settlers of Pennsylvania there was a saying redolent with resignation: "If we have bread, we will drink water, and be content." A Jesuit priest wrote of Maryland: "It abounds with delicate springs which are our best drink." But even the good father's comment can be taken two ways, and in any case he was writing what was really a prospectus to encourage immigration.

If the ships could not bring any significant amount of beer, at least they could carry some supplies of sack and *aqua vitae*. Sack—what we would call sherry—was the great gentleman's drink in Elizabethan times. Readers of Shakespeare will not need to be reminded of Falstaff's devotion to it. On the other hand, it was too expensive for the lower classes, and Christopher Sly, the drunken tinker in *The Taming of the Shrew*, declares that he has never tasted it but has drunk only ale. In Shakespeare's time, also, distilled liquors were just beginning to come in as commercial products. *Aqua vitae*—a generic term, but usually meaning brandy—is mentioned half a dozen times in the plays, but Shakespeare apparently had a low opinion of it, and suggests that it was consumed chiefly by such people as Juliet's foolish old nurse, midwives, and Irishmen.

But *aqua vitae*, and even sack, were concentrated alcohol as compared with beer. They were therefore a godsend to the colonists when shipping space was at a premium. At least enough of them could be brought across to serve for "medicinal purposes," as occasional celebration, and now and then a slug to warm the body against the winter's cold or ward the soul from the chill of homesickness and melancholy. From the very beginning at Jamestown there was a supply of *aqua vitae*, even if not enough for general consumption. It must have proved to be a valuable commodity in a new colony, for in the list of 1623 a gallon of it is put down in the very meager supplies that were to be brought as "victual for a whole year for a man."

Doubtless profiting by this example, other colonies followed the lead. The *Arbella*, bearing the colonists of Boston, had its supply of "strong water." Winthrop records that two of the men tapped a keg of it, and were punished for doing so. Also he records that during a storm, "a maidservant in the ship, being stomach-sick, drank so much strong water, that she was senseless, and had near killed herself." Then, in a somewhat sinister tone, he adds: "We observed it a great fault in our young people, that they gave themselves to drink hot waters very immoderately." One would judge that the supply of liquor on the *Arbella* was adequate.

Even when the colonists were safe in the New Canaan on the shores of Massachusetts Bay, and free of seasickness, they did not give up this liking. In 1633 Winthrop records that entirely too much money was being spent for "strong waters."

Historically, what is most interesting is to see the standard American habits of drink established from the very beginning. Many a European has marveled, when being entertained by an American family, at the strong cocktails before dinner followed by a fine dinner moistened only by water. But if you have room in the ship for *aqua vitae* but not for beer, this is the pattern that is likely to develop. In fact, the commonplace mention of strong liquors in the colonies, even in the first half of the seventeenth century, as compared with the rather infrequent mention in England, suggests that the new-fangled products of distillation were better known in the barren colonies than they were in the wealthy mother country.[1]

2

Once towns and villages had been established and prosperous plantations and farms hewn out of the forest, the brewing of beer was resumed. Salem was only four years old in 1630, when John Winthrop visited there, but he could write: "we supped with a good venison pasty and good beer." This beer may have been brought across in a ship or may have been brewed by some Puritan housewife; there is no record yet of any local brewhouse. There was even beer in Boston in 1631,

[1]John Josselyn, in a book published in England in 1672, thinks it worth-while to insert an explanation that rum is "a strong water drawn from sugar-canes," apparently assuming that his English readers might not know what it was.

a year after its foundation, enough at least for a cup of it to be
passed out to each of some visiting Indian braves. Very soon,
before 1637, Massachusetts had its first brewery.

So it went also in the more established parts of the other
colonies. In New Netherland a brewery was built in 1633, and
in 1642 David de Vries wrote that the people "can brew as
good beer here as in our Fatherland." Only three years after
the foundation of Philadelphia, Penn reported: "Now they
make malt, and malt drink begins to be common, especially at
the ordinaries [restaurants] and the houses of the more substantial people."

In the back-country, however, it was another story—and by
far the greater part of the colonies consisted of back-country.
Not only is beer too bulky and heavy to transport far, but also
it is time-consuming and difficult to brew. The trappers and
hunters and Indian traders of the frontier, the corn- and pork-
eaters of the backwoods—they forgot the taste of beer, just as
their wives forgot how to brew it. For them the alternative remained water or something that was strong enough in alcohol
to make it worth-while to lash a couple of kegs of it on a pack
horse and transport it into the forest.

3

As for these "strong waters," their history in the United
States can be written under four main heads—brandy, rum,
gin, and whiskey.

Brandy came first in time. Along with the heavy sweet wines
such as port and Madeira, French brandy remained a gentleman's drink all the way down through the eighteenth century.
At the popular level, however, it was soon replaced by cheaper
substitutes—either rum or some variety of local "brandy."

The term, indeed, was often used, and sometimes confusingly, for liquor distilled not only from grapes but also from any kind of fruit. An early record of brandy-making is from New Netherland in 1640, but we can hardly suppose that this was brandy distilled from wine, since wine-making itself was not yet established. Much more likely, it was peach brandy.

For a while, indeed, there was much experimentation in the production of native distilled liquors, and home-distilling flourished. A 1683 description of Pennsylvania records: "most people have stills of copper," and specifies that they make "good spirits" from peaches, and also use corn, cherries, wild plums, and wild grapes. The slightly later description of New Jersey cites "peaches, from which last they distill a liquor as in Pennsylvania, much like rum or brandy, in the taste." Unfortunately, all these native developments amounted to little in the long run. If one of them had succeeded, we might have had a really national drink, as the Greeks have ouzo and the Mexicans have tequila. But what chance was there, economically speaking, when the little New England sloops could whip ashore a keg of cheap rum at any landing place?

Peach brandy came the closest to establishing itself. The history of the peach in America is a curious one. It was brought by the Spaniards, and probably trees were taken to Florida, which was settled some forty years before Virginia. As sometimes happens when a new plant is brought into a country, the peach, lacking enemies, flourished and spread exceedingly, northward clear to Pennsylvania. Peach brandy thus became a common drink in the southern colonies, and some pleasant tradition of drinking it still lingers there.

Farther north, where the peaches did not flourish, an apple brandy sometimes attained considerable local hold. Usually it seems to have been produced by distilling, but sometimes by another method that is suggestive of the way in which the colonists faced new conditions of environment and made use of them. An ordinary winter of the British Isles would not produce low enough temperatures to allow any high concentration of alcohol by the process of freezing. But in the northern colonies any winter could be counted upon to have its below-zero nights. The farmer then merely set out his hard cider, and in the morning broke off the ice and threw it away. The unfrozen liquid remained as an alcoholic beverage of high concentration, with strength depending upon the temperature to which it had been exposed. The resultant liquor was known as applejack, and by special association with a particular colony came to be called "Jersey lightning."

By and large, however, all this local "brandy" yielded to rum, the influence of which on the development of the United States has been profound. The raw material of rum is either molasses or else the residue of the sugar cane from which sugar and molasses have been already extracted. Rum is therefore essentially a by-product, and for this reason was extremely cheap as soon as the sugar industry began to develop in the West Indies. Trade sprang up very quickly, and in 1638 Winthrop records that New England ships were carrying dried fish and strong liquors to the islands. Before long, however, the process was reversed, as far as the strong liquors were concerned, and the New England ships were carrying rum to Boston. Soon they found it cheaper to bring back molasses, and manufacture the rum in New England.

Serious-minded Jasper Danckaerts, traveling through the middle colonies in 1679, found bad rum, "which is called by the Dutch kill-devil," to be the bane of the land. He terms it "a liquor that is everywhere," and again," that vile rum," and again, "that execrable rum." Danckaerts was no prohibitionist either; he loved good beer and spoke favorably of peach brandy. But he could not stomach the rum, and in addition its social implications shocked him. He saw it being used to debauch the Indians, at the same time debauching the whites.

Rum was standard, with the Dutch and English, for the Indian trade. In fact, the suggestion has been made that, since the English were able to supply rum more cheaply than the French could supply brandy, the former had an advantage which was not without its influence in the final domination of the continent.

The associations of rum were so universal and so close that Gabriel Thomas, writing in 1698, calls it "rum of the Christians." Doubtless he is a little ironical in so writing, but even irony must have its basis in reality.

Rum remained the great popular drink throughout most of the eighteenth century. In a Virginia village of 1732 William Byrd mentions two taverns, "well supplied with wine and other polite liquors," and then adds, "besides these, there is a rum ordinary for persons of a more vulgar taste." After it declined before the advance of whiskey, rum had been so long synonymous with strong liquor that it remained as a symbol. Thousands of temperance orators inveighed against The Demon Rum. "Rum," wrote Oliver Wendell Holmes, "I take to be the name which unwashed moralists apply alike to the product distilled from molasses and the noblest juices of the vineyard." An alliterative political scarecrow of the campaign of 1884 was: "Rum, Romanism, and Rebellion!" though by that time the actual consumption of rum was small. Even in the Prohibition Era the tradition of its great days, plus its alliterative qualities, gave us "rum row," and "rumrunner."[2]

Brandy for the gentlemen, rum for people generally, peach

[2]Rum-drinking was common along the eastern seaboard until after the middle of the nineteenth century. Thus Whitman, whose atmosphere chiefly reflects conditions around New York City, writes about 1855 of "the liquor-bar lean'd against by the young rum-drinker and the old rum-drinker."

brandy and applejack for local non-conformists—all these formed an unbroken front, and there was little room into which gin could squeeze itself. Gin, short for the name of the Swiss city Geneva, was distilled from the fermented mash of various grains and was flavored with juniper. Later, since the best of it came from the Netherlands, it was often called Hollands. Being based upon grains instead of grapes, it had the advantage, like rum, of being cheap. In the eighteenth century it became the poor man's drink in England. On account of the flavoring herbs it was even considered medicinal.

Gin did tremendous harm in England because it made drunkenness quick and cheap for the first time, and Hogarth's famous picture Gin-Lane eloquently testifies to its ravages. But it made little impression upon the colonies, probably because rum was quick and cheap already. In addition, gin seems always to have been a drink associated with city slums, of which there were as yet few in the colonies. In short, during most of the history of the United States the drinking of gin has been considered almost a depravity, and the drinking of straight gin might be so considered even today.

Only when your crude Dutchman gin becomes Parisianized by being mixed with French vermouth does gin, as a martini, become respectable, popular, and even fashionable. And the vogue of the martini is extremely recent, dating chiefly from the prohibition days of the nineteen-twenties.

Perhaps gin would have flourished better if it had not happened to meet a new and curious competitor. In the year 1682 Thomas Ashe noted that the people of Carolina were making "good sound beer" from corn, and he added: "by maceration, when duly fermented, a strong spirit like brandy may be drawn off from it, by the help of an alembic." This product must necessarily have been a kind of whiskey, although its makers may not have known the name. "Carolina corn" thus makes its appearance, and it is joined by the "good spirits" mentioned as being made from corn in Pennsylvania in 1683.

As already stated, these local experimentations failed at first to meet the competition of cheap rum. About a generation later, however, the situation changed in two respects. First, the frontier had advanced so far inland that it was inconveniently distant from the boat landings where the rum could be put ashore. Second, the Scotch-Irish were arriving from Ulster. These immigrants were partly Celtic in blood, and they had lived in close contact with Celts long enough to learn how to make the national drink known as usquebaugh, which is merely the Celtic way of saying *aqua vitae*, that is, "water of life." Settling mostly in the back-country, they naturally took to making their own whiskey, as they had in the old country. Scotch and Irish whiskey both used barley as the chief base, but for some reason the Scotch-Irish in America used rye.

In the middle seventeen hundreds there was a country of rum along the seacoast and a country of whiskey farther inland, but the whiskey gradually encroached upon the rum. The frontiersmen had to come down to the tidewater towns once a year anyway to get their supplies of salt, ammunition, and ironware, and they found that for those supplies they could barter whiskey as well as beaverskins. Then, the seven years' war of the Revolution must have had a great effect. The British held the sea and many of the seaports, and rum was hard to come by. War, also, is a great spreader of new ideas and new customs. Many an Ephraim Potter or Eben Stubbs of the Marblehead Regiment must have had his first taste of whiskey when he took the proffered flask from some Patrick Wilson or Archy Loughry of the Pennsylvania Line. Moreover, the country of rum could not grow except by colonizing the oyster beds, and the country of whiskey was on the frontier and had all the West open to it.

Farther inland something else happened. In Kentucky the grandsons of the original Scotch-Irish discovered that they could make a good whiskey by using corn as a base. Doubtless, indeed, a little corn whiskey had always been made locally ever since its beginnings in the seventeenth century. But the real center of its manufacture came to be Bourbon County in Kentucky, and it has been known as bourbon ever since.

Shortly after the Revolution five hundred stills were operating in one county of western Pennsylvania, which must mean that almost every farmer had one. The question of whether the federal government could tax this whiskey brought on the so-called Whiskey Rebellion, and helped establish the firm power of the new constitution. These stills were probably manufacturing rye whiskey, the better quality of which passed under the famous trade name of Monongahela, from a Pennsylvania river. Twenty years later the center of whiskey-making had shifted toward the west, and two thousand stills were operating in Kentucky about 1810.

By this time the thing was decided. In so far as it was to be alcoholic, the United States was to be a whiskey-drinking country. This whiskey was to be mostly corn whiskey under the trade name bourbon. Kentucky would be the chief center of its manufacture. But a significant fraction of the whiskey would be rye whiskey, and Pennsylvania would remain the center of its manufacture. A comparatively small amount of Scotch would be imported, for those who could afford it. At the present time about 90 per cent of the "strong waters" consumed in the United States is whiskey.

4

We took leave of beer, so to speak, when that less fiery protagonist had been re-established as a common drink in the more settled parts of the colonies toward the end of the seventeenth century. A good deal of beer continued to be brewed in commercial breweries and to be drunk in the cities. The English tradition of the housewife's brewing of her own beer, however, does not seem to have established itself very widely. In the Northern colonies there is, indeed, rather more mention of cider than of beer. The country people there—and that would include nearly everybody—apparently drank cider very commonly, that is, "hard cider," which in its alcoholic content is about the same as beer.

Farther inland and toward the south, however, neither beer nor cider seems to have been able to meet the competition of water. Having had to drink water at first, the frontiersman learned to like it. When the frontiersman became the farmer and the small-town American, he continued to drink water, or whiskey if he wanted something alcoholic.

Beer-drinking, however, received a tremendous impulse from the great immigration of Germans following 1848. Daniel Dorchester, D.D., writing on the liquor problem in the year 1884, entitles one chapter "The Beer Invasion," and refers to "this comparatively new beverage"—good evidence of how beer-drinking had lapsed. To Dorchester the drinking of beer is a habit brought in by the Germans. He points out that in 1850 the average consumption was 1.4 gallons per person, but that in 1860, after the first decade of heavy German immigration, it had risen to 3.2 gallons. As additional evidence one can note that the Germans established the American usage of the words beer-garden, lager, and bock, and that the great German centers of Milwaukee and St. Louis remain the chief centers of brewing on a national scale. Nevertheless, though great quantities of beer are consumed in the United States it can scarcely be called a beer-drinking country as it can be called a water- or a whiskey-drinking country.

As for wine, that is a long story, and on the whole a very sad one. In the seventeenth century England produced no wine but imported much, and wine production was one of the original ideas in the settlement of Virginia. Wild grapes were known to grow there, and so some French vintners—"vigneroones from Lanquedock"—were sent out. But when European vines were planted, they failed to flourish, and soon died. Actually, they were contracting the disease later to be known as phylloxera, to which the American native grapes were immune.

Only after two centuries and a half, when it was found that European vines could be grafted on American roots, did a wine industry become possible. By that time, to use a military expression, the situation had degenerated, and the establishment of any wine industry at all became extremely difficult. The people of the United States had become not only non-wine-drinking, but even anti-wine-drinking. Wine had come to be considered effete, European, and even degenerate. In some way, as compared with honest whiskey, it was "bad for you." Clyde, the thoroughgoing but obtuse American from Ohio in the play *Life with Father*, characterizes it as "European bellywash." Thus it was fair game for taxes, and in many states has been taxed out of proportion to its alcoholic content.

The California wine industry, established by the Spaniards before 1800, struggled valiantly and was making some progress. Then came prohibition. After prohibition, the beer and whiskey manufacturers could resume work without too great difficulty, but many of the California vineyards had been allowed to go to ruin. Still, from a major center in California and from a minor one along the south shore of Lake Erie, the wine industry has continued to grow since the repeal of prohibition.

Immigration has also had a great influence. Just as most of our drinking of whiskey is to be attributed to the Scotch-Irish, and much of our drinking of beer to the Germans, so the great immigration of Italians has affected our drinking of wine. Granted an original Spanish beginning and important French and German influences, the tradition of our wine-making has much that is Italian about it.

5

On the whole, however, in spite of the interest that attaches to the history of whiskey, beer, and wine, and in spite of the great quantities of them consumed, the most interesting fact about the drinking habits of the United States is that they are so little alcoholic. As against lakes of whiskey and beer may be set seas and whole oceans of water, coffee, tea, milk, and "soft drinks."

Just as by one historical coincidence the American colonies were settled at about the time of the popularizing of distilled liquors, so by another such coincidence they were settled at about the time of the introduction of chocolate, coffee, and tea. These beverages all came to England about the middle of the seventeenth century. Thence they made their way across the ocean.

Chocolate-drinking never became of importance in the colonies, although in neighboring Mexico it is a national habit. On the other hand, both tea and coffee are closely tied up with our history.

Soon after its introduction the British became great tea-drinkers, and naturally this habit was transferred to the colonies. In the early eighteenth century William Byrd drank tea or coffee in the morning, one about as often as the other. Apparently he was something of an exception, and throughout the population in general tea was much more heavily drunk than coffee. It was particularly drunk by women, upon whose consumption of alcoholic beverages society was likely to frown. Even housemaids and farmers' daughters had to have their tea, we are told, and sometimes to the amount of twenty cups a day. It seemed to be a confirmed national habit.

Then the surprising happened. England put a tax on tea, and tea became a political and patriotic issue. Legal tea was not available, and black-market tea not patriotic. At the Boston Tea Party and elsewhere it was destroyed by enraged patriots. Substitutes developed. War followed. For a space of fifteen years Americans could not well drink tea, and they seemed rather to have got out of the habit. After all, it was not a long-established folk custom; it was more like a fad.

After the war tea returned to the American markets, but the American consumer never completely returned to tea. Doubtless the situation is not quite so simple as it might seem, and there were other reasons for the American abjuration of tea. Yet certain curious facts remain. In the middle of the eighteenth century England was devoted to tea-drinking; and it still is. In the middle of the eighteenth century the American colonists were devoted to tea-drinking; the United States now is not. Moreover, the British commonwealths and colonies resemble their mother country. In fact, the greater emphasis upon tea in Canada, as expressed in advertising and on menus, is one of the chief points of difference that strike a traveler when he crosses the line from the United States.

As with wine, logically or illogically, tea is considered slightly un-American. At best, it is a woman's drink. If a man asks for it at an ordinary American restaurant, he will get the tea without question, but he may be sure that he has been put down in the waitress's mind as 1) ill, 2) English, or 3) slightly peculiar.

Coffee, in its history, presents the reverse of tea. As late as 1800 and for some time afterward, more tea than coffee was

drunk, but the proportion of coffee rose as the cheaper Brazilian product came on the market. As the century continued,
British immigration fell off, and continental immigration rose
higher and higher in proportion. Most of the continental Europeans were coffee- rather than tea-drinkers, and some of them,
such as the Scandinavians, consumed coffee very heavily.

In the end, doubtless because of so many mingling influences, the United States has come to assume here, as in so
much else, a halfway position. It is not so exclusively devoted
to tea as are China and England, nor so heavily coffee-drinking
as are Sweden and Greece. In the course of the year the people
of the United States drink about half as many cups of tea as of
coffee. There are interesting regional variations. New England
drinks almost as much tea as coffee. The Pacific Coast drinks
only about one cup of tea to every five of coffee. There are also
seasonal variations, and the consumption of tea rises strikingly
in the summer, particularly in the central and southern states.

The explanation of this seasonal change lies in the popularity of iced tea. This characteristic American drink is sometimes said to have been invented at the St. Louis World's Fair
in 1904, but is actually at least a generation older, and may
well go back to the eighteen-thirties, when ice first came to be
commonly used in American homes. More than a quarter of all
the tea drunk in the United States is consumed in this form.
In the hotter parts of the country during the summer months,
almost all the tea is drunk cold, and this beverage is considered
highly suitable for children, even though they are less commonly given hot tea. Since iced tea, generally flavored with
lemon and sugar, is so common in the United States and so
rarely found anywhere else, it might even be considered the
most characteristic American drink.

The icing of drinks is, in general, a very American habit.

That other American phenomenon, the "soft drink" based on soda water, is also served cold, often iced.

The drinking of soda water from natural springs (sometimes called "beer-springs") was a habit even in frontier times, and the idea of adding a flavoring was an easy one. Soda fountains were appearing in American cities by the eighteen-forties. The continued success of their product, whether dispensed from a fountain or distributed by means of bottles, has not only made the soft drink an important feature of American life, but has also spread American influence widely around the world.

The popularity of the soft drink is not difficult to explain. It rests basically, one would suppose, on what may be called the natural human dislike of water, or at least the widespread like of a variation from water-drinking. It draws support also from the very hot summers that afflict much of our country, and at the same time from the prejudice against the use of alcohol, especially by women and young people, which has often been reinforced by actual prohibition. Soft drinks also had the advantage of cheapness, because they were not subject to the alcohol tax. Cheap as they were, however, they were even cheaper to prepare, and the margin of profit was high. Accordingly, they have offered a tempting commercial opportunity, and have been popularized by tremendous amounts of money spent in advertising.

At the same time, curiously, bottled mineral water has never been nearly so widely sold as in Europe. The American took his with flavoring. Moreover, although he has been subject to great credulity about various health fads, he has not succumbed to the idea of mineral water as a panacea. The elaborately labeled bottle, with its chemical analysis certified by a university professor and its extensive therapeutic claims, appears everywhere in Europe, but is rarely seen on an American table. Apparently the European, habitually a beer- or wine-drinker, can conceive great curative powers to exist in water-drinking, but the American, habitually a water-drinker, is unable to imagine that much will be effected by a shift from one kind of water to another.

At this point, the subject of American drinks might well seem to be nearing exhaustion, but there still remains milk. We can certainly be put down as the greatest milk-drinking country in the world. In fact, most of the civilized peoples consider milk scarcely fit to be drunk at all, except perhaps when mixed with coffee. In the United States, however, the drinking of milk reaches major proportions, and not only among children. There is probably no stranger sight for a European than to see, as he may in any American restaurant, a grown man drinking a glass of milk.

Our tradition is partly hereditary. Both England and Holland were good dairying countries, and the drinking of milk was not uncommon, at least in the country districts. Governor Delaware, reporting on Virginia in 1611, declared that during the last winter the cows had done well: "milk being a great nourishment and refreshing to our people." The Reverend Jonas Michaelius, writing from New Netherland in 1628, complained of the comparative lack of milk there.

The widespread objection to alcoholic drink, and even to coffee and tea, especially for young people, has also emphasized the drinking of milk. Along with this has gone the strong belief in its healthfulness, a belief supported by the advice of doctors and dentists, and reinforced by the scientific production of a safe milk. Some have even expressed the opinion that the drinking of milk is a symbol of American mother-worship, but in view of the many other reasons, this one seems scarcely necessary in addition.

To the present point this discussion of American drink has proceeded without any mention of the one that most Euro-

peans might consider most typical—the cocktail. As this chapter should have demonstrated, the cocktail is not nearly as
characteristic of the United States as is iced tea, "soft drinks,"
and milk. Still, it seems to have been an American invention,
and calls for brief comment.

The word itself, never satisfactorily explained, can be traced
back to about 1800. At that time whiskey-drinking was rapidly
growing more popular, and early cocktails were probably associated with whiskey. Perhaps we can consider it significant
that an "old-fashioned" is constructed on a whiskey base. Since
a great many people actually dislike the taste of whiskey, the
cocktail may have originated in attempts to make it palatable.
One means was to add sugar, and "to take it with sugar" came
to be a common American expression. Bitters could also be
added. With whiskey, sugar, and bitters, we have already the
beginnings of an old-fashioned, and the taste of the whiskey
has been fairly well disguised.

6

A chapter on American drink should not end without some
discussion of American attitudes toward drinking. We have
here a great contrast with attitudes on eating. In general, the
American is tolerant about what is eaten. Short of cannibalism,
and perhaps hippophagy, he has no strong food aversions, and
even cannibalism is probably not restricted by law, since in the
rigor of frontier life the necessity of saving one's life by means
of the body of a dead companion was recognized.

To understand the situation better, we should recall that the
typical early American was a Protestant, and therefore was
likely to know his Bible. In particular, he knew Acts 10, in
which the Lord himself had specifically declared that not only

"fourfooted beasts of the earth, and wild beasts" along with "fowls of the air" had been declared fit to eat, but also even "creeping things."

If there was necessity, then, or if he even felt moved to do so, a man committed no sin to eat any of the strange new beasts of the land, such as an opossum or a raccoon or a skunk. He could even eat frog legs, for a frog was obviously four-footed, and the specific mention of "creeping things" allowed a starving man to eat a rattlesnake in good conscience. Moreover, this tolerance as regards eating seemed to be borne out practically. A man did not develop an insatiable craving for possum meat, nor did he fall into a swinish stupor after a supper of frog legs.

With drink, it was different. Peter had had no revelation permitting him to drink all things. The Good Book mentioned neither rum nor gin nor whiskey, and as regards wine, it could be quoted in both directions. The Lord's first miracle had supplied wine for the wedding at Cana, and such an example was not to be discarded lightly. Paul had written to Timothy: "Use a little wine for thy stomach's sake," and such a suggestion of medicinal use could be, and was, stretched considerably. On the other hand, there were many texts on the other side, particularly in *Proverbs*: "Look not thou upon the wine when it is red," and "Wine is a mocker, strong drink is raging." The words, "strong drink," in fact, suggested even a prophecy of such things as gin and whiskey. Moreover, on the practical side, there were the obvious evils of alcoholism.

As a result, both for religious and for practical reasons, Americans developed an intolerance about certain drinking habits that they never developed about any eating habits. Beginning as an objection to the stronger alcoholic drinks, it spread to wine and beer, passed on to tea and coffee, and has even included certain soft drinks. Various religious sects, notably the

Mormons, have forbidden not only alcoholic liquors, but even tea and coffee. From the opposite angle, the drinking of milk, at least by adults, has been attacked as infantilism, and the term "milk-sop" has been an opprobrious one. There have been confirmed whiskey-drinkers who have professed to look upon the use of water with abhorrence.

7

Yet, when all is said and done, perhaps water remains the first among our drinks. So we may end where we began. The American originally drank water because he had nothing else available. Gradually he learned to like it. The present-day American, no matter what else he may drink, almost certainly drinks a considerable amount of water. It is likely to come to the table at every meal. Even if you sit down at a soda fountain in hot weather, the clerk may bring you a glass of water, automatically, before even taking your order. In schools, in public buildings, on the street, the drinking fountain is a national institution.

In the older days, there was much pride taken in the good taste of local water, and it is still so in country places. The older American, in fact, considered himself something of a connoisseur. "This spring," he would say, "has the best-tasting water in the county." Or, he would say, "Our well has very good water."[3]

In these days of great dams and hydraulic systems, water has been standardized, like so much else. Its taste is likely to depend chiefly upon how much chlorine the sanitary engineers

[3]The American attitude toward water is well indicated by Mark Twain's remark, "Geniuses are like wine; I am like water; everybody likes water." In Europe such a statement would ring strangely.

think necessary to dump into it. No longer is it possible to leave even "Adam's ale" as God made it.

Like our habits of food, our habits of drink have sprung from a complex mingling of hereditary and environmental sources. Both also show a number of native developments. Both are marked by much individuality, and by a willingness to adapt, change, and experiment.

By way of contrast, the next chapter presents the story of American clothing. The interest that attaches to this subject lies, one might say in paradox, in its poverty. In clothing, the Americans have originated and contributed little, and present little that is distinctive.

CHAPTER 7

CLOTHING

When we Earthlings at last begin to colonize Mars, or whatever planet is next in line, we may find it already thinly inhabited by certain indigenous tribes. If so, it is to be hoped that we pay some attention to the already established customs of the country, and assume that these natives are not altogether foolish in the adjustments that they have made to their environment. In particular, we might well pay some attention to their dress, and consider adopting parts of it at least, on the probability that through the course of millennia it has been evolved to suit local conditions.

Probably, of course, we shall do no such thing. Most likely, we shall stick by our own clothing along with our other customs, and shall be vastly uncomfortable and die by thousands before striking off some adjustment. We shall have plenty of precedent in so doing, and shall only be following the general course dictated by ordinary human conservatism and stupidity. Certainly we shall have the precedent of the conduct of those first colonists who came to America.

Take the matter of their clothing. . . . Exactly what they

were wearing, we do not, of course, know precisely. Imaginative illustrators often show them with such things as Elizabethan ruffs and lace cuffs. But however impractical and ignorant they may have been, they were probably not so ignorant and impractical as that! We can scarcely believe, either, that many of them were wearing high boots, though they are often so represented. Such gear is for horsemen, and there would be no horses for a while. But we can at least be sure that they were dressed in some adaptation of the ordinary Elizabethan costume.

As some Indian looked out from his covert at these strange creatures standing on the deck of the ship, he would have seen them, very strangely, almost completely swathed with clothing. Even their hands might have been covered with gloves, and on their heads they doubtless wore close-fitting Monmouth caps or broad-brimmed hats. High collars might even have covered the backs of their necks, so that only with their faces did they establish direct contact with the world. On the upper halves of their bodies, they were wearing close-fitting, long-sleeved doublets or jerkins, most often made of leather or of a stiff material like sailcloth. They wore knee breeches of the same materials, hose, and stout leather shoes.

As for the Indian, he was wearing only moccasins and a small bit of some material such as deerskin to cover what the colonial writers generally term "his privy parts." Whether he wore this for modesty or for protection may be argued. Undoubtedly he wore it merely by tradition, without stopping to analyze why he wore it, any more than the English did for their clothing.

Two long-established traditions of clothing thus met in full career. The Indian's costume, or lack of it, was almost wholly functional. He protected the parts that most needed protection, exposed his skin to the healthful sun and air, kept himself cool in the hot weather, and after a summer shower was not encumbered and rendered uncomfortable by wet and steamy clothing. In the winters he draped himself in deerskin.

English costume also had a functional background. It protected the wearer against the chills and damps of a moist and seldom overheated island. Leather gave some protection against a sword cut, and might turn an arrow. Knee breeches and hose allowed freedom of movement, and shoes protected the feet even better than moccasins did.

But the functionalism of the Englishman's dress was overlaid, almost to the point of being obscured, by other features. His costume was conceived as ornament, and through it he also expressed his rank, wealth, and ability to practice what a later philosopher of the land was to call "conspicuous consumption." His costume was also involved with what is called modesty, and thence passed on into the field of morality, and eventually to that of religion.

All these things being so, can we imagine one of the Jamestown colonists, in the stifling heat of that first summer, coming to his captain with some such words as these: "Sir, we are dying like flies in this heat that never was in England, and have grown so weak with it that we can scarce shoulder our snaphances. Why do we not strip off our smothering clothes, and go as the Indians go, who have learned how to live in this land?"

No, we can be fairly certain that no Englishman ever made such a suggestion. Instead, the more he saw of the Indians' near nudity, the more he wrapped himself in his own clothes as a mark of his civilization and Christianity. And in the following years, as aggressions and wars—now started by one side, now by the other—built up the intensity of race hatred, the clothed and civilized and Christian Englishman stood over against the naked and savage and heathen Indian.

Even men of good will did not minimize this difference of clothing. Thus Jasper Danckaerts equated religion and race and clothing, when talking to a despondent Indian, telling him: "He must not make such a difference between himself and a Christian, because one was white and the other red, and one wore clothes and the other went almost naked."

Thus, during three centuries, before he began to compromise, the transplanted northwestern European cloaked himself in wool and leather, and suffered through the summers and died in the heat waves, but maintained the symbols of his race and religion.

The adjustment, when there was any, had to come from the other direction, when the Indian put on European clothes. As early as 1631, for instance, Winthrop tells of a visiting Indian in Boston who "stayed all night, and, being in English clothes, the governor set him at his own table, where he behaved himself as soberly, etc., as an Englishman." Obviously, the putting on of European clothes was considered an essential part of his Anglicization.

In short, the colonists faced three choices as regards clothing. They could take ideas from the Indians. They could develop their own ideas. They could follow European models. Probably without even realizing that they had any choice or that anything else could possibly be done, they followed European models.

2

Therefore—as opposed to the colorful history of American food and drink—there is very little to be told about the history of American clothing. The first colonists arrived in some form of ordinary seventeenth-century English costume. As the decades passed and modes of dress changed in the mother country, so they changed too in the colonies. Doubtless there was always a lag, for the faraway colonies did not get the new styles very quickly, and most of the colonists were poor and unable to keep up with the latest fashions. But in the long run the colonists followed. In the eighteenth century an American gentleman was not distinguishable from an English gentleman. Both would be wearing three-cornered hats, rather tight knee breeches, buckled shoes, and long coats of some rich color.

This is not to say that there was complete uniformity; there were actually variations according to region, sect, and economic status. New England showed some differences from Virginia, and the descendants of the old Dutch colonists still displayed certain Dutch qualities in their dress, such as that amplitude of breeches for which they were satirized in Irving's *Knickerbocker History*. The Quakers eschewed rich and colorful clothing, and so did the Mennonites and the Methodists.

But there was nothing specifically American about such distinctions. You could not tell an English Quaker from an American Quaker, or an English Methodist from an American Methodist. So it continued, even after independence and into the nineteenth century. A great revolution in men's clothing brought in beavers and pantaloons, and old Major Melville was left wandering around Boston in his cocked hat and knee breeches, to be immortalized in Holmes's poem *The Last Leaf*. But doubtless many a last leaf lingered also in English towns, and in adopting the new costume, the United States was merely following Europe.

One may say, paradoxically, that the strongest testimony for the undistinctive quality of American dress is the lack of testimony. Travelers from other countries, in their accounts, seldom mention clothing at all. They are full of comments upon other matters—food, drink, religious sects. They even tell not a little about housing. But when they mention how anyone was dressed, it is generally to write that he or she was "well dressed," or "poorly dressed," or "fashionably garbed." And even such comment is rare.

It seems to be the same, no matter who the traveler or when he came, or what parts of the country he visited. You can examine Jasper Danckaerts, a Dutchman who came in 1679, or Peter Kalm, a Swede who came in 1748, or William Weld, an Englishman who came in 1795. Or you can examine the writings of any of the innumerable Europeans, especially British, who traveled here in the nineteenth century and went home to write a book about America. They tell next to nothing about dress.

The conclusion is obvious. Travelers, notoriously, write about what is different from their own country. In fact, they have difficulty even in seeing that many things are the same. So, when we find that travelers consistently fail to mention anything at all about American dress, we have very strong evidence that American dress, at any given time, did not differ much from European dress of the same period.

Consider, even, the matter of "wearing" beards, which are a kind of ornament and therefore allied to clothing. The history of pogonotrophy in the United States has not yet been exhaustively investigated, and much of it remains obscure—which is only a scholar's way of saying that he knows less about it than he would like to know. We are safe in asserting, however, that the beard had its greatest flourishing with us, roughly, from 1860 to 1890.

But it was not a native idea. The French seem to have begun the fashion, and in California of the Gold Rush period beards were noted as characteristic of Frenchmen.

Walt Whitman had a short beard in 1850 or a little before. He may have been under French influence in this, as in using such words as élèves, and en masse. He really let his beard grow during the fifties. So did thousands of other Americans. Lincoln was nominated clean-shaven in 1860, and inaugurated with a beard in 1861. Biographers have wondered why he should thus change himself, at the age of fifty-two, and have found no special explanation. Quite possibly he was merely conforming to the custom of the time.

You can view the rise and fall of facial hair very dramatically in illustrations that give, all on one page, the portraits of the presidents, presumably as they were when they occupied the White House. Lincoln is the first with a beard. Johnson was clean-shaven, but then came the deluge. Grant was bearded. Hayes (1877–81) had the longest beard of any president. Garfield was a close second. Arthur, though he had a smooth chin, sported a good mustache and very handsome sideburns. Cleveland, however, had only a mustache. Then came Benjamin Harrison (1889–93), the last, so far, of the bearded presidents. Since him we have had only two mustaches—Theodore Roosevelt, and Taft. Our last seven presidents have been clean-shaven, thus resembling the first fifteen.

The Civil War was the most hirsute in our history—perhaps in anybody's history. A portrait of Grant in 1862 shows him with a magnificent flowing beard, obscuring several buttons on his major general's uniform. He later cropped it to the stubby thing of Appomattox and the White House. Not only the generals but even the men in the ranks were largely bearded, as the song "Till the Boys Come Home" recognizes in the line about their "grim and bearded faces."

But there is nothing peculiarly American in all this growth of hair. Tennyson, Carlyle, and Dickens were all bearded in the same decades as Whitman, Longfellow, and Melville.

And when European beards began to go, so did American beards.

In extenuation of this lack of creativity, in beards and in dress, one can point out that the whole period of the last three centuries has been one of unification and standardization in matters of costume. In 1700 and even in 1800 Europe was diversified and colorful with national costumes, both for peasants and for gentlefolk, but by the opening of the twentieth century these had mostly disappeared. Merely on the basis of costume it has become difficult or impossible to distinguish a well-to-do Swede from a well-to-do Spaniard, or a French shopkeeper from a Greek shopkeeper. The whole trend of the times was therefore against any development of originality in American clothing.

3

A few costumes may be noted that are historical or regional, or the mark of some way of life. Most of these sprang from the frontier, and never made much impression upon the centers of American civilization. They remain now only as fine symbols of the past and of a colorful frontier that has vanished. Such is the fringed hunting shirt of deerskin, as worn by Natty Bumppo and described in the first chapter of Cooper's *Pioneers*. The frontiersman used for it the commonest material of the forest and the one most often employed by the Indians, and from it fashioned a garment somewhat after the European tradition. With such a hunting shirt went often the coonskin cap, with its memories of Davy Crockett. As a good American symbol it was revived by Senator Kefauver in his campaign of 1952.

Linsey-woolsey, woven half of linen and half of wool, was a product of the frontier. Clothes of this material, both for men and for women, were frequently dyed with the native butternut to a characteristic yellow-brown.

There are other costumes, too, to be remembered from the

past. There is the California Forty-niner, with red shirt and knee boots. There is the farmer's wife in sunbonnet, for protection against the summer heat. There is the obsolescent cowboy costume, half Spanish with ten-gallon hat (*sombrero*) and chaps (*chaparejos*) for leg protection in brushy country. All of these, however, are chiefly of the past, and are only revived for the benefit of small boys or some local nostalgic celebration.

4

In the end, then, what can we note as distinctively American or as an American contribution to our present costume?

From the Indians we seem to have taken only one thing—the moccasin. The word itself is an Indian one, recorded from the early years of Jamestown. Easily fashioned from deerskin, moccasins remained in use always on the frontier, where regular-made shoes were difficult to obtain. The tradition was apparently never lost, and the moccasin-type shoe—notable for its comfort—has become increasingly popular in recent years and seems to have established itself.

Blue overalls and jeans, for working clothes, have become as typical of the American workingman as the blue shirt is of a French laborer. They have also become standard wear for the American small boy, and even for many American small girls. From the manufacturing firm of Levi Strauss and Co., one form of such garment has taken the name Levis (never used in the singular), and has supplied a new word.

Only within the last generation have the beginnings of a major revolution in men's clothing been effected, so that we can claim some creative quality. Until 1920 and even later the standard man's costume required a three-piece suit with a tight vest. This still reflected European conditions, where heat was seldom a problem. It also reflected the complete covering of the body in heavy clothing that had become identified with civilization and Christianity. In hot weather the American male had only the choice of wearing proper clothes and being uncomfortable, or of sitting in his shirt sleeves and being comfortable but dressed in a makeshift fashion.[1]

After 1920 the trend toward informality began. Perhaps it may be considered an evidence of the maturity of the country —that our people had begun to think independently in matters of costume. We may also think it an evidence of the maturity of American Christianity that the increasing display of bare skin has been effected without any great fulmination against it from the pulpits.

In the course of this revolution the vest and the stiff collar, one may say, have become obsolete, and also on the way to join the Elizabethan ruff are men's garters, neckties, and undershirts. Hats also—to the great concern of hat manufacturers— have become something to be worn only in inclement weather. To take the place of the stiff uniform of 1920, sport clothes have developed—informal, loose in design, light in weight, cheerful with bright colors. Even materials have changed, and the American is being clothed more and more in plastics, largely the product of his own inventiveness.

The movement toward informality in dress has, of course,

[1] In considering the history of clothing with relation to adjustment to hot and cold weather, we must remember that the individual seems to have immense adjustability, according to the costume to which he is accustomed. Europeans were frequently amazed at the ability of scantily dressed Indians to endure cold. My father, who had been accustomed throughout his life to wear a vest, always appalled me with his willingness to wear a vest in hot weather. A Union officer at Gettysburg tells that he was hit by a spent bullet, but not badly injured because he was wearing three suits of underwear! If I had been wearing three suits of underwear on that hot July day, no one would have needed to shoot me. I would have been dead already.

its international relationships. On the whole, however, the leadership seems to have been American, and thus after three stagnating centuries we at last produce what may be considered a significant contribution in the field of costume.

Women's clothes have also felt the prevailing surge toward informality, and there is a striking and obvious contrast between the tightly, severely, and heavily garmented American woman of the seventies and eighties, and her granddaughter and great-granddaughter of today. This change, however, seems to have followed international trends, more than the corresponding change in men's clothes, and American creativeness is less marked. Even though American designers, in Hollywood and elsewhere, have begun to take the lead, women's fashions seem to remain essentially international.

Of greater importance in women's clothes is the American success at mass production. The result is seen in the frequently expressed failure of the foreigner, the male at least, to tell the shopgirl from the manager's wife. The result is democratic both in its feeling and in its results. It is the effect of machine production, which makes possible the cheap and fairly good imitations of expensive clothes. But the situation is also a result of a unification of taste by literacy and national advertising, which makes the shopgirl actually wish to wear the same clothes that the lady (if we may use such an archaic term) is wearing. Of course, the cheap imitation never deceives a woman's eyes. It does, however, deceive a man—and that is what is important. Sometimes, indeed, there is actually nothing to be deceived about. At times, for instance, by the anomalies of modern economics, two kinds of nylon stockings that not only look alike but are exactly the same, except for the labels, may be sold in the same store. The one will be sold at a high price, so that the woman with money will think she is getting something special. The other will be sold at a low price,

for the benefit of the person who supposedly has to be resigned
to something second-rate.

Although not entirely without interest, the history of American clothing thus yields much less than does the history of
American foods or drinks. The hereditary influence and the
domination of international ideas control the situation, until
in the twentieth century certain native developments, not
without an environmental relationship, begin to assume importance.

CHAPTER **8**

SHELTER

In considering the development of the
United States we are constantly inclined to forget one important fact—the utter and abysmal ignorance of the first
colonists as to how to cope with the wilderness. Transferred
immediately, without experience or schooling, from the highly
civilized countries of England and Holland, they can only be
described as complete greenhorns. They were much more inno-
cent and helpless, in fact, than the average American man of
today would be if placed in similar circumstances. The present-
day American has had some boy-scout training, or gone on a
camping trip, or at the very least he has read in books or picked
up at school some tradition of pioneering. He would be likely,
moreover, to have some knowledge of the dangers of mosquitoes, rats, and polluted drinking water.

The men who landed at Jamestown knew none of these
things; apparently they did not even know how to make themselves comfortable. And being comfortable, we may say, means
a great deal, more, when it comes to founding a colony, than
merely being comfortable. If a man is cold and wet and unable

to sleep well, he soon grows dispirited and listless. Then he wears down physically, and falls sick at the first occasion. Once down, he may never get up. One reason for the death of many of the Jamestown colonists may have been merely their inability to shelter themselves.

Some of them, indeed, had knocked about as soldiers, but a soldier expected to be uncomfortable only for the duration of a campaign and there was excitement to compensate. Besides, most wars were fought in civilized countries, such as the Netherlands, and in his bivouacking a soldier could forage on the country and often get under a roof at night. One of John Smith's great advantages was that he had traveled, if we can believe his stories, in primitive forested countries, such as Transylvania, and had seen how people lived there, and had probably picked up a few of the tricks.

This brief sermon is preached at this point because the difference between the greenhorn and the experienced woodsman nowhere shows up more clearly than in the ability of one and the inability of the other to take care of himself when away from houses and towns, and doing so is primarily a problem of providing shelter.

2

Shelter was like drink. Unlike food and clothing, but like drink, it was too bulky to be brought over in the ships, except in a makeshift way. Tents could be transported, and there were tents at Jamestown, but even before the first hot and humid summer had passed, the cloth was rotten. The settlers erected temporary shelters to supplement or replace the tents, but seem to have botched the job, being quite inexperienced in such matters. Smith describes the "cabins" as "worse than nought." Doubtless they were flimsy structures of branches and bark that gave a shade and shed a light rain, but would be of little help against the downpour and wind of a Virginia thunderstorm.

In New England it was the same story. Bradford sums it up in a couplet:

> And till such time as we could houses get,
> We were exposed to much cold and wet.

At Boston the poorer people spent much of the first winter with little other shelter than tents. They suffered severely, as they naturally would, when trying to live through a Massachusetts winter with no better protection.

Everywhere, therefore, the men set out to provide some kind of quickly made, temporary shelter that would at least be better than a tent. After they had seen Indian houses, the colonists had some models to work by. Smith describes these, not without a suggestion of envy at the savages' ingenuity: "Their houses are built like our arbors of small young springs [saplings] bowed and tied, and so close covered with mats or the barks of trees very handsomely, that notwithstanding either wind, rain, or weather, they are as warm as stoves." Some settlers imitated these structures, and the Indian word *wigwam* was used to describe them.

The dugout was another expedient, although the word in this meaning did not come into use until the nineteenth century. Some of the first Jamestown settlers are described as living in "holes within the ground." The dugouts of the first settlers of Concord, Massachusetts, have become famous by being commemorated in Thoreau's *Walden:* "Old Johnson, in his 'Wonder-Working Providence,' speaking of the first settlers of this town, with whom he was contemporary, tells us that 'they burrow themselves in the earth for their first shelter under some hillside, and casting the soil [earth] aloft upon timber, they make a smoky fire against the earth, at the highest side.'" As might be expected, such elaborated fox-holes were far from satisfactory, and as Johnson continues, perhaps too mildly, "the long rains penetrate through, to their great disturbance in the night season." The same writer applies the word wigwam to these dugouts, good evidence that, as might be expected, it had come to mean any kind of makeshift shelter.

Besides cabins and wigwams, the settlers also erected what they called huts, booths, and cottages. (In the nineteenth century they would probably have been called shanties; now, we would call them shacks.) The very multiplicity of terms probably indicates that these shelters were not particularly one thing or another, but were merely the expedients of hard-pressed people who had no specific answer to the problem at hand. After long centuries of living in towns and on well-established farms, all racial memory of "life in the woods" had been lost. Even in the seventeenth century there were some Englishmen—shepherds on the northern moors, woodcutters and charcoal-burners in the Sussex weald—who knew how to make themselves comfortable on their own. But they were only a few; though the Jamestown lists enter men of many different occupations, they specify no shepherds or woodsmen.

The Dutch were not better prepared. In 1626 a description of the settlement on Manhattan Island indicates that the countinghouse was built of stone, thatched with reed. Then it adds: "the other houses are of the bark of trees." Such structures must have been no better than the huts and hovels and booths of the English.

Obviously one of the first needs of the colonists was for decent houses. The wigwam, easily constructed and proved by experience to be adapted to the climate, might actually have served them very well as a starting point, and they could then have elaborated upon it. But just as the colonists rejected what the Indians had to offer as regards clothing and many other matters, so also they rejected the Indians' system of housing. A wigwam could keep the cold and rain out, but it lacked the associations of civilization and Christianity and home. So, as their models, the colonists kept in their minds the houses of England and Holland.

As for material, the land offered all the wood that a man could ever desire. The English, moreover, had a magnificent and still flourishing tradition of building in wood, for in England there were some forests remaining. The Dutch knew less about wood at the beginning, but they learned.

Strictly speaking, what was available for building was not wood, but trees, and the chief difficulty was not the raw material, but the shaping of it. To serve for the framing of a house, small tree trunks would do, more or less squared up by an ax. Boards for the facing were called clapboards or weatherboards; without too much labor they could be split from billets of some straight-grained wood, such as cedar. The floor could be of dirt. In a pinch, there need be no windows. Since nails were extremely expensive, wooden pins would be used as much as possible, or timbers could be "joined" by mortise and tenon. Thatch of reed or straw, with which all English cottagers were familiar, supplied the roof. The chimney could be built up of small logs, smeared with clay on the inside. In houses of this kind the people of Plymouth were apparently living in 1628, when the Dutchman Isaack de Rasieres visited there and mentioned that the buildings were of "split plank," that is, clapboard.

Such a house might be described as "basic," an early equivalent of our war housing. In one of them a family could live vastly better than in a tent or dugout. It could be improved, too. Next year, clay or some other kind of "daub" could be smeared on, to close the chinks between clapboards and keep the wind out. In a few years, if things prospered, there might even be a wooden floor, and a window with glass panes in it.

The construction of even a basic house involved a considerable amount of labor. Especially if the dwelling was to have any likelihood of permanency, the beams had to be fairly well squared out and truly set. All this involved a great deal of ax- or saw-work. Doubtless, for the better houses, the clapboard was sawn; split clapboard was doubtful stuff, and did not make tight joints. At any rate, from the very beginning in Virginia we find record of clapboard and of sawyers, but not of special clapboard-makers, though these latter are mentioned a little later in New England.[1]

In all this early building there is a predominance of the hereditary factor, although the use of wood was determined by the environment. One should remember also that in the early period, as in any other, there was tremendous variation in the quality of the houses. Just as any present city has its slums as well as its palaces, and just as any town has its right and wrong side of the railroad tracks, so any early settlement had its huts and hovels where its poor and unlucky and shiftless people lived, and also its comfortable or even luxurious houses which

[1] The trade of being a sawyer and of working at the purely mechanical job of sawing out planks in a saw pit was rather common in early times, as is shown by the occurrence of the family name Sawyer. Water-driven sawmills had actually been invented before the seventeenth century, but their introduction into England had been prevented by the hostility of the sawyers, who were afraid of loosing their jobs. In New England, however, where water power was readily available, sawmills were operating vigorously before the end of the sixteen-thirties. In the same decade the Dutch were sawing lumber on Manhattan Island by means of windmills. Thus, as so often in American, labor shortage led to the introduction of machinery, and a certain pattern of life was set from the beginning.

housed its well-to-do gentlefolk. Also, in the backwoods and along the frontier, primitive conditions of housing existed concurrently with advanced conditions in the more settled areas. Even in 1636, when the settlers of Concord spent their miserable winter in dugouts, there were well-built houses in the Massachusetts coast towns. Dates, therefore, mean little, and we always have to ask ourselves where the house was located as well as when it was built.

What was apparently a basic English house of the seventeenth century is described by Jasper Danckaerts. The date was 1679, and the location was at the present site of Trenton, New Jersey. It was a framed house. The clapboards had been split from billets, and were five or six feet long—sharp at one edge, "thick as a little finger" on the other. They were "nailed on the outside of the frame with the edges lapped over one another, generally not so close as to keep you from sticking a finger between them, because of their not being well joined or because of the boards being crooked." Danckaerts declared: "Nearly all the English houses in the country are like this." He adds that to keep out the wind and cold: "the best people smear them with clay." Danckaerts spent a miserable November night in this house, with a northwester howling outside and sending a chilly draft through every gaping crack between the unchinked clapboards. He concluded glumly: "I shall not readily forget this night."

Danckaerts obviously ended with a low opinion of the English as builders, but he was Dutch and may be suspected of nationalistic prejudice. He had the bad luck to have the weather turn cold at this particular time. Besides, this location at the falls of the Delaware was frontier country; Trenton was not really founded there until a generation later. In addition, Danckaerts himself mentions that the house had just been built, and so it had presumably not been finished off as well as it would be later. So, from this single example, we should not condemn all English building practice, though Danckaerts was ready to do so, after his bad night. Still, what he tells us is a severe indictment of split clapboard.[2]

3

In all this discussion of early housing, the reader may have wondered at the omission of any reference to the log cabin. As everyone knows, it is the most typical building of the American frontier, and the conventional imaginative drawing of Plymouth or Jamestown is likely to show such structures. But the truth is that it is simply not so.

Neither the English nor the Dutch built log cabins at first, and apparently did not even know how to do so.

In its origins, the log cabin is very ancient. Doubtless not long after the invention of a good metal ax someone discovered the trick. Vitruvius, the Roman writer on architecture of the first century B.C., tells about the log houses of the Colchians, who lived in a heavily forested country at the eastern end of the Black Sea. His description of how one was built might have been written by Daniel Boone. But if the ancestors of the early colonists had ever known about log construction, the information had not been passed along to the settlers of Jamestown and Plymouth and New Amsterdam.[3]

[2]This house, poor as it was, must have been fairly expensive to build because of the nails that were used to fasten the clapboards to the frame. Because of the expense there must always have been a tendency to economize on nails, and so the clapboards were probably not well fastened.

[3]Log construction of the type with which we are familiar was also used in Japan from an early date, before A.D. 1000. A surviving example of log construction in England is part of the Saxon church at Green-

The Swedes and Finns, who settled on the Delaware River in 1638, were the ones who knew about building log cabins. Of all the colonists they were the only ones who as a group had been used to living in heavily forested country, and they had built such houses there, in the forests of Sweden and Finland.

The log cabin might be called the answer to the frontiersman's prayer. Without it the forested country of the eastern United States could only have been settled with much greater difficulty and delay and hardship.

The advantages of a log cabin over a basic framed house were many. 1) It required only an ax for a tool, and so the frontiersman needed only to carry an ax with him in order to be able to build a house. 2) It required no nails. Each log was held in position by its own weight and by being notched into the logs above and below. This was a tremendous advantage at a time when nails were expensive to buy and often impossible to transport. 3) The construction of a log cabin required some knowledge of the trick, but only moderate skill with an ax, and no other skill at all. 4) The construction of a log cabin demanded, in comparison with the other kinds of houses, very little labor. On one occasion, for instance, there is record that three men built a log cabin big enough to house them all, in two days. It had no window and only an opening for a door, but it was roofed with cowhides laid on pine branches for rafters, and had a fireplace and chimney. In addition to their own labor the men had the help of two cows to snake the logs in. Even so, the expenditure of only six man-days of labor is very little by which to obtain a serviceable dwelling. By using

sted in Essex, but here the logs are split and set upright, palisade-fashion. The details of the history of the American log cabin are too complicated to be presented here.

only small logs a man could handle them by himself, and required no helper at all. 5) A log cabin was much more comfortable than the ordinary frame-and-plank house. The logs were usually from six to eight inches in diameter, and so supplied good insulation. They could easily be "chinked" with moss or mud, and after that treatment the cabin was weatherproof. 6) A log cabin was long-lasting, and seldom demanded repairs. It had no flimsy knife-edged clapboards to warp in the hot weather, and no nails to loosen in the frosts. 7) A log cabin was also, in a small way, a fort. It was not easily set on fire; its logs, if well set and hewn a little on the upper and lower faces, were comfortably bulletproof. Small wonder that it triumphed!

The association of the log cabin with the Swedes and also some of its advantages are admirably shown by the testimony of our indispensable Jasper Danckaerts. The very next day after spending his uncomfortable night in the drafty English house, he came into what we may call the Swedish sphere of influence, at Burlington, New Jersey. Here he lodged in a house "made in the Swedish manner." It was a log cabin, "without a nail or a spike." He adds: "these houses are very tight and warm," and he passed a good night.

By this time, after forty years of Swedish occupation, the log cabin had apparently traveled only a few miles north of the actual Swedish settlements. Doubtless by this time it had reached Maryland along with the deserters from New Sweden who had been escaping into English jurisdiction as early as 1658. Eventually—one might say, like whiskey—it took over all the West and South. Also like whiskey it worked into New England, though it was probably never so common there, at least in the parts that had been settled early.

The lack of a log-cabin tradition in New England is shown by the manner of construction of what is the most famous cabin in our literature. For, neither in its materials nor in its workmanship, was Thoreau's structure at Walden a log cabin. To be sure, he began by cutting down "some tall, arrowy white pines, still in their youth," but, as he tells it, "I hewed the main timbers six inches square, most of the studs on two sides only and the rafters and floor timbers on one side." Moreover, he bought nails to the value of $3.90, and for siding he used boards. Some might say that in not building a log cabin Thoreau was merely, as so often, being a non-conformist. This would be incorrect. In building a basic framed house he was actually conforming to Massachusetts tradition.

But in general the log cabin was triumphant. Its advantages were manifold and apparent. Only in the most treeless of the plains country was it impossible to build, and there it was replaced by the sod shanty. Even in the Great Basin country, where timber was scanty, it paid to build a log cabin, even though you might have to haul the logs for twenty miles. Besides, by this time the tradition was strong. In the mountain states many such houses are still being lived in, though nowadays, if you wish to see log structure in its glory, you must penetrate British Columbia and see the sometimes magnificent ones that run up to two stories. A modern adaptation is the cabin that is constructed in much the old-fashioned way but uses discarded railroad ties. You find them particularly in treeless Nevada.

Although it was unimportant in the earliest years and although it fails to spring from either Virginia or Massachusetts or New Netherland, the log cabin has entered very deeply into the American consciousness, and has supplied one of the most cogent of our symbols. In 1840 the "Log-Cabin and Hard-Cider Campaign" won the voters. In the decades following, log-cabin birth became our equivalent of Norman blood. So great a statesman and so astute a politician as Daniel Webster once made what amounts to a public apology for not having first seen the light within log walls. According to a classic American student's boner, in which truth seems to conquer accuracy: "Abraham Lincoln was born in a log cabin that he built with his own hands."

Most Americans, as they trace their family histories back, encounter the log cabin. My great-great-grandfather, with the assistance of some neighbors, built one in a single day, and on the next day moved into it—a quick solution of the housing problem. His son, as told in the not uneloquent words of *his* son, married him a wife and then: "young, ardent, and full of life and hope, they commenced life in a log cabin on the southeastern slope of the Chestnut Ridge, on a piece of God's earth unclaimed, unturned, and uncultivated." My grandfather was born in that cabin.

Yet, in spite of all that it has been, the log cabin may be said to represent only a major digression. It supplied a serviceable shelter at the primitive level, but there was nothing into which it could develop. Moreover, it demanded excessive amounts of wood, and could be built only when and where wood was to be had for the taking. At the present cost of lumber a log cabin is, in most parts of the country, one of the most expensive constructions that one can imagine.

4

To return, then, from this digression—we left the colonists some years after the first landings, at a time when they were beginning to live in framed houses. As Thoreau's "old Johnson" sums the situation up in 1654: "The Lord hath been pleased to turn all the wigwams, huts and hovels the English dwelt in at their first coming into orderly, fair, and well-built houses." These houses were certainly English in style and planning, but Johnson does not comment upon what must have been to him too obvious and natural to demand comment.

In unimportant details even, these houses reproduced English models. For instance, in some of them the upper story jutted out above the lower story. This had been a device, in a crowded medieval town, to obtain more room by making an aerial encroachment upon the narrow street.[4]

The carry-over of the tradition of this crowded medieval town, together with the habits that it necessitated, was to be of great importance in the American tradition, and in some details we have even yet not entirely escaped from it. Such a town was crowded, primarily because of its encircling wall. A wall was expensive to build, and once built was not likely to be enlarged. Moreover, for defensive purposes, the smaller its circuit the better. As the town grew, additional houses could be built in suburbs outside the wall, but there they were defenseless. Most people, and especially the wealthier citizens, crowded their living quarters inside the wall, until the area became jammed and the timbered houses rose up three or four stories, jutting out as they rose.

Some of the early colonial settlements were built on restricted sites for military reasons. Jamestown stood on an easily defensible peninsula, but it never grew large enough to make the problem of congestion an acute one. New Amsterdam was founded on the tip of an island, and once had a rampart, now commemorated in the line of Wall Street. Boston and Charleston, also, were founded on sites chosen for possibilities of defense. But even these cities were never tightly held in behind

[4]Other reasons for these projecting stories have been suggested, e.g., cantilever (hammer-beam) construction, water-shedding, and convenience in dumping slops. In any case, they appear to be merely traditional in America.

their fortifications, and most colonial towns and villages were free to spread in several directions.

The curious reality, however, is that they did not spread, but remained rather tightly packed. Primarily, lacking any practical reason, we must assume that the colonists continued to live tightly packed together because of mere tradition—that was the way they had always lived, and so they continued. With a whole continent to spread into, they often still built two- or three-storied houses in a continuous row along a street. There were indeed a few practical advantages to this. A single wall might be made to serve for two houses, and each house gave the other some protection from the cold of winter. Moreover, when there was no public transportation and you walked as a matter of course, there were social and practical reasons for a concentrated town.

On the other hand, there was a frightful fire hazard, as long as houses were built of wood, and particularly if they were roofed with highly inflammable thatch. Most of Jamestown burned soon after it had been built. Plymouth had a serious and almost disastrous fire within its first year. Two houses were burned at Boston in 1631, and conflagrations were so frequent in later years that in 1700 a chronicler could write: "Ten times has the fire made notable ruins among us."

The remedy, as the colonists conceived it, was not to spread the houses farther apart, but to employ more fireproof material. Sometimes stone was used, but building in stone is always expensive and slow. Both the English and the Dutch, however, had a strong tradition of building in brick, and brick proved to be practical. So strong was this tradition in Jacobean England that we find bricks made in Virginia almost from the beginning, and they were used in the building of houses at Henrico in 1612. A brick kiln is mentioned as being constructed at Salem, Massachusetts, in 1629. In the same year ten thousand

brick were sent from England to Massachusetts, particularly
for the construction of fireplaces.

Nevertheless, in spite of such early beginning, brick made
slow progress against the competition of cheap timber. A description of Boston in 1657 indicates that it was still built
chiefly of wood. The Dutch at home were even more devoted
than the English to building with brick, and some brick was
manufactured on Manhattan as early as 1628. But as late as
1678 the buildings of New York were described as "most
wood, some, lately, stone and brick." Houses in the towns of
West-Jersey in 1681 were: "some built of brick, some of timber." Even Philadelphia, a silver-spoon foundation from the
beginning, was originally built chiefly in wood, and several
years after its establishment the building of five brick houses
in one summer was unusual enough to be mentioned with
pride by a citizen writing a letter to England.

The turning point was probably around 1700, or shortly
thereafter. By that time the more firmly established American
towns had begun to assume the look that they were to maintain for a century and a half, and to some extent have not lost
even at the present time. The favorite material was brick.
Timber construction was losing in popularity, partly because
of the fire hazard, and partly because timber was becoming
more expensive. The forests in the close vicinity of towns had
been cut down, and transportation of bulky and heavy material
like timber was expensive. But brick could be manufactured
almost anywhere. Brick thus became relatively cheap, especially when its durability and fireproof qualities were taken into
consideration. So we come into the era of brick, whether the
style of architecture is Queen Anne or Georgian or Classical
Revival.

As a result we have the tightly built American towns, remarkably like those of England for the same period. Not in-

frequently, the brick walls of the houses form a solid front, close to the street. The most famous examples of this kind of construction are the early-nineteenth-century "rows" of Baltimore and Philadelphia, but similar constructions are to be found in hundreds of towns. On the whole, it was a thoughtless and traditionally motivated transfer of medieval conditions to a new country.

With even less logic, rural architecture followed urban models. Many farmhouses were built broad, straight, and narrow —as if to face on a street. Moreover, many of them had no windows in their ends, or very inadequate ones, as if assuming that another building was to be constructed against the wall. There was little sense of adaptation to the site.

Too often such a house seems merely a chunk cut out of a city street, and imposed upon the farm. It suggests that life is to be lived indoors. There are no courtyards or patios, and few porches. The comparatively few and small windows suggest a fear of winter cold rather than any attempt to alleviate the fierce summer heat by admitting the breeze. Even the Southern plantation house, with its classical columns emphasizing height, and its porches mere porticoes, often seems something foreign and imposed upon the land rather than something naturally connected with it.[5]

Walt Whitman, whose father was a builder and who himself had worked as a carpenter, gives a good description of the building of an early-nineteenth-century house. Though he elsewhere writes of building in brick, this particular house is of wood:

[5]Nevertheless, as might be expected, there was generally a greater emphasis upon porches, etc., in the South. Weld, traveling through Virginia in 1796, before the flourishing of the Classical Revival, commented: "In front of every house is a porch or pent-house, commonly extending the whole length of the building; very often there is one also in the rear, and sometimes all round. These porches afford an agreeable shade from the sun during summer."

The house-builder at work in cities or anywhere,
The preparatory jointing, squaring, sawing, mortising,
The hoist-up of beams, the push of them in their places, laying
them regular,
Setting the studs by their tenons in the mortises, according as
they were prepared,
The blows of mallets and hammers, the attitudes of the men, their
curv'd limbs,
Bending, standing, astride the beams, driving in pins, holding on
by posts and braces,
The hook'd arm over the plate, the other arm wielding the axe,
The floor-men forcing the planks close, to be nail'd.

These carpenters were constructing the house, it should be
noted, just about as carpenters had been doing in the seventeenth century. They were shaping the timbers on the job—
few and heavy timbers, the hoisting up of which was a labor.
They were cutting mortises and tenons, pushing the tenoned
ends into place and pounding the timbers home with mallets.
They were fastening it all together with wooden pins, driven
in through auger-bored holes, just big enough so that the pins
fitted snugly. Obviously the building of such a house called
for a considerable amount of labor—some of it mere brute
force, but much of it highly skilled craftmanship.[6]

5

Another shift came about 1870. It affected both urban and
rural homes, and may be said to have applied the impulse that

[6]Whitman wrote these lines about 1855, and the type of framing
here described was already obsolescent at that time, because of the
invention of balloon framing. As poets often do, he may have been
thinking of what he remembered from his youth. Besides, balloon
framing was at first considered a cheap and shoddy method of building; as a man who knew his carpentry, Whitman may have preferred
to describe the traditional method.

still motivates our domestic architecture. First of all, the materials shifted back to wood.

Probably this shift resulted more from new economic conditions than from any special change in taste. By this time the railroads had linked the still magnificent virgin forests with the rapidly growing towns and cities, and cheap lumber was again available even at sites far removed from water transportation. Steam sawmills had helped to lower lumber prices. The railroads had also made cheap coal available, and central heating had been developed. People were therefore no longer so much afraid of the winter cold, and could begin to think of avoiding the summer heat. By this time all reason of crowding into restricted areas for purposes of defense had disappeared, and cheap land still permitted diffusion. Streetcars were coming in, and so there was less need to think in terms of walking. At the same time, the scattering of houses reduced the fire hazard and new methods of fire fighting had been invented.[7]

Even all these blind forces, however, could scarcely in themselves have produced the revolution. Somewhere a few individual non-conformists must have disliked the old-fashioned type of living, and begun to experiment. The new type of dwelling, which produced the new type of residence district, and therefore a new way of American living, differed from the old in four respects. 1) It was commonly built of wood. 2) It was not a house in a row, but stood individual and open on all

[7] The development of the so-called "balloon framing" (and its later adaptation, "western framing," or "platform framing") was also of great importance. This method of construction was known as early as 1850, but did not become common immediately. It is now used universally for the construction of framed houses. Its advantages over the older method were cheapness of materials and saving of labor. Without balloon framing the mushroom post-Civil War growth of such cities as Chicago would have been impossible. It seems to have been an American invention, made possible by standardization of power-sawed lumber and by cheap machine-made nails.

four sides. In European terms it was a "villa," although that term never became common in the United States and still carries vague suggestions of European grandeur. 3) The new house was set back from the street. It thus had, being open on all four sides, a front yard and a back yard, and at least small yards on the sides as well. 4) As adaptations for summer, the house displayed more and larger windows, and sprouted porches —front, back, and even side. The porches were often large, and a good deal of living took place on them. Moreover, they often gave on lawns shaded by fine trees so that the house was much more closely linked to the outdoors than it had previously been.

Lest anyone should think that only the homes of the well-to-do are being described, it should be noted that most of the new ideals of the home did not necessarily call for much expenditure. The isolated house with its front porch and front and back yards might be jerry-built, and a street of them might be no better than a slum, but it could still be something different.

The style of architecture in which these houses were constructed need not be our matter of concern. Actually, they were built in almost all possible styles, for American architecture since the eighteen-sixties has been appallingly eclectic. Since the change roughly coincided with the Gothic revival and with the invention of mechanical jig saws, the early examples of these houses were often vaguely Gothic and were hung with elaborate "gingerbread." But questions of architectural style were by no means as basic as the four features already listed. So basic indeed have these become that most American architects merely think within that pattern and imagine nothing else, when planning a dwelling house. In fact, the laws of most American towns and cities require detached dwellings for most of the resident districts, and specify that the buildings must be set back from the street a certain number of feet, thus making a front yard obligatory.

This revolution in the method of shelter has affected the American way of life considerably. The sharp contrast between indoors and outdoors has been broken down, and as the American has come to work more indoors, he has begun to be a little more outdoors in the ordinary course of his living. The new houses, especially since they were often tree-shaded, allowed the American to live more comfortably in the fierce heat of his summers.[8]

The new houses also allowed the American to develop his ego. He was able not only to live more spaciously but also by that very process to live more ostentatiously. Having for so long inhabited a mere undistinguished unit of a block-long brick row, he now wanted to display his individuality. The American architect met him more than halfway. The result has been the greatest flourishing of architectural "styles" that the world has ever seen. Not only the physically isolated house but also the individually designed house has come to be the American ideal, and the American pays extravagantly for it. Even yet the "pre-fab" house fights an uphill battle against this love of individuality.

The change also, if we may put it in such fashion, brought into American life an extraordinary lack of privacy. The new

[8]The refusal of the transplanted northwestern European to adjust to the torrid summers is one of the most notable exemplifications of his traditionalism. It is almost as evident in shelter as in clothing. Even his attempt to adjust by means of windows and porches was a doubtful expedient. The device of a thick-walled, small-windowed house surrounding a patio, designed to keep the sun out rather than to let the breeze in, as seen in Mexico, is perhaps better conceived. The American's final answer seems to be air-conditioning, and this may well transform life in many parts of the country. It represents, characteristically, a complete defiance of the environment, by means of a mechanical device.

house faced outward. Anyone could see what happened on its
porches, and its large windows made secrets hard to keep. The
yards—front, back, and side—were wholly open to the view.
Surrounding walls and high fences were often forbidden by
law and always by convention. The house was conceived, not
only as a dwelling for its owner, but also as a "show place"
for the community. Even the surrounding of one's lot by a
hedge could be construed as an unneighborly act.

The new house was, in fact, an unconscious but therefore
even more striking evidence of a unified society. Men will live
without privacy only when they essentially have nothing to
conceal. Just as the medieval cloister declared that he who
dwelt in it had withdrawn himself from the world, so the new
American house declared that all men were much the same.
Or at least it showed that a man could expose his life to the
gaze of his neighbors because he had nothing to conceal.

The effect of this evolution upon the towns themselves has
been profound. As the houses were spaced more widely the
towns became more diffuse. In spite of public transportation,
"getting around" came to be more and more a problem. Then
came the automobile. As a result the town became more diffuse
than ever, and the automobile became necessary for efficient
life even in a fairly small town.

The utmost diffusion is to be seen in places that have developed wholly or chiefly since the popularization of the automobile. Some western towns merely seem to be houses vaguely
scattered over a landscape.

6

We have not moved very far in our habits of shelter since
the revolution of the later nineteenth century. There has been

some evolution. Urban life has become more common, and in apartment houses people have once more come to live more closely crowded together and yet with much more privacy. The two, paradoxically, seem to work together. The more crowding, the more privacy—because crowded conditions make lack of privacy intolerable. In the individual house also the trend toward privacy is observable. The front porch has largely disappeared, and has yielded to the private, or at least partially protected, court or patio. Hedges and fences have somewhat returned to popularity, although the high cost of stone- and brick-work still restrains the building of walls.

Modern conditions have also produced other effects. Small families and increasing lack of servants have led to the building of smaller and smaller houses. The old four-room downstairs plan called for parlor, sitting room or library, dining room, and kitchen. First of all, the parlor (used only for funerals, weddings, and callers) coalesced with the sitting room or library, and the whole became the living room. Recently, in many modern homes, it has also absorbed the dining room. Even the kitchen is sometimes being treated as part of the general living area, and included as a kind of alcove. In a sense, with small families, no servants, and always rising cost of building, the American family has been returning to the one-room log cabin.

If the modern American dwelling is in some ways returning to this simplicity, it also very largely maintains the structure of the original English framed houses. The house in which this book is being written is located on the opposite side of the continent from Jamestown, Plymouth, and Trenton, and was built in 1950. Yet it employs the same material and basically the same type of construction that were used in those far-off and early settlements, and its carpenters talked, as their predecessors by three centuries talked, of studs and joists and rafters. It is faced with "shiplap" planks nailed to the studs, and these are really nothing but sawn clapboards. The joints are tighter against a northwester than those in the house where Jasper Danckaerts spent his bad night, and the redwood siding is from a tree unknown in either England or New Jersey. But the workman who built that house by the falls of the Delaware would find no mystery in the construction of this rather typical modern American house. Details—the concrete foundations, the "western" framing, and the flattish roof—would puzzle them, but, on the whole, the house is only an exemplification of the Bricklayer's conclusion in Kipling's Truthful Song:

> How very little, since things were made,
> Things have altered in the building trade.

Even though a modern house may be faced in stucco, it still maintains a wooden frame as its basic structure.[9]

But in other respects the modern American home has moved in the opposite direction. The cabin had only its fireplace, with a minimum of pots and kettles. The early houses had little more, but the modern dwelling, conceived as a mechanical complex, is just slightly simpler than a two-engined bomber. It is warmed, let us say, by a gas furnace with electrical control. It may also be cooled in summer by an electric air-cooling mechanism. The cooking is done on an electric stove with a number of automatic controls. The kitchen also has a dishwasher, garbage-disposal unit, refrigerator and freezer, and an electrified collection of toasters, mixing machines, waffle irons, coffeepots, and so forth. The clock is also electric. So, in the laundry, are the washing machine, drier, and

[9]Just as many people would think of the cocktail as the typical American drink, so they might think of the steel-framed skyscraper as our typical building. Actually, such buildings must constitute far less than one per cent of the total. For that obvious reason, they have not been discussed in this chapter.

ironer. Telephone and electric lights and doorbell may be taken for granted. Even the living room has its electrical clock, TV, radio, and record-player. Getting such a unit broken in and smoothly running is likely to require several weeks of time and many visits by servicemen, and may be compared to the shakedown cruise of a warship. Getting it paid for is likely to take half a lifetime.

Yet in all this mingling of environmental influences, native developments, and international ideas, certain traditional and ancestral qualities still remain—anachronistic but undisturbed. Chief among these is the open fireplace. Logically, it is as much out of place as a thatch roof or puncheon floor. It survives, obviously, not for practical reasons, because it is expensive to build and expensive to operate. It scarcely survives even by aesthetic standards, for the blackened brick and the strewn hearth that generally confront us in a modern home are anything but beautiful. It survives, obviously, because the presence of even an occasional open fire brings a deep-seated satis-faction to most people. Before it, they experience, whether consciously or not, some deep upwelling of ancestral feelings, which may have been brought down from the times of the log cabin, or possibly even from the times of the campfire.

By and large, the colonists denied the environment, and practiced their hereditary habits of housing. Only with the revolution that came over housing in the later nineteenth century did the environmental influence become strong—in the use of wood and of space, both made possible by the existence of a well-forested continental country. Some of these new ideas must be credited to native creativeness; there seems to have been little influence of later immigrants. International ideas have operated chiefly at the artistic level. Thus the style of American houses has been Greek, Gothic, or modern, as the civilization of the United States has felt the impact of the international movements known as the Greek revival, the Gothic revival, and modernism. At a more basic level, however, we may maintain that the American home, considered as a place to live, has not been much affected by what has been happening in other countries.

CHAPTER **9**

S E X

An American student—whether ignorant of
the meaning of words or inspired by some Demon of the
Greater Truth—once wrote in an examination about "all the
opportunities for luxury and lust offered by a private home."
Perhaps we may find here the justification for having *Sex* follow *Shelter*. Perhaps, also, as the chapter may demonstrate, sex
in the United States has historically kept close company with
domesticity. Many, however, will doubtless maintain that a
chapter on sex needs no justification at all, and is of enough
importance to be inserted anywhere.

Like the chapter on religion this one, also, must begin with
a disclaimer. Just as, with religion, we have to be content with
an external view, so it must be, even more obviously, with sex.
No professor circulated with his questionnaires at Jamestown
or in seventeenth-century Boston—and he would probably have
been flogged and banished if he had tried any such thing. And
even Dr. Kinsey has reported to us chiefly on the outlets of
sex rather than the deeper feelings connected with it.

Yet, in the long course of centuries, certain tendencies stand out with some degree of clarity. As with religion, merely because we lack a great body of intimate detail, we are not altogether prevented from seeing some general trends and drawing a few conclusions.

The attitudes of Americans toward sex, and their practices, are not well to be understood without a brief consideration of European backgrounds. . . . In the Middle Ages, under the domination of the scarcely challenged Catholic Church, there had arisen a conception that may be called tripartite. First, and best, one might live celibate and virgin, thus emulating many of the most notable saints. Second, and second best, one might live, faithfully, in the married state. Third, and worst, one might indulge, whether married or not, in what is sometimes described as "loose living."

Inevitably such a three-way division reacted against the dignity of marriage. If marriage was at best only second best, an important distinction—perhaps, the main distinction—came to be between celibacy and marriage, not between marriage and loose living. Chaucer's Wife of Bath, in the prologue to her tale, expresses this state of mind excellently. The Church, moreover, had an attitude toward marriage which some have been tempted to consider ambivalent. On the one hand, it elevated marriage to the sanctity of a sacrament; on the other hand, it commonly solemnized marriages not in the church itself but only, symbolically, at the church door.

On the whole, the attitude of the later Middle Ages toward sex may be described as tolerant and easygoing. Prostitution flourished in the cities. The upper classes indulged in a good deal of romantic adultery, and the peasants, in much carefree romping in the hay.

Protestantism affected the condition of marriage in two ways. By denying any special virtue to celibacy and by permitting the marriage of the clergy, the Protestants made marriage the most highly approved state, and so increased its dignity. On the other hand, they refused to consider it a sacrament and frequently treated it as a mere civil contract. The Protestants also admitted—in theory, at least—the possibility of divorce. By and large, however, the Reformation changed marriage less than it changed much else. By that time marriage was already a centuries-old folkway, not to be easily or quickly affected by the ideas of theologians.

If we then consider marriage as a folkway, we can note that by the time of the establishment of the first colonies two attitudes toward it had arisen. Neither of these had special connection with any theology, and pious members of any church might hold to either of them.

First, and more commonly, there was what we may call the "unromantic" marriage, most often "arranged" for the girl by her parents. In such a marriage sexuality was secondarily conceived. The assumption was, we may believe, that as a sex partner any woman or any man was likely to be satisfactory enough. As important individually, and much more important in the aggregate, were the other factors of such a marriage— the adjustment of property through dowries and marriage settlements, the setting up of the conventional living arrangement called a home, the perpetuation of the family.

With such a conception of marriage, infidelity raised no serious problem. Since there had been no great love to begin with, there was less likely to be any great jealousy later. In fact, though adultery was established by English law as a cause for divorce, such a charge could be made to stand against the husband only if his adulteries had become public and notorious. Even adultery by the wife, especially after legitimate heirs had been obtained, might be leniently regarded by society, though less leniently by the law.

On the other hand, the Elizabethan times had some idea of the "romantic" marriage. Such a marriage was conceived as resulting from the mutual attraction of an individual man and woman, sexuality as primary, and property arrangements, living conditions, and the perpetuation of the family as secondary.

From the point of view of the man, we can sum up the two conceptions of marriage briefly. The unromantic marriage is based upon the assumption: "Any normal woman is suitable to share the marriage bed. What is needful, or at least equally important, is a wife to be a good housekeeper and mother, and the possessor of a dowry." The romantic marriage, however, proceeds upon the assumption: "Any woman can be a good housekeeper, and so forth. Or, if she is not, that is not most important. What is needed in marriage is a wife who can bring the transcendent bliss of love."

Obviously the two conceptions are not mutually exclusive. A love match may occur between two young people whom their parents are delighted to join for prudential reasons as well, and on occasion two who are being married for prudential reasons may fall in love besides. Still, the two conceptions, mingled though they may be, represent a basic reality in the life of the last few centuries. Most of us, knowing the Elizabethan period chiefly through Shakespeare's plays, are likely to think of the Elizabethans as dominated by the romantic conception. But Romeo and Juliet, as the tragedy well demonstrates, are actually, and disastrously, flouting the usual practice of their time. Moreover, in some of the plays there is a strong unromantic element that underlies the superficial romantic one. The Merchant of Venice, for instance, is considered a romantic play, but Bassanio obviously has an eye on the main chance, and his first words about Portia are: "In Belmont is a lady richly left." In the long speech that follows he indicates not the slightest affection for her, although he implies (the cad!) that she is

174 AMERICAN WAYS OF LIFE

rather smitten by him. Francis Bacon undoubtedly was correct, for a reflection of opinions of that time, when he wrote: "The stage is more beholding to love than the life of man," and added, "In life it [love] doth much mischief."

On the whole we are probably safe in assuming that the English people of the early seventeenth century generally held to an idea of marriage that was essentially unromantic, and that the colonists were therefore of that opinion. But conditions in America soon produced a change.

2

The first English colony was highly unusual in lacking women entirely. Jamestown has been described as not so much a colony as a camp. But it was not even a typical camp. It completely lacked camp-followers.

As to what solution of the sex problem was attained by these hundred-odd lusty men, we are (lacking any set of answered questionnaires) in ignorance. Probably there was some commerce with the Indian women, but relationships with the tribes were so commonly hostile that there was little opportunity for many of the colonists to acquire concubines. Doubtless the Jamestown colonists behaved about as we should expect of a battalion of United States marines garrisoned on a South Sea island with little chance to fraternize with the natives.

Jamestown was transformed, gradually, by the importation of women for wives. Care was taken that only decent women should be sent out, and at the same time it was specified that they should not be forced "to marry against their wills." Each prospective husband had to pay his wife's passage money.

On the whole, therefore, these women were in an advantageous position. They were in demand. Granted that they accepted the usual Elizabethan idea of the unromantic marriage, they did not expect their prospective husbands to be romantic lovers. Granted that they had survived a moderately well-conducted screening in England and so were not physically repulsive, each woman must have found herself sought after by a number of men, and so was in a position to enjoy the situation and exercise some choice. Moreover, considering the human propensity to become excited over a member of the opposite sex actually present, we can imagine that love, or something to be easily mistaken for it, soon arose in a large proportion of cases.

In fact, the importation of wives, though it rested basically upon the unromantic conception of marriage, might actually do much to create a romantic conception. The drab fact that these women had been recruited and sent over for breeding purposes, much like cows or mares, was probably more than counterbalanced by the fact that they were fewer than the men and thus tended to acquire a romantic quality.

Abnormal though it was, the Jamestown colony set a pattern —men without women—that was to be recurrent and common in American history. The same situation occurred constantly on the frontier. Many mining camps of 1849 were as wholly devoid of women as was Jamestown. Even later, in mining camps and lumber camps and cow camps, women were lacking. On the frontier in general, even if women were not wholly absent, they were comparatively few. As a result, women from the very beginning possessed something in America that they had never possessed in Europe. They had rarity-value.[1] A

[1] In a stable community in Western civilization the numbers of the sexes are normally about the same, but since marriage has traditionally offered more, socially and economically, to a woman than to a man, there are always more men who for one reason or another do not wish to marry. This tips the balance against the women, maintains the dowry system, and tends to make women a drug on the market.

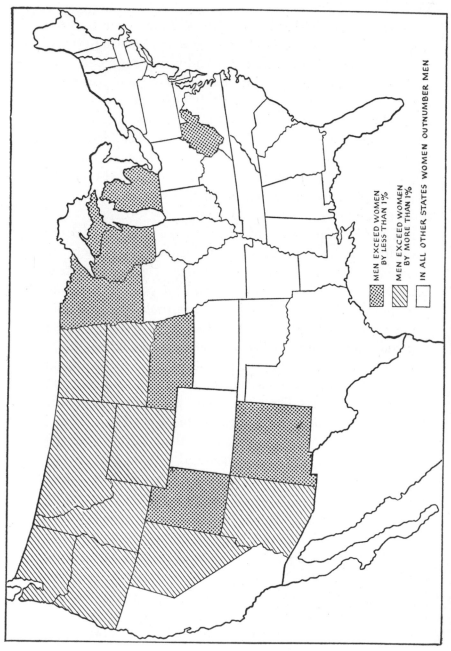

MEN AND WOMEN (1950 *Census*)

MEN AND WOMEN MAP
(1950 Census)

Because women found it more difficult to emigrate than men did, the early colonies had a considerable excess of men. This gave women a rarity-value, and has affected our attitudes toward marriage and our sex habits in general. Early conditions were continued along the frontier and in the newer parts of the country. Even yet, though the total number of women in the United States exceeds that of men, the men are in an appreciable majority in nine western states. Their proportion rises highest in the two least populous states, Wyoming and Nevada. The excess is about 8%.

rarity is prized. Being thus rare, a woman had the opportunity for choice. On the frontier she felt no fear of eventually missing a husband. As the line of a folk song goes: "There's still quite a lot of young men to be had."

The situation inevitably increased the status of marriage. A girl did not have to accept a less honorable arrangement. In addition, the situation worked toward the reinforcement of the ideal of romantic marriage. A suitor was not in a position to demand a dowry when half a dozen other suitors were in competition. Moreover, because of the equalitarianism of the frontier, a girl found little to choose between suitors as far as property and position were concerned, and so was free to make her choice by what the novelists came to call "the dictates of her own heart."

Some still prevailing American attitudes toward marriage thus stem from the original scarcity of women, and so can be traced historically to the original Jamestown colony. The condition has not even yet wholly disappeared. In eight western states there is still an appreciable excess of men over women, and the Eastern girl who goes there, as schoolmarm or in other capacity, has a better chance of getting married than if she stays at home.

3

From the very beginning, the New England colonies differed from Virginia in their pattern of sex relationships, as in so much else. But again, here as elsewhere, the differences were rather superficial.

One difference appears in that the colonists who landed from the *Mayflower* were not a horde of men, but a fairly well-balanced community. Among those one-hundred-two there were eighteen married couples, who with their children totaled about two thirds of the company. What was true of Plymouth was also true of the other Puritan colonies. They were built up around the family, not the individual, as the unit.

But the likeness to the situation in Virginia appears when we remember that about one third of the *Mayflower* company was composed of unattached men. In the other Puritan colonies also men were normally in excess, because unmarried women could not so easily emigrate to America as could unmarried men. So we have, here also, the typical situation, with marriageable girls in an advantageous position.

In general, therefore, the basic pattern remained the same in Virginia and New England, not only because both the colonies had originated from England, but also because the conditions in the colonies themselves were essentially the same.

Thus, though the arranged marriage had some vogue in New England, more romantic ideas soon became prevalent, as they seem likely to do when women are in the minority and thus cease to be considered as chattels and begin to have some freedom of choice. Actual differences between New England and Virginia in the conception of marriage—and eventually these were to be of importance in American life—seem to have arisen chiefly from differences in ideology. In Virginia the Church of England was dominant. The theory of that church as regards marriage was not greatly altered from that of the Roman Catholic. Couples were married by a minister, and marriage was conceived as based on religious sanctions and dissolvable only by death. Practically speaking, under English law and with the blessing of the Church of England, there was no divorce.

The Puritans had broken with that church, and had different ideas. Doubtless to a considerable extent as a reaction against Catholicism, they conceived marriage as a civil matter.

The situation is well established by Bradford's note dating from the first spring at Plymouth:

May 12 was the first marriage in this place, which . . . was thought most requisite to be performed by the magistrate, as being a civil thing, upon which many questions about inheritances do depend, with other things most proper to their cognizance, and most consonant to the scriptures. *Ruth: 4.* and nowhere found in the gospel to be laid on the ministers as part of their office.

In early New England, ministers were actually forbidden to solemnize marriages. As late as 1685 a clergyman, thus offending, was haled to court and required to give his word to desist. Only after 1686, when the New England colonies came more directly under the power of the Crown, was the religious marriage instituted.

The Puritans also allowed divorce. In so doing, they were departing in this as in other ways from the tradition of the Catholic Church and were returning to the Bible. Not only had the Mosaic law allowed free divorce, but also Christ himself had specifically permitted it for the cause of adultery and by implication had allowed remarriage. The Puritans even went a little farther. They recognized desertion as a cause, doubtless assuming that sooner or later desertion meant adultery. Considering marriage as primarily a civil matter, they were even inclined to go farther, and grant still other causes for divorce, such as cruelty.

All this does not mean that divorce was common. In fact, it was extremely rare. Moreover, it was usually coupled with criminal action, so that the divorced person was likely to be whipped and fined, as well as divorced.

In the long run, this New England attitude toward marriage has had a tremendous influence upon that of the modern United States, doubtless in part because other influences joined with it. Thus the separation of church and state was not accomplished primarily because of an attitude toward marriage; but, once accomplished, it assured the triumph of the Puritan idea of the civil contract. Thus marriage exists in the United States primarily as a civil affair. A couple may be married by a magistrate without any religious ceremony. On the other hand, they may be married by a minister or priest, but this ceremony must be legally recorded, so that the minister or priest, even in such cases, may be said to be acting as an agent of the civil authority.[2]

At this point one might attempt to correct the prevalent modern conception that the Puritan, in some way or other, was opposed to sex. This belief seems to be widely held in modern times, and along with it goes that other belief that the Catholic Church favored sex. The actuality is rather the reverse. Naturally, both good Catholics and good Puritans have opposed the expression of sex except when regularized by the marriage bond. But the Catholic Church is the one that has set up the high ideal of virginity, and has forbidden even marriage to its priests. On the contrary, the Puritans had no ideal of virginity as such, and encouraged marriage at an early age. Their ministers also were regularly married, and were among the most enthusiastic practitioners of the Biblical injunction: "Be fruitful and multiply." Although no statistics are available as to the inside workings of a Puritan marriage, there is nothing to indicate that restraint was considered a virtue, and the large numbers of children indicate that sex within marriage was far from being considered sinful.[3]

[2]The modern American attitude toward divorce seems also to stem from Puritan sources. See a later section of this chapter.

[3]The stricter Puritans did not approve of sex on Sunday. The fact that this limitation upon one day in seven was apparently considered something of a restriction suggests a high rather than a low activity.

4

During the later part of the colonial period, in most of the colonies, sex seems to have been about as little of a "problem" as it can well be expected to be in any society. Throughout the South and along the frontier, special conditions existed, but elsewhere we have a situation that may be called Utopian.

In the more settled parts of the northern and middle colonies the situation can well be described merely as "sex through marriage." Both men and women—we should say, boys and girls—were married at such an early age that pre-marital sex problems hardly had a chance to develop. Grooms were generally under twenty; brides were commonly fifteen, and not infrequently fourteen or thirteen.[4]

Because of the tendency of the young man to drift off to the frontier, there was generally no excess of males. The unmarried man was in fact so unusual as to be rather an object of suspicion, and in New England was sometimes subject to a tax. Widowers, and widows, seldom remained single for long, so that one historian has described the situation as producing "universal, early, and repeated marriage."

In general, the attitude toward marriage might be termed "moderately romantic." The well-to-do expected to give marriage portions with their daughters, and therefore to have something to say about whom they married. But there was little tradition of forcing a daughter against her will or even of marrying her without consulting her wishes. Though in Samuel Sewall's eyes Captain Tuthill looked like a very good son-in-law,

[4] I once came across a New Jersey will in which the father stipulated that his daughter should receive a certain inheritance: "when she reaches the age of fifteen, or marries."

Betty Sewall would have none of him when he came wooing in 1699, and her father did not insist. And, at most, the well-to-do were a small class.

Among the general run of people, on the farms and in the villages, marriageable young men and women were likely to follow their own inclinations. Generally, however, they had little enough choice at best. In such small communities you were practically forced to marry the girl next door, and to do it quickly before someone else grabbed her off. Loving may go by liking, but it also goes by propinquity.

As an example of what we have called "moderately romantic," one may quote William Penn's advice. Being a Quaker, he held to the Quaker belief that marriage should spring from reciprocal affection, but the way he put it was: "Never marry but for love, but see that thou lovest what is lovely." And among the lovely qualities of a girl we can be fairly sure that a good Quaker would have included the impending inheritance of a prosperous farm.

Writing about 1775, Crèvecoeur in his *Letters from an American Farmer* generalizes on marriage:

Every man takes a wife as soon as he chooses, and that is generally very early; no portion is required, none is expected; no marriage articles are drawn up among us, by skillful lawyers, to puzzle and lead posterity to the bar, or to satisfy the pride of the parties. We give nothing with our daughters; their education, their health, and the customary out-set, are all that the fathers of numerous families can afford. As the wife's fortune consists principally in her future economy, modesty, and skillful management, so the huband's is founded on his abilities to labor, on his health, and the knowledge of some trade or business.

Crèvecoeur, being French-born, must originally have thought in terms of arranged marriage, and so his approval of American customs is of more significance. As with Penn, however, his attitudes seem to be the "moderately romantic." He fails to mention love.[5]

As for anything except "sex through marriage" this period in the northern and middle colonies has rather little to offer to the pages of history. . . . In Boston, New York, and a few other seaports, a little prostitution was in evidence. This was, however, largely for the convenience of the sailors. In any case, so few people lived in cities that such an urban vice as prostitution could not deeply affect the whole community.

Homosexuality seems to have been so rare as to be scarcely recognized. Laws against "sodomy and buggery" stood on the books, but they were rarely invoked. The whole tradition, both Christian and Germanic, was strongly against homosexuality, and though it was accepted in some Indian tribes, there was nothing to indicate that the practice spread from them to the colonial population.[6]

[5]In this passage Crèvecoeur is ostensibly writing of the Nantucket Quakers, but his use of "us" indicates that he is really referring to American conditions in general. He had lived chiefly in the middle colonies. In that region there was some diversity of marriage customs because of the variety of sects and national backgrounds, but conditions probably did not vary greatly from what has here been presented as a norm.

[6]The name Sodom, in frontier times applied to an occasional village or district, has now been almost banished from the map, but still appears as the name of a village in New York. In spite of the established use of the words sodomy and sodomite, one may doubt whether that specific sin commonly gave rise to these places being so named. They may merely have been notable for general hell-raising. In this connection, note that the word bugger has lost its specific meaning in common parlance, and come to be merely one of general opprobrium. Bradford's note of 1642: "even sodomy and buggery (things fearful to name) have broke forth in this land, oftener than once," suggests in its very language a minimal prevalence. Passages in E. S. Abdy's Journal (1835) indicate homosexuality among the more depraved classes, and he comments on one occasion, evidently as a superlative: "There is a greater regard for decency even in Paris."

In the cities, the keeping of mistresses, a popular eighteenth-century custom in Europe, was not unknown among the well-to-do. Benjamin Franklin, that solid American, was the father of two acknowledged illegitimate sons. Another famous case is that of Charles Henry Frankland, collector of the port of Boston in the seventeen-forties, who became enamored of Agnes Surriage. He first saw her scrubbing a tavern floor, barefooted. He had her educated, and set her up as his mistress, though not without creating something of a scandal. Eventually he married her, and since he had succeeded to a baronetcy, she became Lady Frankland, and a leader of Boston society.

In the colonial time, however, the upper classes were far from numerous, and their aberrations from the sexual norm are not statistically very significant. Much more important are the attitudes toward sex of the greatly predominating rural inhabitants. Perhaps this can best be summed up under a discussion of "bundling."

Unfortunately, there is no subject in American history about which less is definitely known, perhaps for obvious reasons, than about bundling. A current dictionary defines "to bundle" as "to sleep or lie in the same bed without undressing, esp. of sweethearts, as in early New England." This is as much as we can expect from a dictionary, but it obviously stops short of everything that we want to know. The apologists for bundling merely point out that it was a means by which young people could have some privacy and at the same time keep warm, and that since the bed was in the same house, if not in the same room, as the parents' bed, the young lady was actually much better chaperoned than if she were going for an automobile ride or even for a stroll down the lane. To this, the more cynical-minded are likely to say something about human nature, and leer. Since no Dr. Kinsey was operating in the middle colonies during the eighteenth century, we shall never know about bundling.

Lacking any broad statistical base, we can only gather from scattered bits of evidence that the colonial country people took a moderately relaxed attitude toward an occasional premarital lapse. In New England, particularly, the betrothal was solemnized with considerable formality. Doubtless many couples took their bundling more seriously after betrothal. If the intended husband then died or if he proved a rascal and absconded, the girl might be left with an illegitimate child. In such cases she was apparently considered unlucky rather than erring, and was not too deeply involved in disgrace.

Some interesting, though rudimentary, statistics on the matter have been supplied by Charles Francis Adams, in a paper read before the Massachusetts Historical Society in 1891, and based upon the study of church records in the towns of Braintree and Groton. He found that at certain periods the custom existed that newly married couples to whom a child was born before seven months had to confess before the congregation whether they had indulged in relations before marriage, or otherwise the child could not be baptized. Many confessed. Out of a total of about two hundred persons sixty-six did so in the years 1761 to 1775. As the historian adds:

> The entries recording these cases are very singular. At first the full name of the person, or persons in the case of husband and wife, is written, followed by the words "confessed and restored" in full. Somewhat later . . . the record becomes regularly "Confessed Fornication," which two years later is reduced to "Con. For.," which is subsequently still further abbreviated into merely "C. F."

Obviously, at that time and in those towns, the custom of accepting the betrothal as the real marriage must have become

the rule rather than the exception, and only the less enterpris-
ing couples failed to avail themselves of the opportunity.[7]

Doubtless an industrious cynic could collect from this colonial period a considerable list of sex crimes, and other evidences that all was not Utopian. Yet, admitting the frailty of
human beings and of human institutions, we are not likely to
see a better-adjusted period. Because of early and almost universal marriage there was little chance for repressions, and even
a little overstepping of the marriage line was not too rigor-
ously regarded.

The southern colonies, and the frontier regions generally,
offered certain contrasts. The number of slaves in the South
was already large, and that area had also received the greatest
number of indentured white servants. The women, of both
classes, were placed in a difficult position. They could not
easily repulse the advances of the men of the master class, nor
could they demand marriage. As a result, relations with women
of these classes became so common and casual as scarcely even
to be dignified by the name of concubinage. Among the upper
classes, the effect of this system upon marriage was rather less
than might have been expected. The propertied people not
only continued to marry for the purposes of maintaining prop-
erty- and family-succession but also maintained a considerable
romantic conception of marriage.

Among the lower classes, however, the colonial South dis-

[7] We must, of course, allow for couples who indulged but did not
conceive a child. The statistics, however, are far from being satisfactory.
In particular, they cover too short a period. Adams thinks that this
period may have been marked by unusual sex activity because of the
religious excitement (the Great Awakening) of that time. But the
failure to find "C. F." elsewhere and in other times may only indicate
that it was not commonly recorded. Indeed, one would think that
in general decency, especially since confession was considered to have
mitigated the sin, the fault would not have been recorded, except in
congregations that labored under an unusual sex obsession.

played a good deal of what may be called social disorganization. An observer reported of North Carolina in 1737: "The generality of them live after a loose and lascivious manner." A generation later another comment runs:

The manners of the North Carolinians in general are vile and corrupt and the whole country is a stage of debauchery, dissoluteness, and corruption. . . . Marriages (through want of clergy) are performed by every ordinary magistrate—polygamy is very common—celibacy much more—bastardy no disrepute, concubinage general.[8]

Doubtless the unfortunate reputation accorded North Carolina resulted not only from its position in the South but also from its general frontier character. In the backwoods, Indian women were frequently available. Frontier couples might be those who had run away from legal husbands or wives somewhere else, without the formalities of divorce. Few questions were asked. Almost no ministers were available to perform marriages; often, not even magistrates.

The moralist, however, must level his censure against the conditions, not against either the Southerners or the frontiersmen. Those colonists were caught in the toils of a vast economic system, of which the sexual effects were a mere corollary. The sex habits of the frontier, also, sprang out of a kind of economic and geographic determinism. Many a frontier boy and girl, with no minister or magistrate nearer than fifty miles, merely did what came naturally, and then set out to cohabit and raise a family. Practically speaking, they may have made just as good a marriage of it as if they had been blessed by an archbishop. The amazing thing is really that the in-

[8] As one who has many friends in North Carolina and has much admiration for its present status, and particularly for its universities, I regret that this book contains so many derogatory references to its early condition. As a colony, it stood badly in need of a good public relations office. It rarely got any kind of mention except a bad one.

fluence of the easygoing frontier morality did not have a greater influence upon later American life than it actually seems to have had.

5

The nineteenth century, given a few extra years at either end, may be considered a period of transition in American attitudes toward sex.

A quick judgment might be that the importance of marriage declined during this period, and much evidence might be adduced to support this view. The customary age rose sharply until marriages at the age of twenty-five and thirty were commonplace and even first marriages of older people were not surprising. In addition, larger and larger numbers of people did not marry at all. Prostitution increased. Divorces became common, and moralists shook their heads over this "failure of marriage."

But these evidences of the decline of the importance of marriage should not blind us to its advances in the same period. During the nineteenth century the frontier was finally submerged, and with it vanished much of the traditional looseness of living. In the same century, moreover, marriage vastly increased its status among the Negroes. As slaves, in an alien culture, marriage had little of meaning or of value for them. Even if some ceremony was performed, this did not assure them any rights in their children or prevent husband and wife from being arbitrarily and permanently separated at the wish of the master. Emancipation changed the legal status, and allowed Negroes to contract marriages that were fully binding. By the end of the century the respect for marriage among the Negroes had grown so that one would have had difficulty in saying on which side of the color line, in comparable social and economic conditions, the marriage tie was held in greater respect.

The growth of prostitution which marked the nineteenth century was chiefly a phenomenon of the cities, and of the boom towns of the frontier. As our civilization became more and more urban, the "red-light districts" grew more numerous and larger. Some of them, as in New Orleans and San Francisco, acquired a considerable glamour. Cities were necessary for the growth of prostitution, because they gave a sufficient concentration of population to make the business profitable, and also because they offered anonymity and supplied a large floating population of men. Another factor was the generally increasing age at which marriage occurred. After 1840 immigration was also a contributory cause. Many of these immigrants were from European countries in which prostitution was an established part of the way of life. Moreover, the immigrants largely flocked to the cities, and included a large proportion of unattached men. Even in this heyday, however, prostitution never occupied a position in American life comparable to that which it has held in the life of many European countries.

Marriage remained the ideal, and the nineteenth century, on the whole, built up the romantic ideal. The literature of the time is not, indeed, without its mentions of fortune-hunters, and of parents who arranged advantageous marriages for their daughters. But, on the whole, American young people were encouraged to follow their own feelings, and they generally did so. Even after she lost her rarity value, the American girl was not expected to supply a dowry, and a young man was rather more likely to resent any implication that he would not be able to support his wife than to expect aid from her parents.

The so-called Romantic Movement itself, profoundly affect-
ing people's imaginations during the century, was undoubtedly
a powerful factor in reinforcing the idea of the romantic marriage. Probably never before in the history of the world had
so many people been so forcibly impressed with the importance
of the emotional life, particularly with the importance of love.
That passion, which in earlier times had generally been considered a kind of human weakness, was accorded transcendent
importance and endowed with mystical value. In the United
States this conception of love was harmonized with the monogamous marriage, and the assumption was made that "real
love" was both violent and enduring.

At the same time, however, divorce increased steadily. By
mid-century conservative moralists were voicing their alarms.
They cried out that in 1843 there had been 447 bills of divorce-
ment sued in the state of Ohio alone. From Ohio, following
the line of the New England migration, the center of activity
moved on to Indiana, and by 1860 that state had become a
divorce mill. Horace Greeley referred to it as a paradise of free
lovers, where it was possible "to get unmarried nearly at pleasure." In those years it was sometimes possible for a person,
moving to a western state, to obtain a divorce without even
notifying the spouse. It could happen that a man or woman
became divorced without even knowing about it, and there are
records of people who wrote to various courts asking whether
their names had appeared on the records.

Then, as now, attitudes on divorce differed tremendously,
both by religious background and by regional distribution. The
Catholic Church would have none of it, and opposition was
almost as strong in many of the Protestant denominations.
Divorce flourished mostly among the unchurched, but it probably supplied, at the same time, one of the important reasons

for the lapsing of church affiliations. By maintaining their stand against divorce, the churches undoubtedly caused a steady drift away from organized religion.

The East and particularly the Southeast remained conservative, in law and in custom, and comparatively few divorces were sought or granted. The West, that region most thoroughly American and the least permeated by European tradition, was the great area of the flourishing. Thus fostered, the national divorce rate soared, decade by decade, through the century. In 1900, for instance, it was about three times what it had been in 1870.

This increase may seem to belie what has already been maintained—that the nineteenth century was devoted to the ideal of the romantic marriage. Actually, more closely considered, the two would seem really to be in harmony. Divorce frequently indicates not a low ideal of marriage but a high one. When people are married by arrangement, they expect rather little of marriage emotionally. They may therefore drift along indefinitely, and even infidelities, provided they do not become socially notorious, may cause little difficulty. Romantic marriage, however, is founded upon the expectation of great or even transcendent emotional return. When this high ideal is unrealized, a clean break, by means of divorce, often seems the most idealistic solution.

Moreover, in the American tradition, the highest romantic attachment has generally seemed incompatible with an illicit and therefore secret liaison. If this is really the great love, the American seems to think, it should be revealed proudly to the world, and therefore divorce and remarriage become necessary. Those who would count the increase of divorce as an evidence of disrespect for marriage are therefore arguing only from one point of view.

An interesting question of American history during the

nineteenth century is whether there was actually a decline in sexuality. The statement was made, particularly by foreign visitors, who commented upon the "coldness" of American women, and sometimes even of American men. These foreign visitors may, of course, have been judging chiefly by an unwillingness of American women to indulge in affairs, and may have been influenced by a memory of their own repulses. Yet quite possibly some such decline of sexuality may have occurred, especially among the women of the better classes. Romanticism itself sometimes cultivated an idealized love that might become platonic, and this tendency was augmented by Victorian prudery. Toward the end of the century an institution known as "platonic marriage" was actually presented as an ideal, and was even sometimes practiced.

On the whole, indeed, if we had to choose any group as "opposed to sex," it would have to be, not the early Puritans, but the better-class Americans of the later nineteenth century. "Science" itself seemed to have turned against sex, and the medical works available to the general reader emphasized the harmfulness, particularly to the male, of a lusty life. Continence was enjoined upon athletes. Thus, at that period, even when blessed by marriage, the activities of sex felt restraint.

6

Such practices are not, at this late date, susceptible of any statistical demonstration. Far different, plainly evident in the falling birth rate and in other ways, is that great discovery of the nineteenth century—the separation of sex and procreation.

Moreau de Saint Méry, a French émigré, declares in his memoirs that while operating a bookstore in Philadelphia, during the seventeen-nineties, he was the first to offer a contraceptive device for sale in that city, and found a ready market.

A generation later, in 1830, Robert Dale Owen published his little volume, *Moral Philosophy*. It was notable as a defense of the morality of birth control, but it also gave some practical information. It held French practices up as ideal. Although Owen wrote with the expectation that he would be vilified, he later expressed himself as surprised that he had been so generally praised. The book sold rapidly.

Within two years, in 1832, Dr. Charles Knowlton published his *Fruits of Philosophy; or, the Private Companion of Young Married People*. If Owen's approach might be called that of the sociologist, Knowlton's was definitely that of the physician. His small book described the anatomical and physiological backgrounds of human reproduction, and presented four methods of birth control. Although the author was impeccably scientific, he lived in Massachusetts, not in Indiana, as Owen did. Knowlton was three times haled into the courts of his own state, was once fined, and once sentenced to three months' imprisonment at hard labor.

At that time, however, the United States possessed no effective means for book-burning, and the *Fruits of Philosophy* continued to circulate. It went through nine editions in the thirties, and doubtless its ideas were circulated even more widely by word of mouth. Knowlton died in 1850, not much regarded, but he had probably done as much as any man of his time to affect the future development of his country.[9]

By mid-century the falling birth rate was causing great concern. Medical men and learned professors pondered the matter,

[9] His influence in England was perhaps even greater. The famous English birth-control trial of 1877 (Regina vs. Charles Bradlaugh and Annie Besant) involved the sale of his book. In 1928 an article by Norman E. Himes in the *New England Journal of Medicine* was entitled: "Charles Knowlton's Revolutionary Influence on the English Birth-Rate."

sometimes rather naïvely, considering whether passion was failing or fertility declining. Some believed that venereal disease was the villain in the piece. There was a considerable to-do about illegal abortion, which was taking an omnious spurt upward.

From the vantage point of a century later we may feel more confident of a diagnosis. The growing use of contraceptives was most likely the cause of the falling birth rate; abortion represented a kind of second line of defense.

In any case, the birth rate continued to fall. Children were no longer economically advantageous, partly because of a heightened conscience against child labor. Women began to have other ideals than the purely biological one. "Be fruitful and multiply" had served the people well during the colonial period when the land needed peopling. Even so, it had been a wasteful process. Colonial churchyards were filled with the graves of small infants and of young wives dead in childbirth.

The continuing history of the birth-control movement is an interesting one, which has, unfortunately, concerned our historians less than that of the slavery movement, although one is scarcely more important than the other. Like most revolutions it inspired its counter-revolution, and the contest was marked by excesses on both sides. Advocates of birth control were ostracized and persecuted. On the other hand, the sellers of various devices watched the announcements of engagements and marriages, and filled the mails with unsolicited advertisements—surely an invasion of privacy. Largely as a result of such excesses, the mails were closed to materials dealing with contraception, on the grounds of obscenity, after 1873. But the birth rate continued to fall.

7

Sexually speaking, the nineteenth century extended over for a decade and somewhat more into the twentieth. Then, at least if we are to believe the writers of modern novels, came the deluge. As to the date, there can at least be little disagreement. There may, however, be some argument as to just how devastating the deluge really was.

That something happened, anyone who lived through the period will be prepared to testify. Just what happened, and how much of it, and how much continues, are more difficult questions to answer. Fortunately the recent study of American females by Dr. Kinsey, more historically oriented than his previous study of males, supplies some highly important statistical data. For instance, he finds that American women born in the decade of the nineties indulged in extramarital affairs only about half as much as the women born in the following decade, who were thus of an age to feel more strongly the impact of the World War I and its aftermath.

These figures are impressive, but statistics are always slippery. Stating the matter the other way around, we may say that among the women born in the first decade of the twentieth century the percentage who remained faithful to their husbands was only somewhat lower than that of their compatriots of the preceding decade—about 60 per cent as compared with 79 per cent. The comparable male figures would probably not be anywhere nearly so startling.

In the long run, therefore, the "revolution" of the period just succeeding World War I may have to be written off as a comparatively minor one. As our anthropologists point out, nearly all societies have the institution of marriage, and at the same time permit or condone, or even facilitate, certain relaxations from marriage. Quite possibly the revolution represents only a readjustment of these mechanisms of escape, not any basic change in the system of monogamy. The continuing popularity of divorce need not make us doubt such a conclusion, for a high rate of divorce, as we have seen, is not in itself inconsistent with the romantic ideal.

The revolution is still, however, too recent for us to be sure. Kinsey's statistics indicate that during the three decades that have elapsed since 1920 the pattern of women's conduct has remained about the same. The impact of World War II, however, is so recent that he is not able to appraise its effects fully.

Perhaps even more striking than the relaxation of marriage has been what may be called the emergence of homosexuality. It had been strikingly absent from the earlier American scene. Not only was it anathema to the churches and forbidden by law, but also it seems to have been generally unacceptable socially. The strong position accorded marriage gave homosexuality little opportunity, and the conditions of life probably encouraged strong heterosexual identifications. Literature, where we should expect some consciousness of the subject, scarcely supplies any evidence, and before 1920 even seems to be hopelessly naïve on the subject. The notable exception is Whitman, with his poems on comradeship. But even he may not have realized the implications of his writings, and in later life he expressed himself as horrified that homosexual implications had been drawn from them.[10]

[10]But many doubt the denial. At least, however, it shows that even Whitman, whatever may have been his practice at one period, held sufficiently to the American norm not to wish, in later life, to defend homosexuality in theory. The whole subject is a difficult one on which to draw any conclusions because of the extreme reticence, and also naïveté, of the nineteenth century about it. The use of words is confusing also. A virile old army officer, who had served in the Indian

Since 1920, however, homosexual themes have appeared more and more commonly in literature. At the same time, there is evidence that such conduct has become commoner, and it has certainly become socially much less unmentionable and unrecognized than it had been in earlier times.

As for the causes of the new adjustments, there is likely to be a large amount of agreement. All admit that World War I seems to have touched off the revolution. But was it the war itself? Wars are notoriously demoralizing to family life and marriage, but that one affected the United States much less severely than the Civil War, and there is every evidence that the Civil War caused, temporarily, all the derangements that may be expected to result from the continued absence of husbands and fathers and from the general relaxation of conventional standards. Yet the Civil War brought about no striking change in sex habits.

To say that World War I had exposed American youth to the corrupt morals of Europe and thus differed from the earlier conflict is also an oversimplification. The Civil War exposed hundreds of thousands of small-town and country boys to the corruption of camp-followers and city red-light districts, and in particular introduced the Northern soldiers to the special temptations afforded by the slave states.

World War I may probably be considered as supplying the trigger action, rather than the force. By this time, for instance, knowledge of contraception had become widespread, and freedom of action was enhanced by the removal of the fear of social consequences. At the same time, the idea of sin in connection with sex, by no means a wholly restraining factor in

---

wars, was troubled and puzzled in later days about homosexuality. "But," said someone, "surely you had buggery sometimes in the army." "——, yes!" said the oldster. "Is *that* what it means? Naturally, we did! We never bothered very much about *that!*"

any period, was becoming much weaker. Anthropological and psychological studies were beginning to be widely known, and they generally worked not only toward greater tolerance of action in other people, but also toward greater freedom of action in the individual, who came to realize more about the significance of sex and even to fear its repression. "Science," which had previously spoken against sex, now was speaking for it.

Two of the great problems of the nineteenth century—divorce and birth control—seem to have become less pressing in the middle of the twentieth century, in the minds of most Americans. Various churches still oppose both violently, and with some success in their own groups and even in some particular states. But in what might be called their practical aspects the two problems have become less alarming.

After half a century of high divorce rate the United States still seems to be getting along without sinking into the demoralization that the more conservative once feared. Divorce has almost ceased to carry social stigma, even with most people who themselves disapprove of it on religious grounds. Though no divorced person has yet been elected president, one such collected 27,000,000 votes for that office, and many of them came from Catholics and others who oppose divorce in the abstract.[11]

[11]As regards the conduct of people whom they elect to high office, Americans have not been as squeamish as those who talk about Puritanism like to imagine. In 1884 a scandal involving an imputed illegitimate child broke about Cleveland's head in the middle of the campaign. Asked what should be done, he replied, "Tell the truth." When heckled on the subject, he is reputed to have countered: "I have fed and clothed my bastard, can you say the same for yours?" He was elected president. A saying attributed to President Arthur deserves to keep his name from obscurity and to be remembered as a high expression of American individualism: "My private life is nobody's Goddamned business!"

Birth control, also, has ceased to be a sociological bugaboo, and the term "race suicide" has become obsolete. Whatever one may think about the question, one is not likely to oppose birth control on the grounds that the country needs more people. That argument has come to be the special one of dictators needing cannon fodder.

8

In the end some might be inclined to think, "The conclusion is confusion." At the one extreme, they would say, stands the Catholic Church with an attitude toward sex essentially unchanged since the Middle Ages. It upholds virginity as a high ideal, maintains a somewhat mystical idea of marriage as a sacrament, opposes the separation of sex and procreation, admits no divorce. Not far removed from the Catholic attitude is that of many of the more strait-laced Protestant sects. From that point, attitudes and practices range through those of the less strict laymen and laywomen of all churches and on into the ranks of the unchurched. Eventually, if the Kinsey studies are to be trusted, we arrive at considerable numbers of people, at both sophisticated and unsophisticated levels, to whom almost any sex practice, heterosexual or otherwise, is not unacceptable.

Yet actually this impression of confusion is probably somewhat fallacious. Throughout the whole welter the idea of marriage remains remarkably dominant. One has only to listen to the popular songs pouring out from radios and juke boxes. Most of them are love songs, and they stress not only the depth of the emotion but also its permanence. "Forever" is a theme word. Sometimes specifically, and generally by implication, this love is to be realized in marriage. And it is to be "Forever!"

This eternity may in practice mean only a year or two, and may be terminated by divorce, and that, in turn, be followed by remarriage. The importance of marriage, however, is indicated not only by its original occurrence, but also, with many people, by its repetition.

Historically, this importance of marriage is what would be expected from the development of the American people. Not only the early colonists but also the later immigrants were of much the same sex habits. Marriage, heterosexual by definition, was strongly established by religious sanction, legal recognition, and social acceptance. This marriage was conceived as lifelong, as productive of children to the limits of fertility, and as monogamous. Custom, however, allowed the male a considerable relaxation of the monogamous standard, and under certain conditions allowed also a little female deviation.

In the modern United States we may consider that marriage, though it is still conceived as the prevailing way of life, has changed considerably. It is no longer universally conceived as lifelong, or as necessarily concerned with procreation. Considerably greater freedom has been granted to the woman. This does not mean that everyone in the United States believes thus or acts thus, but only that what may be called the general average of opinion and action has shifted in this direction.

The mechanism of these changes is chiefly native development, with some aid from environmental factors and from international ideas. The origins of divorce, for instance, are thoroughly native. It springs from early New England. It has traditionally been more common among the native-born than among the immigrants, and among people of Protestant tradition than among people of Catholic tradition. It has been aided by certain environmental features. Divorce also grows out of the Puritan conception of marriage as a civil contract, and therefore revocable. It arises, moreover, from the idea of the romantic marriage, which in its turn was largely the result of the scarcity of women in the colonial period.

The separation of the ideas of marriage and procreation also seems to be chiefly a native development, though early advocates often cited European example, especially French. America in its colonial period and even later commonly borrowed ideas from England, but the influence in this particular connection seems to have worked eastward across the Atlantic rather than westward. The practice of birth control also developed without much help from the later immigration, or in the face of its opposition. This immigration was largely Catholic, and even yet the distinction between the small families of the "older" Americans and the larger families of the more recent immigrants is a characteristic feature of American life.

Finally, the greater freedom of female action with regard to marriage is also to be considered primarily a native development, although to some extent aided by the environment and by the influence of international ideas. This development also, recent though it is, seems to have sprung more from the older American stock and to have more profoundly affected its mores than those of the more recent immigrants. These later immigrants were accustomed to a system which granted little freedom to the woman, but a broad latitude to the man, for whom it supplied a well-organized system of prostitution. The older American system had granted considerably less freedom to the man, and perhaps a little more to the woman—at least, it permitted her to choose her own husband. The modern American development with its rather rudimentary prostitution and its highly developed system of "amateurs"—so confusing to foreign visiting males—thus seems characteristically native. Similar situations elsewhere, particularly in Great Britain and the commonwealths, probably represent parallel developments rather than influence in either direction.

On the whole, then, though the "average American" conception of marriage may have changed considerably in three and a half centuries and though great diversities of opinion and practice now exist, one is probably still safe in maintaining the dominant importance of marriage in the United States.

CHAPTER **10**

PERSONAL NAMES

In an anthropological account of any tribe, the manner of its giving of personal names is often thought of sufficient importance for inclusion, and so we may fittingly attempt an appraisal of such habits among the Americans.

Names are a part of language, but they represent a highly specialized part, and so cannot be included under a general discussion. In particular, the influence of later immigration and of native developments has been of much more importance for our names than for our language in general.

In our naming habits, as in so much else, we inherit the English tradition, although this differs little from that of Europe in general. In this English tradition, as it was established during the Middle Ages and well before any settlement of America, a personal name was dual, consisting of a given and a family name, in that order. A king or nobleman, or rarely someone of lower rank, might bear more than one given name. But among the kind of people who migrated to America what has later come to be called a "middle" name was so rare as to be almost non-existent. One of the very few examples

to be cited is the curiously named Edward Maria Wingfield,
first president of the council at Jamestown.[1]

2

Since from the beginning the immigrants bore family names
and since those names were already hereditary, the early colonists merely kept the names that they already had, and there
is little to be told. The question has been raised, however,
whether all of the early English immigrants actually had
family names. Such an idea might be suggested by the entry
"old Edward" in one of the first Jamestown lists. More likely,
however, he actually had a family name, and it was omitted
carelessly from the list, or forgotten, after he was dead. More
commonly we find people entered only by the family name,
as in a Jamestown list of 1608, where even two boys are recorded as Milman and Hellyard, not by their given names.
Quite possibly, a few English waifs and strays, especially those
of illegitimate birth, came to America, lacking or not knowing
their family names. If so, they must soon have taken ordinary
names, and did not produce any particularly American flavor.

The only two large groups that have actually had to take
family names while on our soil are the Indians and the Negroes.
The Indians usually bore but a single name, although this was
often long and detailed in description. They tended, however,
to adopt the naming habits along with other European customs. If an Indian was converted, he might take a baptismal
or Christian name, and then bear his old one as a family name.

[1] Wingfield, although by no means an important figure in our history,
has been curiously prominent in this book. He has already been mentioned as accused of brandy-guzzling and atheism, and as the proud
possessor of some of the first chickens.

Thus we could probably account for Caleb Cheeshahteaumuck, who graduated from Harvard in 1665 and died in the next year. But many Indians simply adopted ordinary American family names. When we read of Jim Thorpe or of Colonel Ely Samuel Parker, we cannot tell from their names that they were Indians. In later times, and doubtless in earlier times too, many of their native names were translated, sometimes in simplified forms. Once translated and simplified, such a formerly colorful name tended to become commonplace. Thus an Indian whose name meant "Talking-Crow" might have his name translated and be baptized John, and thus become John Talking Crow. Then his son might be merely William Crow, and would become indistinguishable in a list from anyone of English birth bearing the same family name. An Indian named James Night-Walker could become a mere James Knight Walker. Unfortunately these colorful Indian names seem, on the whole, to be dying out.

The Negroes, when they came from Africa, had nothing corresponding to a family name. While they remained slaves, they generally had no need for one. Being legally chattels, they did not vote, enter into contracts, testify in court, or do any of the other things for which a full name was demanded. Since they lived in small communities, they did not need two names for distinction, and could be called either by the given name, by a nickname, or by the given name with some distinction, such as "Old Joe," or "Big Jack."

But if not before freedom, certainly afterward, the Negroes took family names like other people. In fact, we may say that they took them too much "like other people," and instead of using their own exuberant fancy, they seem to have chosen rather the more commonplace ones. Thus Johnson is the commonest Negro name, and after it come Brown, Smith, and Jones. It looks rather as if the Negro tried to efface himself by taking the name which would not bring any attention to him. The old theory that he took the name of his master seems to have little foundation, as is evidenced by the failure of the names of the great slave-holding families to be very common among Negroes.

Although there is little that can be called a distinctive American creative activity as regards family names, a certain creative process has been at work producing new names from old names by means of radical changes of practically all conceivable kinds. We thus have many names that seem to exist in the United States but not in Europe, such as Yokum, Legree, Goochey, and Lovewear. Only by careful study can a scholar determine that these particular names originated from the German and French names of Joachim, Legaré, Gauthier, and Lavoie. Similarly, the frequent shortening of long foreign names has produced new names which presumably never existed in the old countries. From Calogeropoulos we have Caloyer; from Kalliokowski, Kallio; from Nieninen, Nieni. Translation has also done its work. Frequently it resulted in nothing new, as when a Zimmerman became a Carpenter, or a Jaeger was translated into another Hunter. But when a name was partly translated and partly taken over by sound, the result might be an entirely new name, as when a Breitmann became a Brightman.

The taking of Americanized or partially Americanized names by immigrants is one of our characteristic phenomena. Sometimes this has resulted from a desire to escape from a real or fancied stigma of association with a foreign background. Sometimes it has resulted merely from the nuisance of trying to maintain an unusual name. Sometimes, especially in the earlier years, it merely happened because no one knew or cared much how the name was spelled. The taking of names by immigrants, like the taking of names by Negroes, has generally worked toward a leveling. Whether a man is trying to escape into the crowd or to become one of the group, he is likely to choose a common name. For this reason the number of people called by the traditional British names has risen higher in proportion.

On the other hand, this leveling process has failed to eliminate very many names, and the number of names in the United States is probably much larger than it is in Great Britain or any other country. Thus many a German Mueller has become a mere Miller, but some of them still remain, and others have the form Muller; the result is thus three names in the United States.

The total number of family names in this country has been the subject of a careful study by Elsdon C. Smith, for his *Story of Our Names.* In the Chicago telephone book he estimated that there were 154,750. In arriving at this figure he counted all variations in spelling. He estimated further that there must be about 350,000 different family names in the whole United States. Even if we divide this figure by three to make allowance for mere variations of spelling, the number remains tremendous.

3

With given names, as compared with family names, the Americans have been much more creative. This could be taken for granted. In the vast majority of instances, a man passes his family name to his children without change and without even considering the possibility of change. But someone, commonly a parent, chooses a particular name for each child. Usually this name is a traditional one, but sometimes it may be "made up." Even for traditional names, the storehouse of the past is so jammed with thousands of examples that the problem of choice becomes almost a matter of creation. Therefore, while family names remain stable over generations and through centuries, given names have been subject to fashions and fads, and in the course of a century the "name pattern" of a community may change strikingly.

Our history of given names can begin with Raleigh's colony of 1587, even though it died out and left no descendants. Among the ninety-nine men and boys of that group the commonest names were John (23), Thomas (15), William (10), Henry (7), Richard (7), George (3), and Robert (3). From the same colony we have only sixteen women's names preserved, too small a number for good statistics. There was, as it happened, no Mary among them. But there were three Janes, two Elizabeths, and the other names were common enough, such as Agnes, Eleanor, Margaret, and Rose.

We must, then, return to the list of men to arrive at the name pattern. All the commoner names of these first colonists are in the English tradition. Both John and Thomas are eventually Hebrew, and are from the Bible. John, from the beloved disciple, had been a favorite name for centuries all over Christendom. Thomas, also the name of a disciple, had become a popular and peculiarly English name since the twelfth century, because of the hero-martyr St. Thomas of Canterbury. William, Henry, Richard, and Robert were old Germanic names that had been popularized in England by the Norman conquerors. All except Robert had been borne by English kings, and this had probably helped their popularity. George, a Greek name, owed its place to the fact that St. George had been regarded as the patron saint of England since the fourteenth century. This English tradition of naming was maintained in the southern colonies for a century or more—and, we may add, for women as well as for men.

A more peculiarly American development arose in the Puritan colonies of New England. Originally, the name pattern did not differ greatly from that of the southern immigrants. The ten commonest names of those coming to Massachusetts were in order: John, William, Thomas, Richard, Robert, Edward, Samuel, George, James, and Francis.[2]

The appearance of the single Old Testament name of Samuel alone distinguishes this list from the southern one by giving it a slight Old Testament flavor. But the sons of these immigrants bore very different names. The proportion of Biblical names soared upward, especially those of favorite characters from the Old Testament. Among boys born in Boston between 1640 and 1699 John was still the favorite name. But after it came in order: Samuel, Joseph, Thomas, Nathanael, Benjamin, James, Jonathan, William, and Richard. Thus the first eight names have all become Biblicals, and the once popular William and Richard have been shoved into ninth and tenth place. The second ten names show the Old Testament influence even more strongly: David, Jacob, Joshua, Isaac, Peter, Ebenezer, Ephraim, Edward, Abraham, and Daniel.

With women, also, the use of traditional but non-Biblical names such as Joan, Agnes, and Margaret fell off, and some of them even vanished completely. Girls born in Boston in the seventeenth century were most commonly named, in order: Mary, Elizabeth, Sarah, Hannah, Abigail, Rebecca, Ruth, Lydia, Anna, and Martha. These are all Biblical names, and four of them are from the Old Testament. Some of the traditional favorites managed to appear in the second ten, where we find Ann, Margaret, Joanna, and Jane mingled with Mehitabel, Susannah, Deborah, Bethiah, Rachel, and Dorcas.

Also fairly common for women in the Puritan colonies—

[2]In percentage these stood, respectively, 21.3, 12, 12, 7, 4.5, 4, 3.5, 3.3, 2.2, 1.8. Seven men out of ten thus bore one of these ten names, and one man in five was named John.

totaling about 15 per cent—were "meaningful" names of abstract qualities. Of these, Mercy was the commonest, but we find also Patience, Thankful, Desire, Experience, Charity, Hope, Grace, and many others. Names of this kind, such as Grace, are to be taken in their spiritual or theological sense, not their physical one. Some of the names are presumably to be construed as verbs rather than as nouns, and may be taken as standing for some Biblical admonition such as, "Desire spiritual gifts." Similar names occurred among the men, though less commonly: Increase, Hopefor, Constant, Tremble, Love, Wrestling.

Of all the Biblical names the most interesting is Ebenezer. It is the name of a place in the Old Testament, and seems to have been used as a personal name first in New England. It became one of the commonest names there, and remained so for more than a century.

Although the increased use of Old Testament and of meaningful names was a feature of Puritanism in England also, it was more strongly developed in New England. From those colonies it spread by migration, and our history has become spotted with men bearing such colorful names as Increase, Israel, Zachary, Abraham, Preserved, and Gamaliel. It has affected our legendry, and given us "Brother Jonathan" as a name for a New Englander or even for an American, "Uncle Sam" as the embodiment of the initials U.S., and "Caleb" or "Old Ephraim" for the grizzly bear.

4

After this first burst of creative energy, the Americans went along, North and South, for about a century with little change in their naming-habits. Biblical names continued to give color

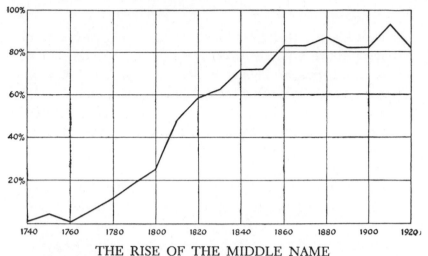

THE RISE OF THE MIDDLE NAME
Percentage of Harvard graduates to bear middle names, 1740–1920

THE RISE OF THE MIDDLE NAME

Dates indicate the decade beginning with the year specified; the percentages indicate the graduates of that decade that bore middle names. Thus in the decade 1780–89 12% of the graduates were officially listed with middle names. Before 1740 only a negligible number bore more than one given name. Harvard was in this respect more conservative than Princeton. Between 1760 and 1860 the steadily rising percentage of Princeton graduates bearing middle names was always higher, sometimes twice as high, as that of Harvard graduates. For men other than college graduates no statistics are at present available, but American baby boys of all groups were more and more commonly being given middle names during this period.

in New England, but elsewhere there was great repetition of a small number of names. This was particularly true with women's names, in the middle and southern colonies, and the excessive use of Elizabeth, Ann, Mary, and Sarah was only saved by the also liberal use of variations such as Betsy, Sally, Nanny, Nancy, and Molly.

The great German immigration of the early eighteenth century had some influence. Johann, often shortened to Hans, was by far the commonest name among these Germans; with Jacob and Heinrich, following. Except where people continued to talk German, these names were rapidly Anglicized, and so increased the popularity of John, Jacob, and Henry. The Scotch-Irish immigration also exerted an influence by building up the already popular James, and adding Alexander and Archibald.

About 1740 the use of middle names began to grow. Probably the Germans had some influence here, for they generally, even as immigrants, bore two given names, of which the first was usually Johann. Another strong influence was family pride, which led to the desire to preserve the mother's family name. Purely practical, as the towns grew larger, was the need to distinguish a man more clearly from others bearing the same names. Once started, the custom grew steadily in popularity until by 1850 the man without a middle name was in a small minority, as he has since remained. The use of the middle name soon produced another typical American habit. Since the full signature of three names was too long for practical purposes, men began to use merely the middle initial, and eventually the typical American was John Q. Public.

In England, on the other hand, such a form is not used. An Englishman has to be J. Q. Public, J. Quincy Public, or John Quincy Public.[3]

[3] Many writers, actors, and others whose names must be publicized either drop the middle initial or use the full name. This may be an

Also serving to produce a distinctive usage was the practice of distinguishing a son from a father by the use of Junior. This typically American practice began in the middle of the eighteenth century when most gentlemen had some knowledge of Latin and were familiar with the use of the term Junior, translated often into English as "the younger," as applied to such Latin worthies as Cato and Pliny. The practice was so well established by 1776 that three signers of the Declaration added the Jr. Again, British custom has been different; the second of a pair of great statesmen is known as William Pitt, the younger.

Still another important movement beginning around 1750 was the rise of the name Charles. Earlier, Charles is hardly found at all in New England, and is rare in the other colonies. After that its growth was not only steady but even spectacular. By 1850 it had become one of the commonest names, and it has remained close to the top since that time. Its curious nickname, Chuck, is typically American.

Almost at an equal pace with the rise of Charles, the use of Biblical names, even in New England, began to fall off. Ebenezer, and even Samuel and Benjamin, came to have about them an old-fashioned aura.

The facts are clear enough; the causes remain obscure. Immigration probably had little to do with such changes. English influence, at the idea level, may have helped the growth of Charles. During these same decades the name was increasing in popularity there, where *Sir Charles Grandison* was a much read novel and Bonnie Prince Charlie had given the name a renewed vogue among those who still held sentimentally to the

---

Anglophile tradition or may be the result of the difficulty involved with the effective printing and display of a single letter. On the other hand, some people—of whom Harry S Truman is a notable example—have inserted a middle initial which does not stand for any name at all.

Stuarts. But most of the other new developments seem to be wholly native and even to run counter to British practice.

Any scholar would be tempted—and doubtless he would be right—to connect some shifts of naming habits with that great revolution in human thought and feeling known as the Romantic Movement. Its full force did not begin to be felt in the United States until after 1800, but from that time on, throughout the whole nineteenth century, the general Romantic influence did a great deal to transform our name pattern. There was a strong German tinge in Romanticism, and to this influence as well as to German immigration may be credited the great rise in popularity of Frederick and Albert, so that Fred and Al became fully Americanized by the end of the nineteenth century.[4]

More clearly Romantic was the revival of many medieval names. Some of these, such as Edwin and Edmund, had never entirely gone out of use, but they now grew in popularity. These names were Anglo-Saxon in derivation, as was Alfred also, which seems to have lapsed entirely but reappeared, in the United States, about 1790, and became common. Many of the medieval names were those of the great English noble families, which might be read in Shakespeare's plays and Scott's novels—Clarence, Howard, Stanley, Russell, Percy, Sidney, Clifford. To this group of names we may also attach Chester, Norman, Arthur, and Roy. To French influence in Romanticism as well as to medieval enthusiasm we can attribute the nineteenth-century growth of Louis, commonly so spelled, rather than in the older English form Lewis. Philip and Raymond are also Romantic and somewhat French in back-

[4]Some of the popularity of Albert after 1840 may be attributed to its increased use in Great Britain, because of the Prince Consort. But Albert appears as an American name before 1800.

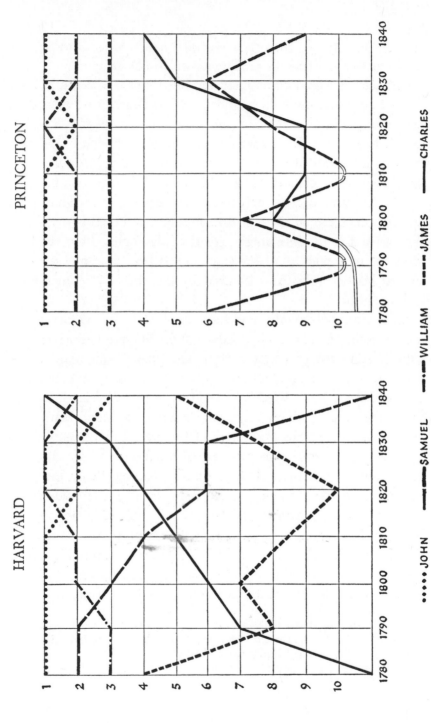

HARVARD

PRINCETON

•••• JOHN   —•— SAMUEL   ——— WILLIAM   ——— JAMES   —— CHARLES

Relative rank of five common names among graduates of classes 1780–1840 by decades

MEN'S NAMES—1780–1850

Dates refer to the decade beginning with the year indicated; numerals indicate the relative standing of the name among graduates of that decade. Thus, at Harvard, John was the most popular name for graduates of the decade 1780–89, and at Princeton the name in fifth place for the decade 1830–39 was Charles. The comparative stability of names at Princeton in this period is to be contrasted with the great changes at Harvard. This is partly the result of the fact that old Puritan names like Samuel were going out of fashion in New England, and that Charles was coming into fashion. Charles did not get in the first ten at Princeton until 1800–09, and it never became as popular as at Harvard. At Harvard, Charles actually stood in first place only for this one decade, yielding place to William and soon to John also. Among American men in general John and William, most often in that order, have generally been the two most popular names. James, a favorite Scottish name, maintained a high position at Princeton through this period because of the Presbyterian background of that college. Although the actual statistics here presented are only for college graduates, they give a fairly good idea of what was happening throughout the country as a whole.

ground, and they became popular enough to make Phil a common nickname and produce Ray as a given name.[5]

Women's names followed the same general course. Charlotte rose in popularity as the feminine form of Charles, but never reached the same ascendancy. Fredericka and Alberta were known even though they never became as common as their masculine opposite numbers. Edith, Mildred, and Ethel show the revival of interest in Anglo-Saxon names. In spite of the shady reputation of her prototype, Guenevere had some popularity, though Elaine is perhaps to be considered the feminine of Arthur. With women also the once popular Biblical names went out of favor. Mehitabel softened into Hetty, and then declined toward extinction. Since family names were at first commonly reserved for men, there could be no close parallel for women to the revival of the English names of nobility. But among the generally Romantic names for women can be included Henrietta, Isabelle, Louise, Rowena, Ginevra, Genevieve, and Mabel, along with Helen, Ellen, Eleanor, and all its other derived forms.

After the Revolution and throughout the following century a growing self-consciousness and ancestral pride led to the transformation of more and more family names into given

[5]Many of these new-fangled romantic names for men acquired a "sissy" connotation, for reasons which are somewhat obscure, but doubtless go deep into folk psychology. One reason certainly was that such names were first given in families with an Anglophile and at least slightly cultural background, and not in tougher-grained families. The assumption of aristocracy in these names, sometimes with a pretension of noble descent, also caused them to be considered decadent and therefore effeminate. In the United States there has been a pretty general feeling that both aristocracy and the arts have something essentially effeminate about them. A reader of Mark Twain will recall that in the most popular of American juveniles the "real boy" is Tom, and the namby-pamby one is Sid, that is, Sidney. These names did not all become popular at the same time. Sidney and Chester date from about 1830; Howard, 1840; Clarence, 1850.

names. Most commonly the mother's family name was bestowed upon one of the sons. The process was rendered the easier since many given and family names were identical in form, such as Thomas, James, and George. There was a tendency to avoid, for given names, the family names ending in -son. Names ending in -s, like Edwards and Roberts, also were not often used. Strongly meaningful names, such as Carpenter and King, seem to have been avoided.

In spite of these exceptions the practice became common. Many ordinary family names came really to have a regular status as given names, and even developed their regular nicknames—Stew for Stewart, and Billy for Wilson. For unknown reasons certain rather uncommon family names became popular for given names, so that they are now usually considered to be such. Here can be mentioned Dwight, Earl, Wayne, and Elmer.

This last name suggests still another process of our naming. It is usually said to be of patriotic origin and to be derived from the family name of two New Jersey patriots during the Revolution. The Elmers, however, were never very famous, and as a given name Elmer hardly appeared until after 1860. Even then it is associated not so much with New Jersey as with the Middle West. Possibly it may derive something from the enormously popular novel, *St. Elmo* (1867).

On the whole, the patriotic factor in naming fails to be, statistically, very important. It has appeared in all periods. Before the Revolution a boy might be named for the king, or some other current hero. The patriotic fervor of the Revolution brought the names of some new heroes into use, and the popularity of Washington himself was a stimulus in producing an upsurge of George. In the same years the name Washington was bestowed upon a goodly number of babies, of whom Washington Irving, the writer, and Washington Allston, the painter, were the most famous. In the same way, Robert E. Lee must have affected the name pattern of the South, though one would have difficulty in saying to what degree, since Robert was a common name, even before his time.

With uncommon names, which should serve better for indicators, the patriotic factor seems small. Zachary Taylor was one of the chief heroes of the Mexican War and became president. But Zachary was an old-fashioned name, on its way out. Though Taylor's popularity was sufficient to cause a number of towns to be called by his nickname Rough-and-Ready, it could not stem the tide against Zachary. Even more striking are the examples of Abraham and Ulysses. Lincoln and Grant were certainly the outstanding northern heroes of the Civil War, but the number of babies given their names seems to have been negligible. Quite possibly, however, these two heroes led to the more common use of Lincoln and Grant as given names.

Franklin, derived originally from the great Benjamin and drawing strength from its use as a given name by one minor and one major president, also seems to be an example of a name establishing itself partly on patriotic reasons. It is also, however, a very handy name to be used as a variant of Frank.

5

In modern times our name pattern is kept stable by certain conservative forces and constantly varies because of certain progressive forces. The continuing stability of our families is the chief conservative factor. Children are commonly named "for someone," and this someone is usually a member of the family. Therefore in each generation there are a great many Johns and Marys simply because there were a great many Johns and Marys in the preceding generation. Because of family tradition a few of the old Biblical names still are preserved, being handed down from father to son or from grandfather to grandson, so that we occasionally still find a Zenas, or Joel, or Seth, or Adlai.

Because the older and more socially established families tend to use the older names, there is also a tendency for them to be used among people who imitate and ape the older families. Thus snobbery acts as a conservative force.

Religion also is conservative. The Catholic Church insists that a child be christened with the name of at least one saint. In their ordinary lives many Catholics are called by some other than the saint's name that they bear, but the practice of the church connects our names with the past. Many Protestant churches also encourage the use of Biblical names, or at least of names that exist in the Christian tradition.

On the other hand, many factors work toward change. The first of these is the mere mechanical one of the size of our population unit. The United States has progressed from a frontier and agricultural period, through a village and town stage, to a condition in which a large proportion of our people live in cities. As the size of the unit has increased, the numbers of people who might bear the same first and last names and might therefore be easily confused have constantly increased. One way to meet this problem was to have a middle name or initial. Another way was to bear an unusual given name. As a result, people with common last names like Smith and Jones are less likely to be named John or William and are much more commonly given a first name, which may, with good luck, be distinctive.

One means by which new names have been supplied is by the taking of shortenings and nicknames as official. This practice, for obvious reasons, has been particularly common among politicians, and in the roll, for instance, of the 83rd Congress we find members listed officially as Bill, Phil, Chet, Kit, Jamie,

Ed. Even in the august Senate one man records himself as Pat, and another as Mike. In addition, one representative records himself as C. W. (Rump) Bishop.

Such informality of name corresponds with the general informality of the middle twentieth century. It is also distinctly of practical use. If a man named John Wilson finds himself confused with another John Wilson, he may escape by adopting officially the name by which he is usually called, thus becoming Jack Wilson.

The tendency to increase the total number of names in use —whether caused by growth in the size of the population unit or by mere love of novelty—is strikingly shown by the increased use of manufactured names. Curiously, these are generally names for women. The phenomenon has been noted also in England, but it seems more characteristically American, and some investigators have thought that its center of usage lies in Oklahoma. No one has, however, supported this conclusion with good statistical evidence, and certainly the custom is common enough throughout the South and Middle West and is far from unknown in any part of the country. At one time it was thought to be particularly a practice among Negroes, but actually it seems to be most typical of those who are sometimes called "poor whites" and those slightly farther up the social and economic scale. It has also been found in bluebook circles and in New York City.

The motive behind this practice can in most respects be considered good. It is merely to place upon the child a new and therefore unique name, which will not be shared with any other person. This is by no means easy. Since most people are rather lacking in imagination, the commonest way of manufacturing a name is to take elements of established names. Thus there are a number of suffixes that indicate or suggest a feminine ending. Here we have -ie, -etta, -ene, -illa, -elle. Then the name manufacturer may select the first part of some standard name, and thus produce Kathetta, Marilla, or Elizene. Or two names may be fused, so that Doris and Lorraine may yield Dorraine. Other names result from abbreviations, or baby talk, or from the mere scrambling of letters. Oddities of spelling also appear in the coinages, and so we have ClarEtta, D'an, El Louise, Johnny-D, and D-etta.[6]

Conservatives may writhe at the linguistic naïveté of such names, and at their occasional bad taste, even to the point of unconscious obscenity. Such names, however, are here to stay, and are a characteristic phenomenon of the American way of life. They certainly represent a creative impulse. Why should our women be named Mary, Jane, and Elizabeth, world without end?

The failure of parents to coin names for their sons is another interesting feature of the times. Generally speaking, men's names are much more determined by the conservative and traditional forces than are women's names. Not only do the latter show these numerous coinages, but also even the more traditional women's names are subject to fashion, showing rises and falls, disappearances and revivals.

Men's and women's names show also another interesting relation. The latter constantly tend to encroach upon the former. Merely by the addition of -ie almost any familiar name for a man can become a feminine—Billie, Frankie, Georgie, Jackie. Especially in the South, family names are given to girls, and when these happen to become popular, the name takes on a feminine suggestion and is no longer used for men. Shirley is a striking example. In a similar way, at least one of the old stand-

---

[6] These coinages have fascinated many scholars, and H. L. Mencken, in his *American Language*, lists several hundred of them. His list, however, like others of the kind, includes a certain number of names that are actually traditional, such as Asenath, and Keturah, which are taken from the Old Testament.

ard names for men has been feminized. Francis was a common Elizabethan name, born by such a thoroughly male character as Sir Francis Drake. But before 1800 Frances began to come into use for women. Francis then declined, and about 1840 the more masculine-looking abbreviation Frank began to take its place.

The suggestion is often made that just as in an earlier period names were strongly influenced by patriotic figures, so now they are influenced by the celebrities of screen, radio, and athletics. Undoubtedly there is some such influence, but it is not so strong as to be easily demonstrated statistically. *Gone with the Wind* was the most read book of the nineteen-thirties, and its two chief feminine characters bore the curious names Scarlett and Melanie. One can now find a few girls bearing these names, but they have certainly not seriously affected our name pattern. Since actors and actresses often take stage names, the reasoning, in fact, often has to be reversed. An actress's name may rise to sudden popularity, not because babies are named after her, but because she herself took the name that was becoming fashionable. The same may be said for heroes and heroines of novels and plays.

Our pattern for given names, we may conclude, is highly complex. It varies, not only according to period, but also according to region, social level, religious affiliation, national origin, and other factors. There is therefore no simple and easy way of demonstrating the exact nature of its variations. The present chapter has attempted to show the chief forces that have affected it.[7]

[7] For comparison with the early lists of the ten commonest names, the present rating (as compiled by Elsdon C. Smith in his work already cited) may be presented, along with their percentages: John (7.3), William (6.3), Charles (3.8), James (3.7), George (3.6), Robert (3.0), Thomas (2.9), Henry (2.0), Joseph (1.9), Edward (1.7). For women the rating is: Mary (4.2), Elizabeth (2.3), Barbara (2.2),

6

To consider the causal background of our present name pattern, that for family names is much simpler than that for given names. Our family names are almost altogether the result of hereditary factors. A few native developments have affected the situation slightly, but on the whole it is simple.

Since our given names are also a part of the language, they too show chiefly the hereditary background. Even in the nineteenth century, when Indian place names were commonly bestowed upon towns, such names did not become popular for people. William Tecumseh Sherman, familiarly called Cump, is an exception. Pocahontas has been an American heroine almost from the beginning, but her name has not been commonly used. Even the popularity of *Hiawatha* as a poem did not break down this taboo. An Indian personal name that has first become a place name has occasionally been used—Tennessee, for instance.

The land, too, has had little influence. Virginia has been a popular girl's name, and its popularity was undoubtedly enhanced by the name of the state. It is, however, a Roman name, and is used also in England. Local patriotism has rarely gone to the point of naming the baby after the home town or the home state.[8]

Dorothy (2.2), Helen (2.2), Margaret (1.8), Ruth (1.7), Virginia (1.7), Jean (1.5), Frances (1.5).

[8]Presumably every American knows that the first English child born in the colonies was Virginia Dare. Not so well known is the fact that the first English child to be born at Jamestown was Virginia Laydon. The popularity of the name, however, is mostly modern. In the eighteenth century it was scarcely used, even in Virginia.

Indirectly, of course, the land has affected naming as it has affected everything else. By its effect upon religion—its making possible so many dissident sects and such a large body of unchurched—the land has worked against one of the traditional forces of naming, and has tended to produce such an American feature as the manufactured name.

Since names are part of language, the English influence has remained strong. In fact, for men at least, our name pattern still resembles quite strikingly that of the first Virginia colonists. The latter immigrants, just as they learned to use English in general, so also learned to use the English form of the name. Such a common Italian name as Giuseppe has usually become Joseph, and exercised its influence only by increasing the use of that already well-established name. Some names, however, have undoubtedly been Americanized to some extent by immigration—for instance, Selma and Olga. Carl, the German of Charles, is one of the few foreign forms that have become well naturalized.

There is great difficulty, however, in separating the influence of immigration from that of native development. The use of the middle name, for instance, may have been greatly influenced by the early immigration of Germans, but might have occurred without their participation. As undoubted examples of native developments may be cited the John Q. Public form and the use of Junior.

Also largely native was the use of Old Testament names in New England, which gives a distinctive flavor to our older name pattern and still survives slightly. The use of family names for given names has its parallel in England, but can also be considered largely a native development. Particularly is this true when the name comes essentially to be used as a given one by people who have no family right to it. The use of such names for girls is another native development, particularly of the South. Typically native is the practice of coining women's names.

Equally difficult to isolate as a factor is the influence of international ideas. We have already had occasion to mention the tremendous importance exerted by that great international revolution, the Romantic Movement. Moreover, some individual names such as Dolores, now one of the first twenty among women's names, probably came into use, not because of immigration, but because of its use in books and motion pictures.

The final word about American names must be a comment on their great variety. As with food and religion, this variety springs mostly from immigration, but also to a considerable extent from receptivity to foreign ideas and a creative native development.

CHAPTER **11**

PLAY

This chapter might about equally well be entitled Recreation, Amusements, Relaxation, Pastimes, Diversions, Leisure, Sports, or Games. The very diversity of words —most of them somewhat vague and all shading into others— shows the haziness of the conception and its complexity. The activities of play merge with those of other fields—for instance, of sex, art, and religion.

Basically, perhaps, we should consider this vague conception to be chiefly a mental attitude. Two people may be doing the same thing; one finds it work, and the other finds it play. Some people even enjoy their work. Others make a work of play, as do professionals in baseball and golf.

The whole conception of the sharp distinction of work and play is perhaps a rather modern one. Among the Indo-European languages there is no common and therefore ancient term, but the word differs from language to language, and seems generally to be derived, secondarily, from one meaning specifically to dance, frolic, jest, or act like a child.

This general discussion is not introduced here for pure love of theory. On the contrary, it has a bearing upon our approach to the history of American play, for of all the topics to be here discussed this one seems the most modern. It is therefore the one that is the least determined by hereditary factors, and the most by native developments and international ideas.

2

Seventeenth-century England had its recreations. Not only was the theater active in London, but also the so-called "strolling players" gave performances elsewhere. There were games of various sorts, such as bowls, football, and field hockey, not well organized perhaps, but none the less fun. The country gentlemen were enthusiastic hunters, and the popularity of fishing is shown by the fact that Izaak Walton was a seventeenth-century Englishman. Among the rowdier spectator sports were bull-baiting and bear-baiting, and even the attendance at public executions. Indoor sports included not only such polite ones as chess, checkers, and the singing of madrigals, but also the more exuberant ones of gaming with cards and dice, and singing bawdy rounds.

Migration to the colonies brought most of these recreations to an abrupt end. In fact, boredom and consequent loss of morale must have been distinct problems. Obviously there could be no theater. Cards and dice could make the passage, but only the most confirmed gamester could enjoy them much when he sat beneath a tree or huddled in a miserable wigwam, and lacked the jollity of some Mermaid Tavern, with its flowing sack, and its Doll Tearsheet. In a country where one might any day go hunting a bear or a panther in the woods, bear-baiting must have seemed tame and artificial, and hardly worth contriving.

Under such circumstances, the traditions must have lapsed rapidly. The social importance of recreation had not as yet been recognized, and so there was nothing of what we have now come to call, somewhat paradoxically, "organized play." Even children's games must have had hard going, because only a small number of children came in the ships, and many of them died in the first years after landing. As a result, the numerous children born in the colonies had few older play-mates from whom to learn games.

In the first years there was doubtless a good deal more play than we have any record of. The chronicler, concerned with what he thought to be the weighty events, was not likely to record that on such-and-such a day some men played football with a pig bladder, or staged wrestling matches to the great interest and diversion of the entire company. As a result, only by a kind of accident do we learn that one day in May, 1611, some of the Jamestown men were playing at bowls, or that on Christmas of 1621 certain of the Plymouth colonists were found "some pitching the bar and some at stool-ball, and such like sports."

Curiously, by modern standards, on both these occasions those in control of the colony suppressed the play, instead of recognizing its morale-building quality. In the early years, both of Virginia and of New England, play had to struggle against the attitude that there was a great deal of work to be done and that to work, not to play, was the appointed and therefore appropriate lot of man on earth. In Virginia, to discourage idleness, Governor Dale forbade bowling; laws were enacted against gaming and against actors, who were officially classified as "idle persons." Massachusetts and Connecticut were much stricter, and banned in particular—dice, cards, quoits, bowls, ninepins, shuffleboard, and "gynecandrical dancing." This last sounds horrific, but it is only a Greek formation, meaning "men and women together."

The New England attitude stemmed largely from the widespread feeling among all the stricter Protestants that pleasure was associated with sin. The Puritans conceived life to be a sober business. They based their conduct upon the Bible, which is a very serious document, not composed by laughing philosophers. In fact, the word *laugh* occurs but rarely in the King James version, and generally refers to unpleasant, scornful laughter. The Biblical verb *play*, if it does not refer to making music, frequently has an unpleasant suggestion of mocking or deriding.

The Puritans also feared play as tending to lead to sin. They objected to dancing as being an incitement to fornication; to card-playing and dicing as associated with swindling and stealing; to the theater because the lives of actors were often not godly; to works of fiction as being lies. They thus committed a classical example of the error of throwing the baby out with the bath.

In addition, Protestantism went hand in hand with the new middle-class idea of "getting ahead." By such a standard, recreation was a waste of time.

This Puritan and middle-class influence, perpetuated by some of the more strait-laced Protestant sects, continued to combat the development of recreation through colonial times and far down into the nineteenth century, and even yet is by no means without its importance.[1]

Much more effective than laws or theories, however, we must judge the environment itself. As compared with England and Holland, the colonies remained primitive. The people

[1]Perhaps the single example in our history of a colonizing effort in which the leaders recognized the importance of recreation was the Mormon settlement of Utah.

lived in isolated and small pioneer communities, most of them under what can be called frontier conditions. As a result, there was little possibility of recreation in our modern sense.

There was much work to be done, and therefore little "problem of leisure." Even the children had their chores. In addition, much of this work was not only physically tiring but also creatively satisfying. A man who clears ground, builds a cabin, and raises corn for his own food is fulfilling his life in much the same way as a man who builds a cabin in the mountains or indulges a hobby of raising zinnias. For the colonial farmer the hunting of game was a practical occupation, but in stalking a deer or turkey he must have had much the same pleasure that the modern hunter attains by bagging his limit. His wife weaving linsey-woolsey for the use of her own family, and his son angling for a mess of catfish, also satisfied many of the imaginative and creative needs that we now fulfill by some more specific indulgence in play.

Another force working against recreation was that of mere isolation. Many recreations are social, and call for a minimum number of participants. Even the most rudimentary forms of baseball, aside from mere "playing catch," demand four or five players. Some thousands of people are necessary for the functioning of a rudimentary theater. Even yet, the people living on isolated farms and ranches have little that can specifically be called recreation.[2]

Nevertheless, except perhaps where isolation was extreme, the frontier does not seem to have suffered for lack of communal recreation. Most of it was at what may be called the primitive level, that is, not recreation as an isolated thing, but recreation connected with some kind of serious occupation, and therefore perhaps all the more satisfactory for not being

[2]One may recall here Robert Frost's line in *Birches:* "Some boy too far from town to learn baseball."

artificial. Much of it was connected with religion, as may be expected in primitive communities. Though people would have denied going to camp meetings to enjoy themselves, the enjoyment was none the less there. At a camp meeting you saw old friends and made new ones, and had a great opportunity for talk and social visiting. You felt the deep satisfaction that arises from group action, and the emotional catharsis was probably even better than that to be obtained from a tragedy, because it had at least the illusion of being produced by reality and not by a dramatic presentation.

Much early recreation was involved with work, conceived as a communal activity. Log-rolling, which has come to have a sinister political meaning, was originally an activity on the frontier, when the neighbors gathered to help a new settler clear the logs from his field. The work itself could resemble a sport, and there could be competition between individuals and groups. After the work was finished, there could be a general jollification, with dancing and singing. Other such events were corn-huskings, quiltings, and house-raisings.

Games seem to have been comparatively few. Horseshoe pitching, which demands little equipment and no more than two contestants, was one game played from early times, and no less a person than John Marshall, the great Chief Justice, was a famous player. Other games were more like contests in practical events, such as shooting-matches and horse races. There were also the rougher sports of gander-pulling, cock-fighting, dogfighting, and just plain fighting.

On the whole, the life of the colonists and of the people in the early farming communities and on the frontier does not seem to have been too unsatisfactory. By modern standards it might seem dull. The same can be said, however, of almost all primitive communities, and one would scarcely go to the extreme of maintaining that everyone in the world was unhappy and bored before the beginnings of professional baseball and TV.

At the primitive level, work and play are less easily separated. If the word *recreation* is not in your vocabulary, you will probably not analyze whether you are having recreation or indulging in more serious activity when you whittle out a wooden spoon (Is this fun, utility, or folk art?), bundle with a pretty girl (Is this amusement, release of the sex impulse, or the first step toward being fruitful and multiplying?), or listen to a hell-fire sermon in church (Is this the equivalent of a soap-opera, or a really practical insurance against hell-fire?).

The gentry—particularly the young blades, with time on their hands and money to spend—naturally had a gayer time. In the cities there were balls and other social diversions, and even plays and concerts. In the country, especially in the South, there were horse races, cockfights, and fox hunts. Yet probably a romantic interpretation has tended to make this life seem more variegated than it really was. William Byrd was a wealthy Virginia gentleman, but his diary shows him living in a manner that most modern Americans would think dull to the point of stagnation. He spent many hours reading, in various languages. A quiet game of cards was about all he had in the way of excitement. And even if Byrd lived more quietly than others of his class, we must remember that the gentry as a whole were not numerous, and that the whole picture of early recreation must represent chiefly the life of the farming folk.

3

The next stage was a curious one. As the frontier moved westward, it left behind it a country of towns and cities. But the frontier, so to speak, took its own recreations with it. Hunting and fishing were not for the city dweller, and a communal house-raising would merely mean the taking away of work from carpenters who needed it. A higher degree of sophistication subtracted much from the enjoyment derived from camp meetings and other manifestations of primitive religion. As a result, the United States of the early nineteenth century seems to have been left an extremely dull place.

The cities, now grown larger, were probably much drabber places than they had been in colonial times, when they were scarcely more than villages and could practice village amusements. Travelers from Europe began to comment upon the deadly monotony of life in the new United States. Everyone, they reported, was working for money, and there was no time for play. Now the American begins to be pictured as the money-grubber, not even taking time to eat a decent meal.

One can, indeed, scarcely doubt from all this testimony that the city-dwelling American of the early nineteenth century was serious to the point of being glum, and seldom took any time off for relaxation. The fact seems to be that he worked because he had nothing to play at. He had the choice between working, and being bored. He might go to a tavern and drink more than was good for him, and doubtless the increasing alcoholism of the period has its proportional relationship to boredom. But there were no baseball games for him to attend or sports of any kind. He had little opportunity to attend the theater or to listen to music. He had no fiestas or saints' days, and few national holidays—and little to do on one of them anyway, except to get drunk. He did not have the infinite Gallic capacity for making a recreation out of eating and drinking, or the infinite Greek capacity for conversation over a thimbleful of coffee. Around 1825 may be called the depth of dullness.[3]

[3] Again we must note that the well-to-do were not so badly off for recreation. The whole nineteenth-century development, in fact, can be

The situation was rendered all the worse by a renascent Puritanism. The drift throughout most of the eighteenth century had been toward greater liberalism in thought and action, but in the early nineteenth century things moved the other way. The now-powerful Methodists, for instance, looked with disfavor on cards, dancing, the theater, and even novel-reading.[4]

Nevertheless the people of the cities, particularly the working people, needed recreation. They needed it more than the frontier people did, because the conditions of city life with its routine work in offices, stores, and factories failed to give any satisfactory mingling of work and play. The distinction between the two became, for the first time, sharp. Now, more than ever before in America, people began to work until the whistle blew or the hands of the clock touched the hour, and while they worked, they worked for their employer, and the money that they earned. To a larger and larger proportion of individuals the labor in itself was neither interesting nor satisfying. The operator of a power loom was not physically exhausted at the end of the day, and neither was he happy or satisfied at the length of cloth that he had mechanically helped to produce for someone else. He needed to have some fun, and

---

conceived as the attempt of the new urban democracy to solve its problem. Very notable is the comparative lack of reference to recreations in Leaves of Grass, even though Whitman was trying to give a whole picture of American life. These poems were mostly written in the eighteen-fifties, but probably reflect largely the period of the preceding decade, when the new urban amusements had not yet dveloped much.

'At least, no one can accuse the Protestant churches of having possessed much of the wisdom of the serpent. By an idealistic but wholly unrealistic opposition to amusements they encouraged a continual drift into the ranks of the unchurched, and bled themselves white. After 1900 their attitudes began to change and they gave recognition to the human need for relaxation, especially urgent under modern conditions of work.

his life came to be split between worktime and playtime, as the life of the frontiersman and farmer had never been.

Inevitably, therefore, new ways and means of recreation developed. About 1825 spectator sports began. Horse racing was the first that drew big crowds. It had always been popular on the frontier and in the country districts; now it became more highly organized, and was brought to the cities. Soon there were regattas. Then the circus developed as a typical form of American amusement. There were more theaters, there was more opportunity to hear music, there was more reading of magazines and novels.

Baseball began to develop. In the eighteen-forties it was a gentleman's game played under the auspices of clubs, and from that beginning baseball organizations are still known as "clubs," even though they have long since ceased to be social. These gentlemen apparently developed a strong desire to win, and so took in members with well-co-ordinated muscles but lower social standing. Thus the game became somewhat popularized. The first gate receipts are recorded from 1858. The Civil War completed the process of popularization, and baseball was a great sport in the camps. After the war it became a national game, amateur and professional.

By this time things were happening rapidly, and America was definitely learning to play. The post-Civil War period saw a tremendous development of sports—croquet, archery, tennis, roller-skating, track, boxing, golf. Intercollegiate football, with twenty-five men to a team, began with a Princeton-Rutgers game of 1869.

Bicycling deserves a special comment, because its history is so typically American. Like so many activities, it began with the kind of rush that entitles it to be called a fad. In fact, it swept the country twice—once for the high-wheel and then for the modern "safety" bicycle. The reception and dismissal of the bicycle shows the American inability to do things by halves. It also shows the difficulty of separating recreation from practical use, because the bicycle supplied both. In 1896 an editorial inquired whether anything since the invention of the locomotive had so materially affected the human race. In 1900 the census declared that few articles ever used by man had created so great a revolution in social conditions. Yet within ten years the bicycle had become little more than a children's toy, disappearing before the advent of the automobile.

A great American triumph was basketball. This was invented by James A. Naismith, in 1891, as a substitute for football and baseball, something that could be played indoors during the winters. Its success was quick and phenomenal. Mr. Naismith had the unusual satisfaction of living to see his game giving healthful pleasure to millions of people in every civilized country and even among semi-civilized tribes.

As the result of all these developments the situation in the United States changed strikingly between 1825 and 1900. Our cities were no longer dull, and our people were no longer devoted wholly to business for lack of anything else to do. Foreign travelers had to change their tune. By the end of the century, if they wished to take an adverse line, it had to be that Americans were pleasure-mad.

Since 1900 the development has continued. In sports this half century has seen, for example, the tremendous development of intercollegiate football, the rise of skiing, the growth of professional wrestling, and a renewed interest in racing, whether of horses, automobiles, or motorboats. It has seen the growth of hobbies—of everything from Little Theatre to photography. It has seen whole worlds of recreation become available with such new inventions as the automobile, the motion picture, radio, and television.

At the same time there has been a change of philosophy.

Sociologists recognize the importance of relaxation; no longer do preachers fulminate against it. Anyone, of course, may realize that an individual may become so greatly interested in play that his work suffers and that many sports have their vicious accompaniments. But such realization does not lead to wholesale disapproval. When the next American colonization occurs—on Mars or elsewhere—we can be sure that the recreational needs of the colonists will not be officially ignored, as at Jamestown and Plymouth.

4

Our modern pattern for recreation is to some extent international, but is also largely specific and unique for the United States. It is certainly not British, and owes rather little to the British tradition. In this respect it may be considered highly unusual, for in the development of every other way of life here considered we have had to emphasize the great and often overwhelming importance of the hereditary factor, which usually must be taken as meaning the British.

This is not to say that this tradition is altogther unimportant in our recreation. American football is now very different from British football, but it goes back to a game played in England from early times and brought to America by the colonists. Even baseball can probably be traced back to rudimentary games in which a ball was struck by a bat. Children's games also seem to be derived chiefly from England, and American tots still sing "London Bridge is falling down."

Yet the differences are more striking. Of the three most popular games in the United States—football, basketball, and baseball—American football certainly differs considerably from English football, while baseball is hardly played in England at all, and basketball is a very recent invention by an American. On the other hand, cricket scarcely has even a toehold in the United States.

An interesting question is whether the spirit of sportsmanship and fair play, so notably characteristic of the British, came to the Americans through the colonial tradition, or was transferred at the idea level in the nineteenth century. Doubtless it was to some extent transmitted in both ways, although a neutral observer would probably conclude that its transmission has not been complete. The typical American intensity as manifested in the desire to win, whether displayed by player or spectator, often seems to approach the excitement of a bloodlust. The hurled pop-bottle and the cry, "Kill the umpire!"—even though neither need often be taken seriously—are symbolic of an American temper rather different from a British temper.[5]

But if the influence of the British tradition has not been of first-rate importance in the development of our recreation, neither has that of the other immigrants. The Germans brought with them their turnvereins, and their love of gymnastics. But the ritualism and the drill-like quality of marching- and gymnastic-exhibitions failed to appeal to the Amer-

[5]This raises a large question, and one scarcely to be solved by a passing comment. The American is on the whole, most people would agree, more violent and excitable than the Englishman. This cannot be written off as resulting from the admixture of Italian blood. It was characteristic of the American even before the time of the "later immigration," and is probably most noteworthy in the South, which has been least affected by this immigration. More likely it is a carry-over from the long period of immersion in the violence and extremity of frontier life. Quite possibly, it is to be considered a survival rather than a development. The Elizabethan Englishman seems to have been more excitable than the modern Englishman, and the American may merely have preserved this trait, as he has preserved various archaisms of language.

ican. The popularity of golf and of skiing seems to have little relation to immigration of Scots and Scandinavians.

The environment has had a certain influence, but not a predominating one. The Indians played various games, but only lacrosse has been taken over from them, and it is a Canadian game, scarcely played in the United States. The hot summers have made swimming popular, and such an archetypal American figure as Benjamin Franklin was an enthusiastic and skillful swimmer. "The old swimming hole" remains as one of our great nostalgic symbols. The cold winters of the northern states soon made skating a pastime, particularly among the Dutch. Its popularity allowed the thoroughly American Emerson to write without fear of being misunderstood: "In skating over thin ice our safety is our speed." Thoreau in *Walden* was even more colloquial, for the same idea of taking a chance on the ice, when he put it: "Let us not play at kittly-benders."

Hunting and fishing have undoubtedly remained great American sports because we originally took over a continent that was well stocked with fish and game. Even the development of baseball is in some degree dependent upon the environment. Baseball is a game that is highly wasteful of space. Though it has become popular in crowded Japan, its development was much easier in a country having plenty of room. The term "sand-lot baseball" indicates that it was played largely on the vacant lots that were such a characteristic of the loosely built American towns that developed after the Civil War.

In the whole evolution of play, however, the most important factors are undoubtedly native developments and international ideas. Baseball, American football, and basketball—all were either originated or chiefly developed within the United States. The circus and the rodeo are essentially native. The tremendous interest in travel seems to be a natural development out of the foot-loose conditions of the frontier, plus the easy op-

portunity for travel supplied by a large country without cus-
toms- or immigration-barriers, and with no necessity of
speaking a foreign language.

Even that characteristic American social gathering, the
"party," seems to be a native development. Foreign travelers,
before 1800, noted what seemed to them the curious American
custom of having people gather together and sit around without any focus of entertainment such as music or cards, merely
entertaining themselves by means of an often desultory conversation. The cocktail party, since in addition it makes use of
an American invention in drink, may therefore be put down
as doubly American.

But the influence of international ideas has also been great.
Generally these ideas have spread at the leisure-class level.
Americans traveling in some foreign country learned some
game or observed some custom and brought it home with
them. Or else, by reading, they learned that some new sport
was fashionable abroad, and then brought it to the United
States. Thus golf came from Scotland; croquet and tennis,
from England. The waltz came from Austria and the polka
from Bohemia and the tango from Argentina. Bridge seems to
have originated in British India; even poker came from France,
and, it is thought, eventually from Persia. In fact, just as every
part of the world has supplied some delicacy for the American
table, so every country has supplied something to our rich fare
of recreation.

Even so, we need not consider ourselves necessarily a debtor
nation. We have sent baseball to Japan, and basketball to all
the world. And, as a popular play lets us be sure, the cocktail
party has penetrated to England.

5

In the development of recreation the United States owes a great debt to its leisure class. Though moralists and Marxists may fulminate, the idle rich have served a highly useful social function in spending their money freely to develop new means of amusement. Baseball began with gentlemen's clubs, and became popular and even plebeian. Football was originally an ivy-college sport. Golf began with the country club, and went on to the municipal links. The automobile started as a rich man's plaything.

This is natural enough, since the people who had leisure were able to take the time to develop new amusements, and were also able to spend the necessary money in experimentation. Their purpose, indeed, was to amuse themselves, and not to benefit the country. But has any social class, as a class, ever been motivated by any other fundamental idea than its own good?

The development of leisure and of recreation have necessarily advanced with equal pace. Hard-working "dawn to dusk" farmers and farmers' wives in the era of scythes and hand churns had no time for recreation. Neither did the city laborer when he worked a twelve-hour day. When men came to have more leisure, they needed more recreation, and they developed the means. The process will undoubtedly continue in the future, as social conditions change. Even now, increased longevity coupled with early retirement makes recreation for older people a much more important consideration. . . .

The high development of the idea of the team may perhaps be claimed as American. The British have a fine sense of cooperation in sports, but their sense of teamwork and of specialization often seems somewhat rudimentary to an American. In most American sports it is not important that a man on a team should be able to do all things well, or even several things well; he must be able to do one thing supremely well. Logically, since there are nine men on a baseball team and a game is played in nine innings, the team might be expected to rotate its positions so that every man played one position for one inning. But such an idea is so thoroughly un-American that even its suggestion seems slightly subversive. The height of specialization was reached in the two-platoon football system when some men played only on the defense and others only on the offense. . . .[6]

Somewhat analogous to the specialization of the individual is the specialization of play itself. This is to say that it has become more and more sharply differentiated from work. An individual must shift cleanly from one to the other, and no longer, as in frontier times, is he likely to be doubtful whether some occupation, such as hunting, is work or play. Only gardening, carpentry, and a few other occupations may serve as pleasure-giving hobbies and at the same time make money, or at least save money.

Still another phase of specialization is represented by the sharp differentiation between spectator and participant. An old story relates how a shah of Persia, visiting Paris, was taken to a ball. Looking at the vigorously exercising couples and remem-

[6]The idea of the team has been transferred out of the field of recreation, and World War II saw military operations often conducted by combat teams. The analogy with American work is also close. The American factory cultivates the specialized workman much as baseball cultivates the specialized player. It is a far cry from the ideal of the fully rounded man. It is a far cry also from the village handy-man and the Yankee jack-of-all-trades. Just as to succeed in his life work the American must become highly specialized, so also he must do in his sport.

bering his dancing-girls at home, he remarked: "Can't these people hire someone to do this for them?"

As if following the suggestion, the Americans have hired people to play baseball for them, and quite often even to dance for them. "Spectator sport" has become a regularly recognized term, and we have not only "sport clothes," but even "spectator-sport clothes." Some see in this development a fine manifestation of democracy, and point out that the spectator has a magnificent opportunity to identify himself with a group. Others, more pessimistically, point out that the periods of the great development of spectator sports have not been those of democracy, but may be found in the periods of the later Roman and the Byzantine empires.

As pointed out at the beginning of this chapter, play is a vague conception, and shades off imperceptibly into many fields. Since holidays have come more and more to be associated with recreation, we pass to a consideration of holidays.

CHAPTER **12**

HOLIDAYS

In spite of a slight change of spelling, *holi-day* scarcely conceals, even from the most casual, that it was originally *holy day*. Anthropologists seem to agree that such a day was, in the beginning, devoted to the placation of some force of nature or the worship of a god. The idea that men and women needed a rest from work and that they would thrive better if they had a break in the endless monotony of repeated days—all this, it is believed, has been a secondary growth. The shift from one conception to the other, however, seems to have been universal, and was probably soon effected.

If, then, about 15,000 B.C. some tribe was sufficiently developed to devote a special day to primitive religious rites, we may imagine that they gave up their ordinary occupations for that day, and devoted themselves to heavy eating, vigorous dancing, and doubtless other activities that a moralist would describe as more natural than edifying. By the time, however, that the year 14,999 B.C. had rolled around, the idea of the feasting and dancing and fun-making was doubtless, in the minds of some members of the tribe, beginning to loom larger than the idea of religion. Such seems to be the evolution of the holy day into the holiday, and nowhere is the process better illustrated than in the development of the United States. The whole history of the American people can be written in connection with their holidays—their origins, the shifting means of their celebration, the rise of one as against the decline of another. The holidays reflect both national unity and regional divergence. Some, like Thanksgiving, are legally established; others, like Halloween, rest upon folk custom. Some, like Christmas, are very ancient; some, like Father's Day, are very recent. All have a place. Whether we consider the contemporary scene or range backward through the centuries, without holidays the life of the American people would be a poor and insipid thing.

2

The most important American holiday is Sunday. In fact, it might be said to be fifty-two times as important as any other holiday. Its weekly recurrence creates a basic rhythm of life, and the ordinary American can scarcely imagine a civilization without a Sunday.

Yet neither in racial tradition nor in Western civilization is the observance of Sunday very ancient. The primitive Germanic tribes knew nothing of it, and neither did the classical Greeks. The seven-day week seems to have originated in Babylonia for astronomical reasons—since the five then-known planets, plus the sun and the moon, add up to seven. The ancient Israelites took the week from their kinsfolk the Babylonians, and made their own great contribution by dedicating the Sabbath as a day of rest. With the establishment of the Roman Empire the practical idea of the week spread widely.

The Christians, however, shifted their "holy day" from the seventh to the first, partly because that was the traditional day of the Resurrection, and partly to avoid seeming to follow Jewish customs.

In A.D. 321 Constantine established Sunday as an official day of rest. Later emperors went even farther, and restricted public amusements on that day. By the year 600 things had gone so far that Pope Gregory the Great protested against the closing of the baths on Sunday.[1]

During the Middle Ages church and state alike insisted that people attend religious services and abstain from work on Sundays, but did not frown upon play. As a result we have what is still sometimes called in the United States the "Catholic" or "continental" Sunday.

The first Protestant theologians could make out little case for the observance of Sunday, considering it to exist chiefly under the Jewish dispensation. Whereas the Catholics only worshiped and played on that day, many of the early Protestants saw no objection to working also. But practical rather than theoretical considerations seem to have saved Sunday for the Protestants. The body needed a day for rest, and the soul needed a day for worship.

In England, where the established church never went to extremes, the Catholic tradition of the Sunday was preserved throughout most of the sixteenth century. Only toward the end of that century did the stricter Protestants, then coming to be known as Puritans, decide that their consciences required them to observe a strict Sunday. This Puritan influence had its effect on the Church of England as a whole, and just at this time the American colonies were founded. The United States

[1]It is too great a leap of the imagination to connect the well-known traditional American custom of the Saturday-night bath with this closing of the baths on Sunday.

thus began under a conception of a Sunday that is perhaps best expressed in the language of the *Shorter Catechism:*

Q. 60. How is the Sabbath to be sanctified?—A. The Sabbath is to be sanctified by a holy resting all that day, even from such worldly employments and recreations as are lawful on other days.

In Virginia a law for the observance of Sunday went on the books as early as 1617. Regulations in the New England colonies were severe. Only in New Netherland did something of the continental tradition of Sunday maintain itself.[2]

The heavy immigration of Presbyterian Scotch-Irish after 1700 only emphasized the Puritan strictness of Sunday observance. Although John Knox had enjoyed his Sunday game of bowls with a good conscience, Presbyterianism had become stricter in the generations that followed him, and the Presbyterians in the New World were no backsliders.

Legally and theoretically, therefore, the American Sunday remained for at least two centuries a day to be devoted to attendance at church, to private worship and meditation, and to rest. Nevertheless, practical considerations prevailed. Animals must be fed, and so must people—although the food should be as far as possible prepared on the preceding day. Emergency labor might be performed, and if it was a case of

[2]Jasper Danckaerts, who was rather Puritanical for a Dutchman, gives an account of a Sunday on Manhattan Island in September, 1679, which indicates that a good deal of relaxation was allowed on that day. Among others whom he found enjoying themselves in what he chooses to term a low pot-house was apparently an old fellow of sixty-five named Jean Vigné, reputed to have been the first white child born on Manhattan. He happens to have been in some distant degree a great-uncle of mine, and I treasure him as a counterpoise to the large numbers of Puritans and Presbyterians that crowd my family history. He was not a disreputable character, as might be imagined from Danckaerts's account, but had served on the municipal council of New Amsterdam. I cite the fact to demonstrate that Sunday relaxation was allowable in early New York, even for a respectable citizen.

defending the blockhouse against Indian attack, no one considered that the loading and discharge of firearms violated the Sabbath.

By and large, although most Americans now look upon its extremes with disfavor, the tradition of Sunday observance had far-reaching and beneficial effects. It was, for instance, an inestimable boon to slaves. It was a bar against excessive exploitation of any laborer. It even protected the employer from himself, requiring him to cease from his labors for that one day of seven.

The excesses of Sunday observance were probably less important in actuality than they seem in retrospect. "Blue laws" may stand on the books, but they are notoriously hard to enforce, and frequently become a dead letter. Probably the old-fashioned Sunday rested most heavily upon the children of pious parents, and such youngsters too often had their natural activities curtailed without being channeled into other directions.

Upon the unchurched and in all the frontier districts the restrictions rested but lightly. The prohibition against work was of course likely to be popular even with the unchurched, but they were more ready to take the day as an opportunity for amusement.

Nevertheless, Sunday remained officially a day of gloom, until well on in the nineteenth century. By 1850 heavy immigration of Irish and Germans was beginning to have its effect. They brought with them Catholic and continental ideas of keeping Sunday. The Civil War must have had its influence, for in the midst of a campaign no general stops for Sunday. In the western states, as they were admitted from 1850 onward, legal restrictions against either work or play on Sundays were at a minimum. Nevertheless, as far as work is concerned, labor policies and general custom distinguish Sunday as a holiday just as firmly in the newer as in the older states.

In the course of our history the day has thus passed from a primarily religious to a primarily secular holiday. In the seventeenth century it was justified as a day to be set apart and thus sanctified before the Lord. In the twentieth century it is justified partly on traditional grounds, as a "right" of the workmen, and partly on rationalistic grounds, as a healthful and restorative break in the weekly routine, probably enabling a workman to produce more in the six days than he would in the unbroken seven.

In recent years Sunday has actually begun to expand backward into Saturday and thus produce the weekend, and many people work only five and a half days or even only five.

In the end, the chief sanction of Sunday and of the expanded Sunday that is the weekend rests upon tradition. Sunday is something that merely exists, and the reasons for its existence have become secondary. Like most traditional institutions, moreover, it is without accurate scientific basis. Just how much leisure should a modern man or woman enjoy? Should it be one day in seven or one day in five? If it should be two days in seven, should these days join to form a weekend or be distributed? Or should the individual be allowed some option? Whether there can be any real answer to these questions is, however, of little importance. Tradition has become so strong that any attempt at change on rational grounds would almost certainly be ineffective.

3

Aside from Sunday, the early colonists were rather poorly equipped—if we may use such a word—with holidays. Of patri-

otic holidays they had none at all. They did not celebrate the
signing of the Magna Charta or the defeat of the Spanish
Armada. Their closest approach to a secular holiday was May
Day, but its roots also were religious. Christmas was a great
English holiday, then as now displaying both secular and religious traits. But, on the whole, English holidays of the seventeenth century may be said to have been in a transitional or
decadent state. Protestantism, though it had finally decided to
take Sunday over, still looked askance at the other traditional
festivals of the Church, and searched the Bible in vain for any
justification for the dates of Christmas, Easter, Epiphany, and
the other great religious days. The Church of England continued to observe them, and they were therefore celebrated in
colonial Virginia. The stricter Protestants, however, eschewed
these festivals altogether, and considered them mere corrup-
tions fostered by Popery and partially veiled continuations—as
they certainly were—of pagan celebrations.

In addition, one may say that holidays—in spite of being
mere ideas without tonnage—are less easily transported across
an ocean in ships than are seed-wheat and livestock. Just as
the exiled Israelites lamented by the rivers of Babylon: "How
shall we sing the Lord's song in a strange land?" so many a
colonist must have looked out across the waters of James or
Hudson and wondered how he could sing Christmas carols or
celebrate Twelfth-night. On May Day, in England, one went
to the woods for garlands and flowers, but in Virginia the forest, dark and hostile, pressed close in. The land itself must also
have had its influence. May Day in England was a festival to
mark the opening of spring, when the blood first ran warm,
and lad and lass thought of love. But in Carolina the spring
came earlier, and by May 1 the land might already have been
for a month under the blanket of sultry heat.

Essentially, however, the history of each holiday is a thing in itself, and each one suffered different adventures.

4

Of the days observed with legal sanction everywhere throughout the United States, Christmas is not only the most important from nearly every point of view, but it is also the most ancient. Although it is now celebrated a few days after the turn of the sun at the winter solstice, it was originally—no scholar doubts—a midwinter festival. Its origins lie deep in prehistory. Bede records: "The ancient Anglian tribes began the year on December 25th when we now celebrate the birthday of the Lord." In Rome before the Christmas Era it was the day of "the unconquered sun," which was included in a great week-long festival. During this Saturnalia—a word still preserved in our dictionaries to mean "any period of unrestrained revelry"—the Romans celebrated with feasts, merry-making, and the exchange of presents. During the first centuries of the Christian Era when Mithraism and Christianity were rival religions, December 25 was celebrated as the birthday of Mithras.

Since the Biblical accounts give no date for the Nativity, the early fathers speculated about it. Gradually, as the power of Mithraism faded and as the church began to take the old folk festivals over, Christmas was made to coincide with December 25. It became the great festival of the year—partially Christianized, partially retaining old customs, such as the lighting of the yule log, the relic of a prehistoric fire ceremony.

With origins thus, in plain record, not at all scriptural or even apostolic, Christmas was under severe attack as soon as the theologians of the Reformation turned their attention to it. The Church of England kept the observance of Christmas,

but the Puritans, finding it nowhere in the Scriptures, rejected
it as a Popish corruption of true Christianity. They also rejected it as a folk holiday, since it had come to be celebrated
rather wildly, after the manner of the Saturnalia, with much
drinking, card-playing, and dicing, and a general letting down
of conventional standards under the appointment of a so-called
Lord of Mis-rule.

In the colonies, therefore, there was a wide split. In Virginia, and in other colonies where Church of England influence was strong, people continued to keep Christmas after
the traditional manner, in so far as they were able. The Germans and Dutch also celebrated the day. But the Puritans
would have none of it.

A famous passage of Bradford's *History of Plymouth Plantation* describes an incident of 1621. "On the day called Christ-
masday" the governor summoned everyone to work as usual.
Many of the colonists, however, were not Puritans, and these
were all for having a holiday. They excused themselves, raising
the argument (always a strong one with a Puritan) that their
consciences troubled them about working on that day. The
governor then told them: "if they made it matter of conscience,
he would spare them till they were better informed." These
individuals then organized some games in the governor's absence, only to have him turn the tables on them when he returned. "So he went to them, and took away their implements, and told them that it was against his conscience, that
they should play, and others work." The account concludes
with the sentence: "Since which time nothing hath been attempted that way, at least openly."

The Puritans, in short, not only did not keep Christmas,
but also were definitely anti-Christmas. Such an attitude
accounts for Samuel Sewall's gloating over the way in which
Boston continued "business as usual" on December 25. His

entry for that day in the year 1685 ran: "Carts come to town and shops open as is usual. Some somehow observe the day; but are vexed. I believe that the body of people profane it, and blessed by God no authority yet to compel them to keep it." As late as 1722, when the old order was beginning to change even in New England, he could still write: "The shops were open, and carts came to town with wood, hoop-poles, hay and so forth as at other times."

The Presbyterians in general agreed with the Puritans in their objection to Christmas, but no colony was dominated by them, and so their influence was less marked.

In the long run, however, Christmas triumphed utterly, and an investigator would have difficulty in finding any of this ancient prejudice still alive. Christmas is a legal holiday in every state. It expands, moreover, into a whole season, and its pre-eminence is recognized by the phrase "the holidays." Just as Sunday has become the weekend, so Christmas has spread backward to include Christmas Eve, and has reached forward almost to join hands with New Year's. Although there is no legal sanction for a vacation, probably less work is done in the week between Christmas and New Year's than at any other time in the year.

Not only is Christmas the greatest of American holidays, but it is also, by all odds, the most complex. Because of the custom of giving gifts, it is of major commercial importance. Many a retailer counts upon shifting from red to black on the basis of "Christmas trade." Few people remember, however, that this exchange of gifts can be traced clear back to the Saturnalia. As with other customs, Christianity offers its own explanation, in this case pointing to the gifts brought to the Christ-child by the three kings.

Christmas, which is literally "Christ's mass," is celebrated by special masses, and even by services in the Protestant churches, but it is more a folk holiday than a religious one, and preserves much less of a religious character than does Easter. It is therefore just as wholeheartedly celebrated by the unchurched, and even by many Jews, as by anyone else.

The international character of Christmas is one of its interesting features. The singing of carols is an English tradition. Most of the well-known carols are English, but carols are also sung in most of the countries from which Americans have originated. The Christmas tree represents the adaptation of a German custom. The crèche, scarcely yet naturalized, is chiefly French and Italian. Santa Claus, as his name indicates, is the Saint Nicholas of the early Dutch colonists; he originally brought gifts on December 6, and was later drafted for service upon the greater holiday. Along with him came, apparently, the custom of hanging the Christmas stocking. The conventional figure of the modern Santa Claus, however, seems to be largely an American development—stemming from Clement Clarke Moore's poem of 1823, A Visit from St. Nicholas. The custom of sending cards was introduced from England about the middle of the nineteenth century, and has grown to be a major feature of Christmas since 1900.

Through everything Christmas remains primarily a family holiday. It is not an outstanding day for the restaurateur, for on it the scattered members of a family are likely to be gathered in to sit around one great table, children and grownups together, to feast upon a Christmas dinner.

5

Of all the other holidays that are both national and legal only New Year's goes back to a pre-American origin. In its antiquity, however, it is far from comparable to Christmas.

The date at which the year should be supposed to begin was in dispute for a long time. An ancient tradition was that the world was created in March, and that therefore the year began at that time. Accordingly the Ram is still listed first among the signs of the Zodiac. In English tradition March 25, the approximate date of the spring equinox, was held to be the begining of the year until long after the first American settlements, but it was not a time of great festivity. Our celebration of New Year's Day stems largely from the Dutch. The Netherlands had settled upon this day long before England did so, and the celebration of January 1 became an occasion for great festivity.

New Year's has thus never been primarily religious. The watch-night services held in some churches with the offering of prayers for a prosperous year seem to be a modern innovation.

In general, New Year's in the United States lies under the shadow of Christmas and has comparatively little character of its own. It is a day when a man is free from work to do whatever he pleases, and when New Year's resolutions—seldom taken seriously—are in order. Only two traditional and conventional features seem to linger in its celebration.

One of these is "seeing the New Year in." In thousands of restaurants and night clubs and in millions of homes people await the stroke of twelve and the first blowing of whistles. Sometimes they await the moment gaily and hilariously, but just as often they sit doggedly. Then finally—whether all too soon or at long last—midnight comes, and with it the only occasion in the course of the year when anyone is privileged to make all the noise he can in the middle of the night without being in danger of arrest for disturbing the peace.

The other traditional feature of New Year's is its alcoholic quality. A drop too much at Christmas or Thanksgiving, with the children present, smacks a little of bad taste, but New Year's is a grownup's occasion. Again we draw from the tra-

dition of the Dutch colonists. In early New York open house
was the rule, and every gentleman made his round of calls, at
each house receiving his drink of punch from the ladies. With
such a custom in vogue, sobriety was not a virtue for a gentleman on that day, and was scarcely, indeed, a possibility. In
accordance with this tradition New Year's remains the only
American holiday that seems to emphasize eating less than
drinking. The eggnog party remains an institution for the
afternoon. And if even the judge gets a little hilarious, it is not
to be held against him, but rather to be put down as a double
manifestation of that ambiguous phrase "the spirit of New
Year's."

6

Of the holidays to originate on American soil Thanksgiving
is the oldest. It is also in many ways the most thoroughly
American.

In simpler days, before debunkers and scientific historians
became strong in the land, American children were taught a
simple, charming, and quite satisfying account of the origin of
Thanksgiving. As the story ran: "The Pilgrims at Plymouth in
the autumn of 1621, after they had gathered a plentiful harvest,
out of gratitude for that abundance, celebrated their first
Thanksgiving Day; they ate wild turkeys, and the Indians came
in to feast along with them; this was the origin of the celebration."

Now, certainly, this story went too far, after the manner
of stories for children, in making a simple matter out of a
complex one. Certain it is that the Pilgrims held a harvest
festival in the autumn of 1621 and feasted themselves. Since
the record stands in black and white that the governor "sent

four men on fowling," we may suppose that turkey was the principal meat at the feast. Moreover, King Massasoit came with many of his braves. The trouble is: 1) that this is not specified as a Thanksgiving, and 2) that no continuous tradition has been recorded of the celebration of the autumn feast. These loosenesses in the argument gave the debunkers a chance to throw doubt upon the whole matter. Moreover, they can point out that the establishment of special days for Thanksgiving was a Puritan custom, and that these days were not limited to autumn.

In some cases, however, it is possible to debunk the debunkers, and this is possibly one of them. Their case rests chiefly upon that weakest of all foundations—"argument from silence." The fact that there is no continuous record of Thanksgivings, in a time and place where there were no newspapers and very little written record of any kind, is of small importance. If there is no record of Thanksgiving days for some time in church and legal documents, what of it? Holidays may be very real without ever being official. Halloween and April Fools' Day have managed to get along for centuries without having legal status. Moreover, what if Thanksgiving did lapse for a year or even for several years? The tradition of the holiday can be kept alive for a long time in the individual human memory.

And this "first Thanksgiving" has about it so many features of the later festival that it cannot be lightly dismissed. Let us enumerate them. 1) It was an autumn festival. 2) It celebrated the harvest, as our day still does, with its decorations of corn and pumpkins. 3) Even if not a Thanksgiving in the religious sense, it had about it much of that suggestion. 4) It was celebrated with a great feast, as the day is still typically celebrated. 5) The chief meat at that feast was fowl, and that fowl was almost certainly turkey.

The debunkers can point out that the first Thanksgiving proclamation definitely to mention the harvest is that of 1668. This is, indeed, forty-seven years after 1621, but is less than the span of a human life. Some men and women not yet fallen into dotage were doubtless still alive at Plymouth in 1668 who as boys and girls had feasted on turkey in 1621. Such a memorable occasion is not to be forgotten. Is the mere absence of records enough to convince us that there was no autumnal celebration of Thanksgiving in individual Puritan families during those years of silence? Or even if the tradition had lapsed wholly, may not the institution of the harvest Thanksgiving of 1668 be a revival, stimulated by those who were old enough to remember the Thanksgiving of the first autumn?

November 25 was the day appointed in 1668. After that time the record is not continuous, but it is closely enough so to raise few doubts. Plymouth seems to have been the point of origin for Thanksgiving; thence it spread. During the eighteenth century, autumnal Thanksgiving days were appointed regularly in Massachusetts, Connecticut, and New Hampshire. Annual appointments were in harmony with the Purtian reluctance to establish any regular holy day except Sunday. Such appointments also ensured that the Thanksgiving would not fall upon a Sunday; Wednesday and Thursday were the days chiefly used.

Although occasional Thanksgivings were appointed by Congress during the Revolutionary War and the War of 1812, the spread of the autumnal festival seems to have proceeded state by state. New York, which had received a heavy migration from New England, adopted the custom officially in 1817. Before the outbreak of the Civil War it had spread to all the northern states and many of the southern ones. In 1863 President Lincoln appointed August 6 as a Thanksgiving Day for the victory of Gettysburg. He later proclaimed November 26 of that year as Thanksgiving Day, and since that time the Presidential Proclamation has been annual. Fortunately the establishment of the national Thanksgiving Day during the Civil War did not make it a sectional holiday in the minds of the Southerners. It is celebrated in all the states.

In its origins Thanksgiving Day must thus be considered partly a Puritan substitute for Christmas. It was also largely religious—a kind of Puritan substitute for a Catholic saint's day. Church services originally loomed large in the observance, and they are still held. In the early nineteenth century some state governors refused to appoint such a day on the grounds that it was a state interference with religion. Its proclamation by Lincoln is only another illustration of the curious way in which the federal government has managed to recognize religion without becoming involved with religion.

In later years Thanksgiving, like almost all other American holdays, has become secularized. As New Year's Day gives license to drinking, so Thanksgiving Day gives license to eating, and we have the traditional dinner, with its foods that have become symbolic of the American past—roast turkey with bread stuffing flavored with native herbs, cranberry sauce, mashed potatoes, pumpkin pie. There is also the permission, or almost the compulsion, on this one occasion of the year, to play the glutton—for now the corn has been gathered and the barns are full, and now the Indian summer is over and the war bands no longer are threatening, and now a man needs some fat under his ribs before the north winds begin to blow from Canada.

7

Two holidays sprang from the years of the Revolution. . . . The vast significance of the Declaration of Independence was recognized immediately, and John Adams wrote on July 3, 1776, that July 2 would be celebrated in the future. He happened to be wrong as to the date, but he was remarkably right in the rest of his prediction. The very next year the anniversary was celebrated with the ringing of bells, bonfires, fireworks, parades, and illuminations.

The most remarkable feature of the Fourth is that it has no roots in the farther past and no religious connections. It is wholly patriotic, that is, secular. Although such holidays have since that time become common throughout the world, they were not customary before 1776, and undoubtedly the American celebration has had much to do with the establishment of similar days in other countries.

But if the Fourth was not religious, it originally had about it something of a sense of dedication. Doubtless to some extent because a holiday was associated with religion, the celebration of the Fourth elevated patriotism almost to a religious level. The typical early observance of the day included a public gathering at which the Declaration was read and an oration on a patriotic theme was delivered. The analogy to a church service with its reading of the Scripture and its sermon is an obvious one. As time went on, the dedicatory features of the celebration tended to die out. The Declaration's long list of grievances against George III became outdated, and could scarcely seem otherwise than slightly ridiculous. As the nineteenth century waned, oratory went out of favor. Just as the religious element departed from Thanksgiving, so the high dedication of patriotism faded from the Fourth.

The other characteristic features, the noise and the fireworks, had existed from the very beginning, doubtless because the celebration was inaugurated in wartime. This feature grew and flourished until the occasion became a small boy's one day in Paradise. Then, about 1900, the total of annual deaths from fires and explosions rose so high that an inevitable movement toward a safe-and-sane Fourth resulted. Gradually the day lost its second distinctive feature, and lapsed into an ordinary summer holiday of picnics and baseball games. . . .

The colonials, as loyal subjects of the Crown, had celebrated the King's Birthday before the Declaration of Independence; the analogy to the celebration of Washington's Birthday is close, especially when we remember that many Americans wished to make Washington a king. Sporadic celebrations of the day are recorded from 1783 onward. In 1790, when Washington was president, the celebration took a more official turn, and Congress adjourned on that day. Even Washington, however, did not escape altogether from party politics, and the celebration of his birthday was for many years a Federalist rather than a national custom.

In 1832, however, occurred the centenary of his birth. By this time party lines had been redrawn and the Federalists had disappeared. The star of Washington had risen and shone brightly, unobscured by partisan fogs and smoke. At this time the celebration of the day began to spread widely.

Although February 22 is now a legal holiday in every state except Idaho, it lacks special ritual. The holding of a birthday ball is perhaps the most characteristic means of observance. The day has as its symbols the hatchet and the cherries—even though everyone agrees that their connection with Washington is only a shoddy fiction of Parson Weems, which actually represents the young George as an intolerable little prig.

8

The nineteenth century saw the establishment of the various days associated with the Civil War, and of Labor Day.

The Civil War holidays are of particular interest as showing the survival of sectionalism. Not one of them has managed to become fully national, although February 12 is celebrated in thirty-four states and May 30 in forty-four.

The graves of soldiers had been strewn with flowers and otherwise honored, often without distinction of blue or gray, even during the years of the war. General John A. Logan, Commander in Chief of the Grand Army of the Republic, appointed May 30, 1868, for "strewing with flowers or otherwise decorating the graves of comrades." Unfortunately, the use of the word "comrades" seemed to exclude the graves of Confederate dead, even though in actual practice they may often have been honored. There seems to have been no special reason for the choice of the particular day, except that it was not close to any other holiday and that flowers were readily available at that season. Known as Memorial Day or Decoration Day, the holiday was rapidly legalized after its beginning in New York in 1873. It was never an occasion for the celebration of victory, but was rather a mournful remembrance of the fallen.

Since it could be used to honor the Confederate dead, it was adopted in some form by all except four of the southern states. On the other hand, beginning with Florida in 1891, ten southern states legally established a special Confederate Memorial Day on June 3, the birthday of Jefferson Davis.

As the Civil War has receded into the past, there has been a tendency to make Memorial Day an occasion for the remembrance of the fallen in more recent wars. As in the beginning, however, it is a day for the memory not of victory but of grief.

The great division of the Civil War shows itself also in the split between Lincoln's Birthday and Lee's Birthday. The former is legally established in thirty-four states, including the three seceding states of Arkansas, Tennessee, and Texas; the latter, in twelve states, including all the seceding ones, plus Kentucky. Four states thus legally observe both days; six states, neither. As with Washington's Birthday, the celebration of Lincoln's Birthday dates largely from the year of his centenary, in 1909. . . .

The history of Labor Day is brief, but not without its interest. The idea was suggested in 1882 by Peter J. McGuire, a man not otherwise much known to fame. McGuire was interested in the labor movement, which at that time was just beginning to achieve some effective organization. His idea was that there should be a day dedicated to the laboring man. With considerable shrewdness he selected a date halfway between July 4 and Thanksgiving. The first Labor Day was celebrated in New York City on September 5, 1882.

The idea seemed to please everybody. Laborers approved, because they thus got another holiday, and because their movement was accorded some official recognition. Employers seemed to have raised little objection, because the day was sponsored by conservative rather than radical labor elements.

Rather curiously, far-off Oregon, removed from the centers of organized labor, was the first state to make the holiday legal. This was in 1887, and the same year saw the official recognition by four other states, including New York. In 1894 Congress recognized it for the District of Columbia and the territories; by then it was observed nearly everywhere, and it has since come to be one of the five holidays that are legal in all the states.

The parade of laboring men was an early feature of the day. These times, however, the last thing the average American workingman wants to do on a hot September day is to march along a sticky asphalt street. Instead, he is off with his family

GOOD FRIDAY MAP

GOOD FRIDAY MAP

In thirteen states Good Friday is a legal holiday, and in one it is a legal holiday from noon to 3 P.M. The patchwork character of the Good Friday map is difficult to explain, but may be taken as typical of the variations that often exist among the states. Since the importance of the day is emphasized by the Catholics, its establishment in the traditionally Catholic states of Maryland and Louisiana may be thus explained; but it is not established in the traditionally Catholic state of New Mexico or in the now strongly Catholic state of Massachusetts. Yet it is observed in the strongly Protestant state of Tennessee and in the traditionally Puritan and anti-Catholic state of Connecticut. In the latter it is to be explained as a survival of the annually appointed spring Fast-day (still observed in New Hampshire) which in the eighteenth century was a kind of counterpart to Thanksgiving, and eventually was identified with Good Friday. Since the day is observed by the Lutherans, its legal status may be thus explained in North Dakota and Minnesota, which have received heavy Scandinavian immigration. As for Arkansas, we need only comment that it is the most be-holidayed state of all, observing everything possible, including both Lincoln's and Lee's birthdays. The other states are doubtless to be explained by some local influence.

in the car for a day at the shore or a weekend in the mountains. Since Labor Day always falls on a Monday, a long weekend is assured.[3]

Like most American holidays, Labor Day has thus lost its dedicatory quality. It has become an occasion when a man is relieved from work and is allowed to do whatever he wishes. Because it occurs near the end of summer and makes a long weekend, it has come to have something of the season-marking quality of an English bank holiday. "After Labor Day" the resorts are less crowded; children come home from camps and are made ready for school; cities begin to lose their summer languor and to quicken their pace. . . .

November 11, most recent of the holidays established legally in all the states, was first proclaimed by President Wilson in 1919. He declared that the day was established: "with solemn pride in the heroism of those who died in the country's service and with gratitude for the victory." In its very name, Armistice Day, there was a prophecy of the future. It was called neither Peace Day nor Victory Day. Inaugurated when the sense of victory was already becoming bitter with the realization of an uncertain peace, Armistice Day has remained a halfhearted holiday. For a while it was celebrated with parades of veterans, with public meetings, and religious services. Sometimes business was suspended for two minutes at the hour when the firing had ceased. But when the outbreak of another conflict proved that Armistice Day had indeed celebrated only an armistice, such celebrations approached the point of mockery. As a commentator upon American holidays concludes for his entry of November 11: "Not generally observed since World War II."

[3]Parades were a great feature of nineteenth-century secular holidays. All the organizations—military, fraternal, and other—turned out and marched in their assigned places. Sometimes there was even a final section of "citizens generally." One wonders who was left to look at the parade.

9

This chapter must come somewhere to a close. Yet how could one fail to mention a few others? . . . There is Easter, greatest of church festivals, bearing the name of a heathen goddess, escaping the necessity of legal recognition because it falls upon a Sunday. Some remnant of the ancient springtime festival lingers in the custom of "Easter clothes." Because of the buying of clothes, Easter is second only to Christmas as reflected in the retail trade. Parades have ceased to be an important feature of secular holidays, but the "Easter parade" still continues, though the term was doubtless first used in parody.

Two widely observed holidays are associated with the later immigration. . . . Columbus Day, commemorating his landing on October 12, was first established as a legal holiday by Colorado in 1905, and is now legal in forty-one states. It was propagated largely by the Knights of Columbus, and thus has a certain Catholic background. Because of the national origin of Columbus, it is a favorite Italian holiday. On the other hand, Saint Patrick's Day lacks legal establishment, but approaches the status of a national celebration because of the widespread and contagious enthusiasm of the Irish.

Also without legal sanction five ancient folk holidays manage to maintain themselves with varying degrees of vitality. . . . April Fools' Day, when harmless deceptions are in order, seems to be Celtic in origin, perhaps a spring festival of Lug-the-Long-Handed. Though it is obviously one of those occasions when ordinary standards of conduct are relaxed or reversed, the exact reason for its particular kind of foolery seems to be forgotten.

May Day also is Celtic—the great fertility festival of Beltane.

It was the most famous of the old English folk festivals, but its excesses had apparently become too great, and it was dying out in the seventeenth century. It never seems to have been of much importance in the colonies, and its present existence is probably due to a nineteenth-century revival. It is now thoroughly emasculated, and is celebrated chiefly in girls' schools.[4]

Halloween, on the contrary, is still observed with considerable vigor, and is the only holiday on which boys have a license to play pranks. It is the faded survival of another Celtic festival. The symbolism of witches may have some connection with its occurrence at the approach of winter—the time when the powers of darkness begin to be strong.

Valentine Day still continues the faint tradition of a spring fertility festival, and the exchange of sentimental valentines between boys and girls maintains a dim memory of the ancient significance. In recent years the day has even come somewhat to have a new life, much cultivated by the retail stores, as an occasion when a husband gives a gift to his wife.

Most vestigial of all is Ground-hog Day—February 2, when the ground hog, we are told, emerges from his hole, and if he sees his shadow, returns there in the knowledge that winter will last forty days more. This is the most shadowy (in two senses) of any of our holidays. Though it is solemnly reported by newspapers across the whole country, it has neither legal status nor ceremony nor symbolism, and it preserves only the merest fiction of a superstition. It was once Candlemas, an important church festival, but it is actually much more ancient. Its origin has been traced to primitive beliefs in immortality connected

[4]A famous incident of New England history is the setting up of a maypole, with attendent celebrations, by Morton and his company at Mount Wollaston (or Merrymount) in 1628. The Plymouth men sternly repressed this incipient transfer of May Day license.

with the mysterious reappearance of the bear after his hibernation. It thus goes back to the religion of tribes inhabiting the forests of northern Europe, and may be as old as Christmas. . . .

On the contrary, Father's Day and Mother's Day are creations almost of yesterday, but have established themselves as part of the American way of life. Commercially, for their influence on the retail trade, they rank only below Christmas and Easter.

As for state holidays and local holidays, these are legion. Individually, moreover, an American is granted the privilege of celebrating his own birthday and the anniversary of his marriage.

10

As with others of our customs, our holidays thus show great diversity in their manner of genesis. Christmas, New Year's, and the minor folk holidays are of Old World origin. Most of the others represent native developments. The special influence of later immigrants is seen in Saint Patrick's Day and Columbus Day. Our only important international holiday of modern origin is the singularly unfortunate November 11.

Historically, most of our holidays have arisen at the instance of particular people or of particular groups. They began little, and grew. As they grew, they tended to escape from special interests and to become more universally and also more vaguely American.

In recent years commercialism has undoubtedly been one of the chief factors in directing the course of American holidays. Mother's Day and Father's Day, for instance, have been a great boon to the retail trade, and have certainly been estab-

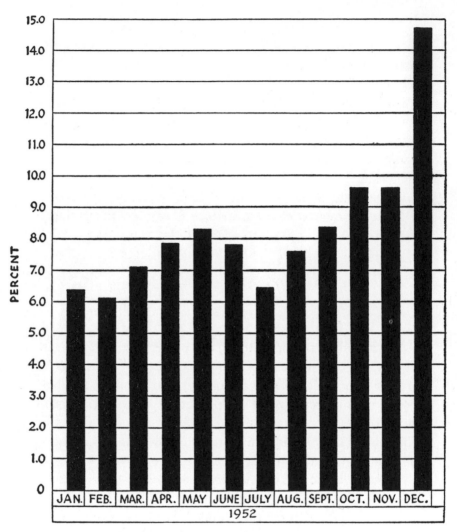

Percent of total annual department store sales transacted by months
in the U.S.

(Source, U.S. Department of Commerce)

RHYTHM OF THE RETAIL YEAR

The rhythm of the retail year reflects the environment, particularly the climate, to some extent, but in the minds of retailers is largely tied up with holidays. This is most obviously shown by the great December peak (representing really only the first twenty-four days of the month) that is "Christmas shopping." The minor peak in April, May, and June reflects Easter, Mother's Day (second Sunday in May) and Father's Day (third Sunday in June), and also the buying done in preparation for the summer holidays. July is low, because many people, particularly women and children, are out of town on vacations and because the hot weather discourages such an activity as shopping. The Fourth, especially since firecrackers have generally become illegal, does not stimulate buying. "After Labor Day" in the first week of September, trade improves. January and February are low, partly as a reaction after the Christmas trade, partly because storms and snow discourage shopping. By trying to build up Valentine Day (February 14) as an occasion on which a husband buys his wife a present, stores are attempting to improve February, at present the lowest month.

lished through advertising. Nevertheless, they could scarcely have been so successful if they had not built upon something basic in the American character. Moreover, in modern civilization, commercialism cannot be denied. Advertising becomes one of the means of folk transmission.

Perhaps the most discouraging feature about American holidays is their tendency toward leveling. By a kind of erosion they all seem to be becoming the same thing. What people do on the Fourth of July is likely to be just what they do also on Decoration Day and Labor Day. Thanksgiving and Christmas retain some individuality, but even they have lost their religious aspect and are being leveled to the general sameness. A holiday has simply become, for most Americans, a day when one is free from work. By thus giving the individual some leisure and punctuating the monotony of life, the holidays serve a useful purpose. To regret that they have lost almost all their association of dedication and consecration is merely to regret that such qualities seem largely to have disappeared from modern life.

Only in their origins do holidays still maintain at least a decent fiction of being holy days. A mere cold-blooded attempt to establish one about the middle of June because there is no national holiday in that month would be contrary to the American tradition. It would have to be tied patriotically to June 14 as Flag Day.

Perhaps only in the schools does a real sense of the dedication of holidays still linger. Children are taught their significance, and even comparatively minor holidays are celebrated with appropriate ceremonies.

CHAPTER **13**

ARTS

In all of our modern vocabulary there is no concatenated polysyllable so difficult to define and so provocative of debates and controversies as is that simple three-letter word—*art*. As Chapter 11 had occasion to point out, the activities of mere recreation may shade into those of art, so that what one person may consider art may seem to another to be only amusement.

The present chapter, to avoid such controversy as far as possible, will confine its discussion to the traditional major fields of literature, music, and sculpture and painting. Even within such limitations the Devil's question, "What is art?" has not yet been answered, and the present chapter will be forced to make the usual straddle by concerning itself partly with folk art and partly with sophisticated art.

To consider, historically, the position of the arts in American life, one must begin, as elsewhere, with the colonists. The English people of the early seventeenth century, like all peoples, had an artistic tradition. In music they had folk songs, such as ballads and carols, and in their singing of madrigals they reached what was a rather high level of musical sophistication for their times. In painting and sculpture, however, the English had made little advance. By all odds the strongest artistic tradition among the English was that of literature. In poetry and the drama, and even in prose writings, the Elizabethan age had made its great contributions.

Colonists, thus conditioned, were plunged into the new environment of a forested wilderness. The frontier has been said to represent a return to savagery. In some respects the fate of the frontiersman was even worse than that of the savage, and this may be said with respect to the arts. Many primitive tribes have a strong artistic tradition, which they can maintain by means of the materials at hand, and as a part of their established way of life. The colonists, however, were facing new conditions that were hostile to the perpetuation of the old traditions of art. Many among them, for instance, must have been used to attending the theater, but there was no possibility of a theater in America. Not only was the established artistic tradition thus broken, but also the colonists were generally separated into small units, sometimes mere families, and they had little leisure in their new environment. Finally, many of them were members of churches that opposed various forms of art.

As a result, sculpture and painting may be said to have been extinct in the early colonial period. Music, at least in its more sophisticated forms, was also extinct. Only literature maintained itself. The writer seems always to have been held in respect, and the colonists continued to write both prose and poetry, even with some degree of sophistication. Seventeenth-century colonial prose closely resembles British prose of the same period, and the poetry also uses the same forms and most of the same conventions. These conclusions would hold most strongly for the New England colonies, which were by far the most literate. But even in comparatively unliterary Virginia some unknown rhymer could turn out quite a passable poem in pentameter couplets on the death of Nathaniel Bacon in 1676.

There was also, even on the very frontier, a tradition of oral storytelling. Sometimes the themes were traditional ones brought from the old country, such as the folk-epic of Jack the Giant-killer. Sometimes the themes were those of the frontier itself. The importance of this tradition is hard to appraise, because few of the stories have been preserved in written form, and even when so preserved have probably been much altered. But the frontier storyteller should not be forgotten, for in the work of such a great writer as Mark Twain this influence is an important factor.

By and large, however, though Americans may be proud that the colonists preserved the literary tradition, the actual production of the period is comparatively unimportant. It could scarcely have been otherwise, considering the scanty population, the lack of literary centers, and the dearth of outlets for publication. Many of the best colonial writings remained in manuscript for many years, and were not actually printed until the nineteenth century, or even the twentieth. Here are to be included such outstanding examples as Bradford's *History of Plymouth Plantation*, Edward Taylor's poems, all of William Byrd's writings, and Franklin's *Autobiography*.

2

Independence produced no sudden change. After 1776 almost half a century elapsed before we note any particular upsurge in American artistic archievement.

In this connection 1820 is an interesting date. This was the year in which Sydney Smith, the English critic, leveled his famous taunt: "In the four corners of the globe, who reads an American book? or goes to an American play? or looks at an American picture or statue?"

Although apologists for the United States have raised voices of protest against Smith's rhetorical question, he was correct enough, for all practical purposes. Yet, curiously, he had asked his question at about the last possible year. Even in 1820 Irving was beginning to have British readers. Before the decade had passed both Irving and Cooper were known throughout Europe, and one might say in the four quarters of the civilized earth.

Two features of this artistic emergence should not pass without comment. First, the date is significant. In connection with recreation we have had to comment upon the new interests in spectator sports and other activities that began in the decade of the twenties. Obviously Americans were beginning, at this time, to have more leisure, and they could thus pay more attention both to recreation and to art. Second, the particular artistic form was literature. This is what we should expect from the colonial tradition.

Since 1820 American literature has never ceased to maintain a tradition, and it has never suffered what might be called a serious recession. American literature has contributed its world figures, such as Poe, Whitman, and Twain. Beginning with Sinclair Lewis in 1930, five American-born writers have been awarded the Nobel Prize.

As compared with the other arts, literature has certainly remained the dominant means of artistic expression for the people of the United States. One can even maintain that "wanting to write," or more specifically, "wanting to write a novel," is one of our almost universal ambitions.

The reasons for this desire to write lie deep in the conditions of American life. First, there is the long tradition, stretching clear back to colonial times. Second, writing requires little equipment, as compared with either painting or sculpture or music. Third, it requires—or seems at least to require—little technical training. No one would think of trying to paint a mural or compose a symphony without years of study, but people think nothing of trying to write a novel merely by sitting down and beginning. (They often seem to be surprised when they fail, but the curious thing is that they occasionally succeed.) Fourth, writing can be economically rewarding, and thus holds out the same lure as the gold mine, even if no greater chance. Fifth, just as it is more likely to be economically rewarding than is music or painting, so writing is also generally held in greater honor.

Finally, alone among arts in the United States, writing has been equally attractive to men and to women. It has never been considered effeminate, and many of the most virile American heroes have been ardent and successful devotees of the pen. One can begin with John Smith and continue through Benjamin Franklin, Thomas Jefferson, and Theodore Roosevelt, clear to the present. On the other hand, writing has offered an outlet for women from the time when Anne Bradstreet began to write poems soon after her arrival in Massachusetts in the early seventeenth century. A typical figure of American life is the housewife who attempts to earn a little money and fame by stealing some time from her dishwashing and writing a novel. And occasionally, as the examples of Harriet Beecher Stowe and Margaret Mitchell demonstrate most brightly, she has written it.

3

The history of American music is not comparable with that of American literature. The Elizabethan tradition of part-singing, if it made the transatlantic passage at all, must have

soon lapsed under colonial conditions, and lutes and organs
were expensive and difficult to maintain. By merely learning to
read and write for purely practical ends, the colonial mastered
the basic technique of literature, but music had no such close
connection with practical life, and music teachers were scarcely
to be found at all.

Some of the early German congregations cultivated choral
singing, and even rendered the works of such masters as Haydn,
Bach, and Handel. Most of the American churches, however,
gave little encouragement to music, and many of them restricted it. Some churches allowed only the singing of psalms;
some permitted no musical instruments; a few banned music
altogether.

Musical culture began to develop—again the date is sig-
nificant—about 1820. In that year the Boston Philharmonic
Society was organized, and in the next year came the first
American performance of a Beethoven symphony.

Since there was no tradition and since no large immigrant
group was involved, this new movement is to be credited
chiefly to the influence of international ideas. It thus was
neither native nor popular. From the very beginning, then,
we find the gap between "highbrow" music and "popular"
music.

This gap was partially bridged during the later nineteenth
century, and with better luck might have been completely
bridged. That period saw tremendous interest in music. Moreover, this was an interest not merely in hearing music, but in
rendering it.

Anyone surveying the American musical scene of about 1880
might well have been highly optimistic. He would have seen
a nation in which both listening to music and singing and playing music were not merely socially approved but were beginning to be a part of the normal way of life—were, in fact,
rapidly becoming the accepted tradition. The piano resounded

throughout the land. The observer of 1880 might well have
thought that before long the Americans would take the next
step and begin to compose music. Then that art would assume
a comparable place to literature. In fact, the observer could
even have concluded that with the appearance of such a song
writer as Stephen Foster the movement, naturally commencing
with the simpler art forms, had already begun.

He might even, projecting himself forward to the mid-
twentieth century, have imagined an American people paying
homage to Bach and Beethoven and occasionally listening to
their works, just as they paid homage to Shakespeare and Milton and occasionally read their works or saw them presented.
He could have imagined this people, however, really interested,
not in music of the past centuries and of foreign countries,
but in the music of their own contemporary composers.

But it has not so happened. The present-day American—
granted that he listens to "serious" music and reads "serious"
books—rarely reads an older book after he has left the class-
room, and rarely listens to "serious" modern American music.[1]

The failure of music thus to develop may be attributed to
several historical factors, such as professionalism, feminism,
mechanization, and immigration.

To begin with, as soon as professional singers and instru-
mentalists began to tour even the small towns, people learned
that their local young ladies could not really play very well and

[1]The question can be raised as to whether jazz is to be considered
"serious" music. Certainly many people so take it, and it is just as
certainly American, a notable Negro contribution. It has also exercised
a considerable influence abroad. At present it seems to hold a position
on the line between a folk art and a fully recognized art. In a somewhat
similar position is the work, most widely known through musical shows,
of such composers as George Gershwin and Cole Porter. Yet, to date,
it may be doubted whether any American composer has managed to do
what numerous American writers have done, that is, to attain first-class
"serious" rating and wide popularity.

that the tenors and basses of their local glee clubs could not really sing very well. This rapidly discouraged the young ladies and the tenors and basses.

Moreover, from its beginning, the nineteenth-century interest in music had been largely be-feminized. Its symbol came to be one young lady singing "The Last Rose of Summer" to another's piano accompaniment. Thus arose a cultural paradox. Literature, in which women often participated with great success, remained an art to which an American male might devote himself without much suspicion of effeminacy. But music, in which women had never traditionally accomplished much, became—for a generation at least—an art that an American male scarcely dared cultivate.

Perhaps of most importance was the mechanization of music. David Ewen in his excellent book *Music Comes to America* writes: "The greatest force in making America a country of music lovers was unquestionably that of mechanization." One would not argue with such an authoritative statement, and doubtless Mr. Ewen chose his words carefully. "Music lovers," yes; "music producers," no.

Just as the growth of professionalism had discouraged the amateur, so the growth of mechanization, some years later, struck at the professional. As late as 1910 hundreds of little orchestras played in theaters and restaurants, and hundreds of little bands rendered selections in parks and at beaches. Where are they now? Instead, we have the record delivering through the radio and the juke box, and millions of people listening to the music of a few musicians.[2]

Immigration has also had a great effect. In the later nine-

[2]Like so much else in recent times, the responsibility for music has largely been turned over to the schools. High-school bands and orchestras multiply and flourish, and are giving to a large number of Americans the musical training that they might formerly have gained in small professional orchestras.

teenth century the immigrants were largely from countries where music was much more intimately a part of the tradition than it was in the British Isles. No one can doubt the great effect upon our music of the coming of the Germans, Italians, Scandinavians, Slavs, and Jews. The general judgment would be that this effect has been extremely good. But there is possibly another side. These immigrants brought with them what may be called an international music, but this is also, it may be argued, an alien music. It was not British, much less American. It has been grafted upon the American tradition, but perhaps the graft has not altogether healed. Given another generation or two, and things may change. But at present the musical situation may be partly the result of a sophisticated tradition implanted by immigrants upon an older population group not yet prepared for it.

The present situation is therefore peculiar. In some ways it is almost Utopian. Partly by listening directly to professional musicians, but much more by listening to records and radio, the average American has an easy opportunity to hear almost any kind of music, to the limit of his leisure. There is also every indication that Americans listen to an amazing amount of "good" music, and enjoy it. In a sense, what more could be asked? Many people, in fact, view with admiration the recent growth of our appreciation of music, and look upon the situation almost with smugness.

Viewed from another angle, as compared with our literary culture, our musical culture is stagnant, non-creative, and—relatively speaking—dead. The situation is much the same as that with spectator sports. Just as we watch a few skilled professionals playing football or baseball, so we listen to a few skilled musical professionals. Not many people attempt to sing or play, and only a negligible number attempt to create music in the real sense, that is, to compose it. Our music has no tra-

dition of a Harriet Beecher Stowe or a Margaret Mitchell, and
so we lack that hundred thousand people who might be trying,
annually, to write a symphony, or even a light opera. As a
result, we do not give ourselves any real chance of producing
an Emily Dickinson of music. ASCAP, the all-inclusive organization of American musicians, was reported recently to have
only about sixty "serious composers."

The United States thus has never had and does not now
have any strong tradition for the composing of music. It had
once a strong tradition for the rendition of music, but this has
now largely been lost. At the present time a remarkably small
number of Americans can play any instrument or carry a part
in a song; a great many of them cannot even carry a tune, or
whistle one. Yet, at the same time, the number of listeners to
the best of music runs into the millions.

This is not healthful for the living American composer, who
from his professional work can earn little or nothing, and generally has to work at some other job in order to eat. In fact,
it might be said of the American composer that he really does
not exist at all. Certainly, sixty in a population of a hundred
and sixty million is a negligible number. The great majority of
those who might now be producing a significant American
music have almost certainly given the matter up as a bad job
and gone off doing other things.[3]

[3]Recently I had some contact with a young composer whose situation
seems typical. 1) He was supporting himself and his family by teaching. 2) He had temporarily gained some free time for composing by
being awarded a fellowship. 3) He had no expectation of earning any
money from composing, and expected to have to devote the bulk of his
time and energy to teaching. 4) He was composing for a band, although
more interested in orchestra, because: "If you compose a band-piece,
you have some chance of having it played; if you compose for an
orchestra, you have hardly any chance."

4

The history of our painting is somewhat comparable to that of our music, and may therefore be discussed more briefly. There is no continuous colonial tradition. In the eighteenth century portrait painters began to have an opportunity, and a school of such painting developed. But just as the invention of the phonograph restricted the opportunity of the professional instrumentalist, so about half a century earlier the development of photography killed the opportunity for the portrait painter. In the nineteenth century—again the analogy with music is close—the young lady busied herself with pencil, or water colors, or even oils, as part of her education. Once more, we may note, it was the young lady rather than the young man.

The result of her efforts was unimportant, except in so far as it was negative. For, just as happened with music, painting came to have a certain flavor of effeminacy. An American man who took up painting was likely to be regarded as at least a Bohemian trifler, if not definitely effeminate.

In many respects the situation became—say, by 1900—even worse than with music. Although there is always a certain amount of hypocrisy in the appreciation of any art, the enjoyment of music in the United States seems to be on the whole genuine, even though often not critical. At an art exhibition, however, the proportion of hypocrisy seems to rise considerably higher, and there seems to be less real enjoyment and more attempt at criticism, much of it hypercritical if not hypocritical.

Recent years, however, have shown a certain change, and in some respects the situation of painting seems now healthier than that of music. The difference may lie in the discovery of primitivism. Art galleries begin proudly to display the works of early, untrained American artists. Grandma Moses becomes almost as famous as Margaret Mitchell. Thousands of people realize that painting is something at which they can express themselves, without laborious and expensive years spent in mastering techniques of color-mixing and brushwork. There has been a similar interest in sculpture.

Such popular participation—not mere spectatorism—must certainly be putting new vigor into painting and sculpture. Perhaps in another generation we shall see the effects.

5

The present chapter has, so far, been considering art as a social phenonemon, rather than as a matter of masterpieces produced by a few outstanding artists. Objection may rightly be taken. The production of one Beethoven is doubtless more to be desired than the production of a million second-rate composers.

The present discussion, however, is actually proceeding upon the theory that only under proper conditions can a Beethoven be produced at all. Some indeed may hold that geniuses produce themselves and will undoubtedly and inevitably so appear, in spite of all difficulties. Such a belief is certainly not capable of demonstration, and seems very unlikely, by mere common sense. If you want a crop of good wheat, you create for it as favorable an environment as possible. Otherwise, it is impossible. Even so, your wheat crop may fail, but you at least have given it a chance.

Thus considered, the present discussion has not been alien to the problem of the production of great artists and great masterpieces. We have, in the past, achieved an environment in which millions of people have "wanted to write," and so those millions have experimented and labored, from them a few great figures have emerged, and we have a literature that has attained a respectable position by world standards. But our social tradition has stimulated and encouraged rather few people to paint pictures and carve statues and even fewer to compose music, and in these fields of art we have had little production that has had much impact upon the world, or even upon our own people.

Considered in its social relations, the production of great masterpieces would seem to require, first, a social tradition that stimulates many people to try, and second, some adjustment in the way of life so that the promising writer or painter or composer may integrate himself with society at least to the extent of being enabled to produce, and thus go on to develop his creative faculties. Ideally, the process would be one of elimination, with the most fit encouraged at each stage to continue and the least fit channeled into other lines of activity. Practically, no society can ever possess a perfect system for the judging of art, much less for the judging of potential artists. Much must be left to chance, and individual initiative.[4]

At this point we may ask: "What kind of adjustment has American life traditionally provided to permit or encourage the highly creative individual to attain full fruition?" We may elaborate the question by another: "How well has this highly creative individual been integrated with society as a whole?"

[4]There is another theory, which is, in general, that the true artist is necessarily the rebel, the misfit, the non-conformist. While it may be admitted that a certain amount of discontent and revolt, or possibly "a maggot in the brain," is good for an artist, just as a few fleas are said to be good for a dog, history seems rather to indicate that many, if not most, of the great artists have maintained a good adjustment to society, though they may have objected to many of its details.

As to the social and economic adjustment provided for the creative individual, we may answer that we find, in our past and in our present, all four of the different adjustments that may be found at other times and in other places.

First, we have "the artist as amateur." This is essentially the adjustment of the artist in a primitive society. In a savage tribe some individual composes the songs or tells the tales, but at the same time does his full share of the hunting or of the field work and expects no special compensation for his creative activities, except perhaps now and then a choicer cut of the communal kill or a warmer spot by the fire.

Second, we have "the artist as performer." This may be taken to represent a later stage, appearing in what are sometimes called "heroic" societies. Epics, ballads, and lays were recited or sung by some bard or minstrel, who earned his living primarily by entertainment, and only secondarily by the ability to create the material that he used in his role as entertainer.

Third, we have "the artist as recipient of patronage." This stage is characteristic of feudal and baroque society, and flourished in Europe from the later Middle Ages, through the Renaissance, and into the eighteenth century. Much of the world's greatest art—whether poetry, painting, sculpture, or music—has been produced under this system.

Fourth, we have "the artist as businessman." Thus conceived, he produces his wares and sells them in the open market. This adjustment seems to be the most recent, and is characteristic of modern democracy.

Of the four adjustments, the "artist as performer" is least characteristic of the present time. Specialization has rendered this solution obsolete. The great composer of music is not likely also to be the concert pianist, or even to possess the dramatic flare that is needful for a great conductor. The true poet is not necessarily a good reciter of poetry, and may just as likely be a shy man who makes a very bad public appearance. In the United States the artist as performer has functioned chiefly from the lecture platform, and for an occasional individual lecturing is still lucrative. In the later nineteenth century it was much more important, and nearly all our important writers of that period gave it a try. Such a commanding figure as Emerson supported himself largely by lecturing. In the twentieth century Vachel Lindsay depended upon the income from his recitals of his own poetry, and Carl Sandburg has sung folk songs to his own guitar from one end of the country to the other. But these are the exceptions.

Patronage has never flourished greatly in the United States, and has declined in modern times. During the nineteenth century the federal government assumed a certain responsibility, though wholly informal, toward writers. As a kind of patronage, a writer sometimes received an appointment that was moderately lucrative without being onerous, so that he could continue to write without being under too great economic pressure. Irving, for instance, was attached to the embassy at Madrid; Hawthorne, Howells, Harte were consuls. The lapsing of this tradition many indicate that government service now offers fewer sinecures, but it may also be taken as an indication of the shrinking respect for the writer. During the depression of the nineteen-thirties the WPA assumed some responsibility for the starving writer, musician, and painter, but this was only on an emergency basis. Governmental patronage of the arts, never strong, has now declined almost to nothing.

A little private patronage continues to exist. We see it in the modern proliferation of fellowships, grants-in-aid, and prizes which are offered by foundations and donors. Our possessors of great wealth have, however, rarely possessed also the desire, much less the taste, to further the production of art, and have also lacked the hereditary rank that made patronage graceful and natural for a Renaissance noble or eighteenth-century prince. Moreover, the American artist shies away from the idea of being "kept," with the inevitable suggestion that he who pays the piper calls the tune.

The artist, however, very frequently functions as the amateur. He has, thus, certain advantages. Not expecting to support himself by his art, he can remain free from the dangers of commercialism. Working at some ordinary job, he maintains a valuable contact with society. On the other hand, after putting his hours in as a teacher, insurance agent, janitor, or newspaperman, he may lack the time and energy to consummate himself as an artist. One may question whether a part-time artist can attain full greatness. If the amateur has been lucky enough (or unlucky enough) to be born well-to-do, he gains some advantages, with certain losses. Lacking the economic spur, he is likely to end a mere trifler. The rich man, moreover, loses contact with common earth and common people, and so is rendered all too unlikely to be able to interpret such a country as the United States.

Most commonly, we have "the artist as businessman." He produces, and sells. Thus conceived and thus conceiving himself, he has the great advantage of attaining economic dignity, according to the standards of his society. He stands on his own feet, and theoretically asks no favors of anyone.

But here too he has troubles. The chief is that he is the smallest of all small businessmen. The writer is generally at the mercy even of his publisher, and the publisher too, by modern standards, is a very small businessman. Not only is the writer or artist individually minute, but he is negligible in numbers. He constitutes no significant voting bloc, and therefore exercises little political influence. As a result, though the artist is conceived as a businessman, he has had the greatest difficulty even with such obvious questions of justice as copyright laws. None of the ordinary governmental aids to business are available to him. For instance, governmental loans are available to "business." But a writer who needs financial help in order to complete a book cannot get a loan from the government. Farmers have various aids such as "price support," but the artist has nothing comparable.

Or, take the matter of public libraries. The American people have become devoted to public libraries with an almost religious intensity. They believe that books should be made available to the people. A writer's book is therefore placed upon the shelf immediately, and he receives a royalty (perhaps, thirty-five cents) for that single copy. A hundred or more people may then read and enjoy that book, but the author receives nothing more for it. Thus we have a kind of curious halfway state-socialism. One cannot imagine it applied to automobiles or cotton. The consumption of literature, so to speak, has been socialized; the production of literature remains a matter of completely *laissez-faire* economics. Considered as a businessman, the artist thus is in an extremely difficult position.[5]

6

In addition to enduring an unsound economic position, the artist in the United States is not held in the highest position of honor. He is accorded neither the respect nor the adulation shown to a motion-picture actress, a TV comedian, a champion athlete, a senator, or even an atomic scientist. Perhaps for this

[5] A great anomaly of our history is that Andrew Carnegie, one of our outstanding examples of individual initiative and free enterprise, did so much to destroy the free enterprise of writers by socialistically founding free libraries. What would *he* have thought if someone had started to go around supplying the public with free steel?

reason, expatriation has been a continuing phenomenon. There have been notable examples among writers (Henry James, T. S. Eliot). Many other writers, though living abroad for considerable periods, returned to the United States and never really lost touch (Irving, Cooper, Twain). The tendency has probably been even stronger among painters.

Moreover, the position of the writer seems to be declining. The American people once showed its appreciation for such literary figures as Longfellow, Whittier, and Emerson by naming many schools in their honor. In the four quarters of this land how many schools have been named for a twentieth-century writer?

What may be put down as one of the scandals of our time is that the obvious justice of some relief from income tax for a successful first book was originally granted, not to some needy and obscure beginner at writing, but to a glamorous military hero, who was already receiving a high salary and was certain, in any case, to make a large amount from his book. There could scarcely be a better incident to illustrate the present-day lack of regard for the artist.

If our society, then, offers little economic reward to the artist and at the same time holds him in comparatively small honor, what can we expect? We may ask, "Why do we not have more good books?" The real question is, "How do we manage to have as many good books as we do?"

The situation also furnishes a good enough explanation of why the artist, in the modern United States, is usually in revolt against society—a Bohemian, a non-conformist, a radical. He has little respect for society, one may guess, because society has little respect for him and even fails to grant him the economic opportunities afforded to others. The situation, of course, is not so simple as this, but such a statement may serve as an approximation. As a result there is a growing tendency

for modern art—whether sculpture, painting, music, or literature—to withdraw itself farther and farther from the main
stream of modern life.

This chapter has been written on the theory that art as a
way of life is not merely to be conceived as a matter of the
masterpieces of the past viewed by people in museums, or of
classical music, or of the great books of previous eras, no matter
how deeply appreciated by no matter how many people. The
question here considered has been twofold. First, we have
given some attention to what may be called the process of
folk art, that is, the participation of a people in creation.
Second, we have considered the problem of the production of
masterpieces. In both, we have been interested in art not only
as appreciation but also as production.

In general, the tradition of artistic expression in the United
States, with its emphasis upon the written word, is strongly
hereditary, following the English tradition, which never wholly
lapsed during the colonial period and under the conditions of
the frontier. The other arts suffered such a lapse. Being re-
stored under the influence of international ideas during the
nineteenth century, they have not even yet been able to
affiliate themselves so closely with the American way of life
as has the traditional art of literature. Even today, by its literature much more than by the other arts, the United States
exercises a world influence.

CHAPTER **14**

CONCLUSION

This sort of thing might go on forever.[1] Chapters could be written on business and work, education, government and politics, law, place names, family relationships, and many other topics. Readers, however, are finite, and so— even more certainly, I say at this point—are authors. Accordingly, to use a good American phrase, let us pick up our marbles. . . .

As to the mechanisms producing various phases of the American way of life, Chapter 1 postulated, primarily, environment and heredity; secondarily, native developments and international ideas. It is now possible to summarize the effect of these factors, individually.

Environment, whether acting directly or indirectly, seems to have been at its most potent, rather curiously, in establishing our drinking habits. Our heavy use of water, of iced drinks, and of strong liquors, and our comparatively small consumption of wine, all seem to be based upon environment.

The environment has also exercised a strong influence upon

[1] Well, for a long time, anyway.

food and upon religion. It has been of less importance in shelter, arts, language, sex, and play; upon clothing, strangely, it exercised scarcely any influence at all, until recently. Finally, environment may be said to have been of negligible influence upon personal names and holidays.

The Indians, considered as a special phase of the environment, have notably affected our food habits; language, less strongly; the rest, scarcely at all.

Since heredity may be considered the other chief factor, its influence is somewhat the reverse of environment. It has dominated in language. It can also be called the chief controlling factor in the determination of most of the other ways of life here considered. In fact, only in play and drink does the hereditary influence seem definitely subordinate to any of the others.

Native developments have exercised their strongest influence upon play, where they may even be said to dominate. They have also been an appreciable factor in most of the other fields. Their influence has probably been least in clothing and religion.

International ideas have nowhere been dominant. They have exercised their most important influence, throughout a considerable part of our history, in clothing. Such ideas have also been of some importance in food, play, and arts. Their influence has been slight upon language, religion, drink, shelter, names, and sex; negligible, upon holidays.

Some attempt at a comparative appraisal is likely to be involved with prejudice and to be influenced by specialization. A geographer will incline to emphasize the influence of the environment. A scholar of German ancestry, reared with a pride in the tradition of the forty-eighters, will be likely to see Germanic influence written large. The cosmopolite will emphasize international ideas—everything from French cookery to modern architecture. The grass-roots American will focus upon native developments.

In this connection, I can claim no immunity from prejudice and individuality. Like other Americans, I have sprung from a particular heredity and been subjected to a particular training. At the moment, however, I have a special advantage for such an appraisal, in that to write this book at all I have had to study many subjects outside my own field of specialization, and to assume many different points of view. In fact, to make the present appraisal, all I need now to do is to sum up what has already been presented.

The result of reviewing, quantitatively, the previous chapters would seem to bring out most strongly the importance of the hereditary element in American life. What we do, in fact, seems to be done chiefly because of hereditary habits brought to the country by immigrants, and all our patriotic wishes to emphasize American originality cannot change history.

In addition, the strongest hereditary influence is the earliest, that is, the northwestern European. If the study were extended into other fields, this conclusion would probably not be altered. In government, for instance, the influence of the English parliamentary system is overwhelming. In jurisprudence the English common law remains our basis. So it would probably go in most of the topics to be investigated.

On the whole, this is not surprising. Those who came first established the pattern, and those who came later, arriving only a comparatively few in any one year, tended to conform to what they found already established. The process is most strikingly exemplified in language. It failed to function when the first comers had failed, as with religion, to establish anything approaching a unity.

If the pattern of the life of the United States is thus so strongly determined by hereditary factors, we should be inclined to reject the often-voiced dictum that we are a "new people," and that we have a "new culture." Our roots run back just as far as those of any other people. We speak an Indo-European language. Our predominating religion is just as old as the predominating European religion—because it is the same one. In fact, a general conclusion that emerges strikingly from the evidence is that the United States is much more definitely like Europe than different from Europe. . . .

I introduced this book with a quotation from the poetry of Archibald MacLeish, whose writings I treasure particularly for their interpretation of his own country. But one of his lines— provocative though it may be—seems to me indefensible in the light of the non-poetic evidence here collected:

It is a strange thing—to be an American.

Perhaps the sentiment might be accepted if we could extend the generalization farther, and write:

It is a strange thing—to be a human being.

For, surely, to be a member of the human race is for any thinking man to realize that he is one of a species that is strangely unique in the history of the world, and the conscious realization of this position and its possible responsibility may even be somewhat terrifying.

As for the strangeness of being an American, MacLeish is apparently thinking much in such terms as those presented in this book, that is, that American culture is composed of a mingling of heredity and environment, so recently achieved that the different strands may be separated in the light of history.

Yet any such conception of strangeness has validity only in a comparative sense. Is it stranger to be an American than to be one of some other nationality? Is it not strange also to be a

Greek, and sit—forever and inescapably—in the intellectual shadow of the Parthenon? Is it not unspeakably strange to be a Russian, and be hurled out of serfdom and into near domination of the world within a century? Is it not, once anyone starts thinking about it, a strange thing to be an Englishman, or a Pakistani, or an Eskimo?

The ordinary American, like the ordinary person of any other nationality, sees nothing strange in his life. To him, the other fellow is strange.

Strangeness, in so far as it represents a quality of uniqueness and individuality, is nothing that any nation should be ashamed of, but should rather treasure. Whether Americans in their common ways of life possess this quality more than it is possessed by those of other nationalities may be left as a question for debate. The present volume has attempted to present some of the evidence. . . .

In certain respects the theme of this book may be considered a humble one. It has dealt with various topics of unglamorous and everyday nature, such as our full-dress historians and philosophers have rather pointedly passed over, as if not worthy of their attention. Much of the material has been dug out of original sources because no scholar has previously bothered to collect it.

But in other respects the theme of the book is a proud one. It deals with what must be considered one of the central problems of our history—perhaps even the most central of all—that is, how and to what degree has that miracle been performed by which from emigrants and exiles out of many nations has been fused, in the end, one nation.

AUTHOR'S NOTE

About half of the chapters of this book were first presented to the public as lectures that I delivered as Professor of American Literature and Civilization, under the Fulbright Act, at the University of Athens in the winter of 1952–53. These chapters, however, have been rewritten and expanded from the original lectures.

In thus attempting to interpret my own country for Greeks, I necessarily looked for the unities of American life and emphasized them. This was not so difficult in Athens as it would have been in any particular city of the United States. Seen from a foreign country, the differences between the various regions of one's own country tend to disappear, and the national unity to appear stronger.

My treatment has, thus, to some extent run contrary to the tendency of modern research, which has been to specialize upon periods, regions, and social groups, and thus to emphasize a confused and almost infinite diversity. The book, therefore, will probably be criticized adversely by specialists for too great simplification.

Perhaps my best course would be merely to soften criticism by readily admitting that the book contains much simplification, against which the reader should be warned. It also asserts many generalizations, against which the reader should again be warned.

Yet, having presented the book to the reader, I would leave him in a poor position if I merely ran away before a possible attack of specialists. Neither is it my own honest conclusion that I should. Particularization and generalization are complementary methods of approach to truth. Neither attains truth fully, but each serves a purpose, and the errors of one are perhaps not more heinous than those of the other.

I take comfort also from a recent conversation with a prominent geologist. "As long as you are making your reconnaissance map," he said, "you get a result that is useful and illuminating. Once you try to put all the details in, the whole thing becomes confused and loses significance." I hope that this book has analogies with the reconnaissance map.

As for my acknowledgment of sources, I should declare that the book rests, first of all, upon my own experiences of life in the United States, over a period of more than half a century. Secondarily, it rests upon what I may call without great exaggeration a lifetime of reading and study and thought in the fields of American history and literature. Only in the third place does this book rest upon specific reading and note-taking performed for the special purpose of writing it.

Nevertheless I would be ungrateful if I did not acknowledge certain sources, and the reader may also wish to extend his reading further. I therefore mention with great gratitude and with a recommendation to readers: H. L. Mencken: *The American Language;* M. M. Mathews: *Dictionary of Americanisms;* three excellent works by W. W. Sweet on the history of American religion; Richard Osborn Cummings: *The American and His Food* (unfortunately beginning only with the national period); Ernest Pickering: *The Homes of America;* James Marston Fitch: *American Building;* Arthur W. Calhoun: *A Social History of the American Family;* both the Kinsey reports (which scarcely require further identification); Elsdon C. Smith: *The Story of Our Names;* Foster Rhea Dulles: *America Learns to Play;* George William Douglas: *The American Book of Days.*

What is essentially startling, however, is the lack of books on most of the subjects here treated. For this reason most of the material here presented has been drawn directly from original sources, particularly from colonial records and travelers' accounts. Most of these sources are made clear in the text, although I have not thought it necessary in a book for the general reader to clutter the pages by giving chapter and verse for each quotation and every allusion.

A chapter differing somewhat from the others is *Personal Names.* Its numerous detailed statements and statistical summaries are largely based upon my own compilations of many thousands of names, including full studies of the Harvard and Princeton alumni lists. I hope eventually to publish a book on the history of American given names. So far all my data are in MS., except for a monograph: *Men's Names in Plymouth and Massachusetts in the Seventeenth Century* (University of California Press, 1948).

For help and counsel I wish to thank, among my colleagues at the University of California: James D. Hart, David W. Reed, Carl Sauer, Henry Nash Smith, Theodosia B. Stewart, Francis J. Turner, and Winfield Scott Wellington. I am also under a debt of gratitude to Reginald Biggs, Joseph Bransten, Howard Cady, Howard Carver, Elizabeth Hutson, and Gair Sloan. For many courtesies I thank the librarians of the University of California Library and of the United States Information Service Library at Athens.

For permission to use copyrighted material I am indebted to Houghton Mifflin Company for permission to quote from *Land's End* from *Collected Poems 1917–1952,* by Archibald MacLeish.

George R. Stewart
Berkeley, California,
January 5, 1954

INDEX

INDEX

Omitted from the index are 1) casual and allusive references and names used merely as examples, 2) names that occur too frequently to be advantageously indexed, e.g., American, United States, English, Puritan, and names of regions such as New England and the South.

DATE DUE

MAY 1 3 1997			
DE 15 '09			
GAYLORD			PRINTED IN U.S.A.